Helen Hunt Jackson

Bits of Travel

Helen Hunt Jackson

Bits of Travel

ISBN/EAN: 9783337205706

Printed in Europe, USA, Canada, Australia, Japan

Cover: Foto ©Andreas Hilbeck / pixelio.de

More available books at **www.hansebooks.com**

BITS OF TRAVEL.

By H. H.

BOSTON:
JAMES R. OSGOOD AND COMPANY,
Late Ticknor & Fields, and Fields, Osgood, & Co.
1872.

Entered according to Act of Congress, in the year 1872,
BY JAMES R. OSGOOD & CO.,
in the Office of the Librarian of Congress, at Washington.

UNIVERSITY PRESS: WELCH, BIGELOW, & CO.,
CAMBRIDGE.

CONTENTS.

	PAGE
A GERMAN LANDLADY	1
THE VALLEY OF GASTEIN	34
THE AMPEZZO PASS AND THE HOUSE OF THE STAR OF GOLD	62
A MAY-DAY IN ALBANO	82
AN AFTERNOON IN MEMORIAM, IN SALZBURG	89
THE RETURNED VETERANS' FEST IN SALZBURG	95
A MORNING IN THE ETRUSCAN MUSEUM IN THE VATICAN	103
ALBANO DAYS	111
A SUNDAY MORNING IN VENICE	117
THE CONVENT OF SAN LAZZARO, IN VENICE	124
ENCYCLICALS OF A TRAVELLER	131

A GERMAN LANDLADY.

PART I.

IT was by one of those predestinations which men call lucky chances that I came to know the Fräulein Hahlreiner. An idle question put to a railway acquaintance, and in a moment more had been spoken the name which will stand in my memory forever, calling up a picture of the best, dearest, jolliest landlady in all Germany.

Up two such flights of stairs as only victims of monarchies would consent to climb we toiled to find her. There was a breeze of good cheer in the first opening of her door.

"Is the Fräulein Hahlreiner in?"

'I are she," laughed out of the broad red lips and twinkled in the pretty brown eyes. We had not suspected it, for she looked in no wise like the proprietress of an apartment to let, — more like the happiest and best-natured of chambermaids; untidy a little, it must be owned, but so picturesque in every word and motion, that one would not have risked any change, even to additional neatness. The rooms were just what we wanted. Who could have believed that, while we were journeying sadly away from beloved Tyrol, there stood waiting in the heart of Munich just the beds, the sunny windows, the cheerful parlor, that would fit us? The readiness of one's habitations is a perpetual marvel in the traveller's life: it is strange we can be so faithless about accommodations in the next world, when we are so well taken care of in this. It took few words to make our bargain, and few hours to move in; in a day we were at home, and the big, motherly Fräulein understood us as if she had nursed us in our cradles. How her presence pervaded that whole floor! There were thirteen rooms. A German baron with wife and two children, to whom he whistled and sang and shouted twelve hours a day, like a giant bobolink in a meadow, had some of the rooms. Two mysterious Hungarian women, who were secret and stately and still, and gave dinners, lived on the corner; and we had all the rest, except what was kitchen, or cupboard, or the Fräulein's bedroom.

It is wonderful how soon it seems proper to have kitchen opposite parlor, unknown neighbors the other side of your bedroom wall, dishes washed on the hall table, and charcoal and company coming in at same door. When we learn to do this in New York, there will be fewer deaths from breaking of bloodvessels in the effort to be respectable.

No artist has ever taken a photograph of the Fräulein Hahlreiner which could be recognized. Neither can I photograph her. I can say that she was five feet seven inches high, and fat to the degree of fatness which Rubens loved to paint; that she was fifty-two years old, and did not look as if she were more than forty; that she had hazel brown eyes, perpetually laughing, a high white forehead, two dimples in her left cheek which were never still, and hair, as free as the dimples, too long to be called short, too short to be called long, always floating back in the air as she came towards you: on great occasions she had it curled by a hair-dresser, — the only weakness I ever discovered in the Fräulein; but it was such a short-lived one, one easily forgave it, for the curl never stayed in more than two hours. I can say that, in spite of her fatness, her step was elastic and light, and her hands and feet delicately shaped; I can say that her broken English was the most deliciously comic and effectively eloquent language I have ever heard spoken; I can say that she cooked our dinner for us at two, went shopping for or with us at five, threw us into fits of laughter at eight by some unexpected bit of mimicry or droll story, and then tucked us up at bedtime with an affectionate "Good night. Sleep well!" But after all this is told, I have told only outside truths, and given little suggestion of the charm of atmosphere that there was about our dear Fräulein and everything she did or said.

The Munich days went by too quickly, — days in the Pinakothek, days in the Glyptothek, days in the Art Exposition, with its two thousand pictures. We had climbed into the head of the statue of Bavaria, roamed through the king's chambers at the Nymphenburg, seen one hundred thousand men on the Teresina meadows, and the king giving prizes for the horse-races; and now the day came on which we must leave Munich and each other.

My route lay to the north, — Nuremberg, Rhine, Rotterdam, London. For many days I had been in search of a maid to go with me as far as Rotterdam. The voluble Madame Marksteller, who supports a family of ten children, and keeps them all in kid gloves and poodles by means of an intelligence office, swept daily into my room, accompanied by applicants of all degrees of unsuitability. It grew disheartening. Finally I was reduced to the choice between a pretty and young woman, who would go with me only on condition of being my bosom companion, and an ugly old woman, who was a simpleton. In this crisis I appealed to the Fräulein.

"Dear Fräulein, why could not you go with me to Rotterdam?"

"O my dear lady, you make me go to be like fool, to think of so nice journey," said she, clapping one hand to her head, snapping the fingers of the other, and pirouetting on her fat legs.

But all sorts of lions were in the way: lodgers, whose dinners must be cooked.

"I will pay the wages of a cook to take your place, my Fräulein."

A country cousin was coming to make a visit; a cousin whom she had not seen for twenty-five years. She might stay a week.

"Very well. I will wait till your cousin's visit is over."

"But, my lady, I fear I make stupid thing for you. I knows not how to do on so great journey."

"Ha!" thought I, "I only wish I were as safe from stupidities and blunderings for the rest of my life as I shall be while I am in your charge, you quick-witted, bright-eyed old dear!"

The country cousin, I fear, was hurried off a little sooner than she liked.

"I tell she she must go. My lady cannot wait so long. Six days in Munich are enough for she," said the Fräulein, with a shrug of the shoulders which it would have cut the country cousin to the heart to see.

On a windy noon, such as only Munich knows, we set out for Nuremberg. If I had had any misgivings about the Fräulein's capacity as courier, they would have been set at rest in the first half-hour at the railroad station. It was evident that anything she did not know she would find out by a word and a smile from the nearest person: all were conciliated the minute they looked into her ruddy face. And as for me, never in my life had I felt so well presented as by the affectionate tone in which she said "My lady."

Trusting to Murray, I had telegraphed to the Würtemberger Hof for rooms. At nine o'clock of a dark night the German crowd in the Nuremberg station lifted up its voice, and said there was no Würtemberger Hof.

"There must be," said I, brandishing my red Murray, with my thumb on the spot. Crowd chuckled, and said there was not.

"O my lady, wait you here while I go and see," said the Fräulein, bundling me into a chair as if I had been a baby. Presently she came back with, "My lady, she do not exist these now four years, the Würtemberger Hof. We go to the Nuremberger Hof, which are near, and he have our telegram."

Out into the darkness we trudged, following a small boy with a glass of beer, and found, as the Fräulein had said, that the Nuremberger Hof had received our telegram, and had prepared for us two of the cleanest of its very dirty rooms. How well I came to know my Fräulein before the end of that rainy day in Nuremberg!

"O my lady, am I to go where you go and see all?" she exclaimed in the morning, when I told her to be ready at nine to drive with me. "O, never did I think to see so much." She had evidently had in the outset a fear that she would see little except at the railway stations and hotels. She little knew how much pleasure I anticipated in her companionship.

They are cruel who tell you that a day is time enough to see Nuremberg. It is a place to spend two weeks in; to lounge on doorsteps, and peer into shadowy places; to study old stones inch by inch, and grow slowly wonted to all its sombre picturesqueness.

As we stood looking at Peter Vischer's exquisite carvings on the shrine of St. Sebald's, I pointed out to the Fräulein the bass-relief representing St. Sebald's miracle with the icicle. She looked with cold, steady eyes at the finely chiselled fire which was represented curling upward from the little pile of broken icicle, and then said, "Do you believe, my lady?"

"O no, Fräulein," said I; "I can't quite believe that icicles ever made so good a fire as that, even for a saint. But I suppose you believe it, do you not?"

"O no, I not. The Church ask too much to believe. If one would believe all, one cannot do," said she, in a tone of timidity and hesitation quite unusual for her;

and a moment later, still more hesitatingly, "Have you read Renan, my lady?"

I started. Was this my German landlady, who spent most of her time over her cooking-stove, asking me if I read Renan? "Yes," I said, "I have read most of his books. Have you?"

"O yes, and I like so much. My confessor he say he no more give me —" (here she halted: the long word "absolution" was too much for her, and she made a sweeping gesture of benediction to indicate it), — "he no more give me — so — if I not put away that book; so I go not to him, now, two year, because I will not make lie."

"But then you are excommunicated, are you not, if you have not been to confession for two years?"

"Yes, I think," cheerily, quite reassured now that I must be as much of a heretic as she, since I too read Renan; "but I will not make lie. I will have my Renan. Then I read, too, the book against Renan; and he say St. Paul say this, and St. Peter say the other, but he go not to my heart. I love the Jesu Christ more by Renan as in what the Church say for him."

Strange enough it was to walk through the still aisles of these old churches, and, looking up at the dusty stone saints, to whom incense is burned no longer, hear this simple soul repeat over and over, with great emphasis, "I love the Jesu Christ more by Renan as in what the Church say for him."

Then we went down into the old dungeons under the Rathhaus, through chilly winding galleries, into stone chamber after stone chamber, rayless, airless, pitiless, awful. The Fräulein grew white with horror. She had never believed the stories she had read of torture-chambers and dungeons.

"Ach, mein Gott! mein Gott! and this is what might be to-day if Father —— had the way; and they tell us we lose the good old times. I will tell to all peoples I know I have seen the good old times under the ground of this Nürnberg!"

When we came out again into the open air, she was so pale I feared she would be ill. She sat down trembling on the stone stairs, and drew a long breath: " Ach Gott! but I am thanks to see once more the overworld."

It was almost wicked, after this, to take her to the still worse dungeons under the city walls, which are literally hung and set full of instruments of torture, and in the last of which is kept the famous Iron Virgin. In the first chambers were milder instruments for punishments of common offences, many of which have been used in Nuremberg within seventy years, — grotesque masks to be worn on the street by men and women convicted of slanderous speaking ("Ha, ha!" laughed the Fräulein, " there could not be made enough such masks to be weared in Munich"); and a curious oblong board with a round hole at each end, into which husbands and wives who quarrelled were obliged to put their heads, and live thus yoked for days at a time. This pleased the Fräulein greatly. " Think you, my lady, this would be good?" she said, sticking her fat fist through one of the holes, and opening and shutting it, — " think you they would love theirselves (each other) more?"

But her smiles soon died away, and she was paler than in the Rathhaus dungeons. This great hearty woman, usually ruddy as a frost-bitten apple in December, and stronger than most men, grew white and trembling at the first look at the horrible instruments of torture with which the other chambers were filled. Indeed, it was a sight hard to bear, — racks and wheels and pulleys and weights and thumb-screws, helmets and cradles and chairs set thick with iron spikes, and at last, in the lowest dungeon of all, the Iron Virgin. I held the poor Fräulein's hand. For the minute I was the protector, and not she. The woman who was our guide recited her story with such glib professional facility, and pulled out bars, and shoved back the doors, and showed the sharp spikes, all with such a cheery smile, that to me it robbed the cruel stone statue of much of its atmosphere of the horrible. I even felt a morbid impulse to step into the image's embrace and let the spiked doors be partly shut on me; but for the Fräulein's sake I forbore, and hurried her out as quickly as possible into her "overworld."

"O, never would I live in this Nürnberg, my lady," she said; "at each step I see ghost; and see color of that water," she added, pointing to the sluggish river: "it are black with the old sins."

How she laughed the Nuremberg jewellers into selling me oxidized silver cheaper than they meant to! How she persuaded the stolid Nuremberg "cocher" to drive faster, at least ten times faster, than was his wont! And how, most marvellous of all, she convinced the keeper of the Nuremberg cemetery where Albert Dürer was buried, that it could do no harm for me to bring away a big bunch of bright sumac leaves from one of the trees! I should as soon have thought of appealing to one of the carved Baumgartner burghers on their stone slabs to give me permission; but the Fräulein was too much for the keeper. He turned his back, so as not to seem to condone the offence, and satisfied his conscience by calling out, "Enough, enough, you have taken enough," several times before we were ready to stop picking. How quickly she saw and how keenly she felt the best things! Not a line of Adam Kraft's or Peter Vischer's carving was lost on her. Not a single picturesque face or group escaped her. Much more I saw, in that one day of Nuremberg, for having her by my side; and very short I found the next day's railroad ride to Mayence, by help of her droll comments on all that happened.

Curled up in one corner were a fat old German and his wife, and opposite them an officer with his young

bride. The officer and the burgher talked incessantly with great vehemence. I saw that the Fräulein listened with keenest attention; it was evidently all she could do to keep quiet. At the first opportunity she said to me: —
"O my lady, he are ultramontane, the fat man; he are Senator; they talk always about our government. I like so much to hear what they say; but the fat man, he are such fool."

The Senator's wife looked like a man in woman's clothes, — hard-featured, bony, hideous. As night came on she proceeded to make her toilet; she took off her boots, and put on huge worsted shoes, bound with scarlet; on her head she put a knit cap, of cranberry red; above that, the hood of her gray waterproof; above all this, a white silk handkerchief, tied tight under her chin; on top of all, her round hat. The effect was like nothing in earth but a great woollen gargoyle. The Senator looked on as complacently as if it were the adorning of Venus herself.

"O my lady, have you seen what she make for mouth when she speak?" said the Fräulein. I had not, for we were on the same side of the carriage. "My lady, you must see. I will make that she speak for you," said the malicious Fräulein, drawing nearer to the unsuspecting victim, and asking some question in the friendliest of voices. I forgave the unchristian trick, however, at sight of the mouth in motion.

After the Senator and the officer had both left the carriage, the Fräulein told me the substance of their discussion; political questions seemed familiar to her; she had her own opinion of every candidate; and O, how she did hate the ultramontanes! "O my lady, this Senator he wish to have for president a man who make always his walk backwards. Never he go forwards."

It took me some seconds to comprehend that this

was the Fräulein's English for a conservative, the thing she hated with her whole heart.

The sun shone brightly on the fields and woods. She exclaimed with delight at each new mile: "O, how I like to see smoke go up from house!"

"O, find you not the world nice, my lady? I find so nice, I could kiss the world. Always people say, this world are bad world. The world are good world. It are mens that are bad."

Then she would startle me again by farmer-like comments on the country.

"O, here are all such poor wood country; I would cut down such poor wood, and make land for other thing.

"Now begin to be more good stone, here.

"O look, my lady, what nice farm with much meadow for coos." (Never could I persuade the Fräulein to say *cows*.)

At last I said to her: Fräulein, you talk like a farmer."

"Ach, my lady," and her face grew clouded, "I make farm for eleven year. I am great farmer. That is all what I love. O, I could die, some time, I such hungry have for my beautiful farm."

By this time I was prepared to hear that my Fräulein had at one time or another in her life filled every office for which German towns have an opening, from burgomaster down; but that she had been a farmer I never suspected.

"You must tell me, Fräulein, all about it, when we are on the Rhine. We can talk quietly there."

"Yes, my lady, I tell you. It are like story in book."

For a few moments she looked dreamily and sadly out of the window; but her nature had no room for continued melancholy. Soon she began to laugh again, at sight of the slow, ditch-like Main, on which unwieldy boats and sloops were wriggling along.

"O my lady, this river go all the way as if he think each minute, 'I go no farther.'"
Match that who can for a hit at a sluggish river.

At one of the stations I saw her talking with a conductor on another train bound back to Nuremberg.

"I ask for my cousin. He are ober-conductor on that train. I send him note. He can see me when I come back. He will be in Heaven when he get my note." And her face twinkled more like the face of fifteen than of fifty. I looked inquiringly.

"He are my cousin; but I love he not; but he write me every year, for tirteen year, 'Will you marry me?' and I write to he: 'Thank you, thank you, but I think not to marry you, nor any other man. Live well, live well.' And he speak no more, till come same time next year; but always he say to all peoples, that he will me marry. He wait till I be glad of he. But I think he wait till I die. And his mother she hate me, because she wish that he had wife to take he out of her house. He make her cry so much, so much. He is so — how do you say, my lady, when peoples is all time like this?" and in an instant she had utterly transformed her face, so that she could have passed any police officer in the world, however he had been searching for her, so cross, so glum, so hateful did she become from eyebrows to chin. Never off the stage, and rarely on it, have I seen such power of mimicry as had this wonderful old Fräulein.

"He are always like that, my lady, all time, morning, noon, night, all year; and he say every day to his mother, 'Hold tongue! I will not have wife, if I cannot have Caroline.'" This last sentence she pronounced with a slow, sullen, dogged drawl, which would have made the fortune of an actress.

"O Fräulein," I said, "you ought to have been an actress."

"Yes, my lady, I think," she replied, as simply as a child, with no shade of vanity in her manner. "I would be rich woman now. When I was a child, a great manager in Augsburg he ask my grandfather to give me to study with his daughter. He say I make good, and be great player; but in those days no people liked artists like to-day, and my grandfather he are so angry, and he say, 'Go away; come no more in my house.'"

Thus laughing and listening, and looking out on the pleasant meadows of the Main, we came to Mayence, and at Mayence took boat to go down the Rhine. This was the Fräulein's first sight of the Rhine. All the tenderness and pride and romance of her true German soul were in her eyes, as the boat swung slowly round from the pier, and began to glide down the river. And now began a new series of surprises. From Mayence to Cologne there was not a ruin of which my Fräulein did not know the story. Baedeker was superseded, except for the names of places; as soon as I mentioned them to her she invariably replied, "O yes, I know; and have you read, my lady, how," etc. The Johannisberg Castle, given to Metternich by his Emperor, the cruel Hatto's Tower, the Devil's Ladder, the Seven Virgins, the Lurley, the Brothers, Rolandseck and Nonnenwerth, — she knew them all by heart; and for the sake of hearing the time-worn old stories, in her delicious broken English, I pretended to have forgotten all the legends. Nothing moved her so much as the sight of the two rocky peaks on which the two brothers had lived, and looked down on the Bornhofen Convent in which their beloved Hildegarde was shut up.

"O, each brother, he could see her if she walk in that garden," she said, with tears in her eyes. "Now, it come no more that a man love so much, so long, so true."

Just beyond the Brothers we passed the great Marienburg water-cure. Reading from Baedeker, I said: "Fräulein, that would be a cheap place to live; only twelve thalers a week for board and lodging and medical attendance."

"O no, my dear lady. It are not cheap, for there be nothing to eat. At end of eight day the man from Wassercure he shall be so thin, so thin, it shall shine the sun through him."

Throughout our whole journey the Fräulein's astonishment was unbounded at the poor fare and the high prices. In her beautiful goodness, she had supposed that all landlords were content, as she, with moderate profits, and anxious, as she, to give to their guests the best food.

"O my lady, find you this chicken good?"

"Not very, Fräulein. What is the matter with it?"

"O, the bad man, the bad man, to ask for this chicken one gulden. He are old chicken, my lady, and he are boiled before he are in oven. O, I know very well. O, I win much money by this journey; never before had I courage to give old chicken. Now I give!"

Much I fear me that from this time henceforth the lodgers in my dear Fräulein's house will not find it such a marvel of cheap comfort as we did.

"O my lady," she said one day, "if you come again to me, you shall all have as before. But to other peoples, I no more give beefsteak for fifteen kreutzers. I will be more rich, I have been ass."

By dint of the Cologne and Düsseldorf line of steamboats, and the Netherland steamship line, and endless questioning and unlading and lading, the Fräulein and I and the trunks at last came to land at Rotterdam. We had a day at Cologne, a night at Düsseldorf, and one never-to-be-forgotten night on the river. At Düsseldorf, we wandered about the streets for an hour and a half seeking where to lay our heads. Here the poor Fräulein had on her hands, besides me, an English barrister and his wife, who could speak no German, and who drifted very naturally into our wake. What a procession we were at eleven o'clock of the darkest sort of night, nobody knowing just were he was going, each person thinking somebody else was taking the lead! Suddenly the porters ahead of us plumped our trunks down in the middle of the street at the feet of two men with lanterns.

"Really, aw, now this is, aw, the most extraordinary place for a custom-house, aw, 'pon my honor," said the English barrister, whose name was not Dundreary.

"Have you meat or sausages?" said the biggest man, flashing his lantern-light full into our dismayed faces. "O mercy, no!" shouted we with bursts of laughter, and such evident honesty, that he let us go, contenting himself with punching the sides of all the carpet-bags.

"O Fräulein, did you tell that man you had no sausages?" said I, sure she could not have eaten up the six I saw her buy at Cologne.

"My dear lady, he say, 'Have you meat or sausage?' and I say, 'No, I have no meat.' I not make lie, I make diplomatique."

From Düsseldorf to Rotterdam it was a day and a night and half a day. The Rhine stretched broader and broader. The shores of Holland seemed slowly going under water, and the windmill arms beat the air wildly like struggling arms of drowning monsters. It was as cold as winter in the cabin: and it rained pitilessly on the deck. The poor Fräulein read all the magazines which I had bought for her in Cologne, and an old comic almanac which she borrowed from the steward, and at last curled herself up in a corner and went to sleep in despair. The night differed from the day only in being a little colder and darker, and in the Fräulein's having a red-flannel petticoat over her head. When I waked up and saw her pleasant great face in this ruddy halo of fiery flannel, I felt as comforted as if it had been a noonday sun.

It was at noon of a Thursday that we came, as I said, to land at Rotterdam; but this is hardly the proper phrase in which to describe arriving at a place which is nine parts water. Venice seems high and dry in comparison with it; and the fact that you go about in boats at Venice, and in cabs at Rotterdam, only serves to make the wateriness of Rotterdam more noticeable.

"O my lady, it are all one bridge from one water to another water," said Fräulein, as we drove up and down and across canal after canal to find the house of Moses Ezekiel, the Jew, who is a money-changer. It rained dismally, but the Dutchwomen were out on all the doorsteps, with pails of water, scrubbing and wiping and brushing and rinsing, with cloths and mops and brooms, as if they were enchanted by some soap-and-watery demon. Windows shone like mirrors; door-handles glittered like jewels.

"O, how they do are clean, these Dutch!" said the Fräulein, taking account with a housekeeper's eye of all this spotlessness.

How sorry I grew as the hour came for me to say good by to this dear, honest, droll, loving woman I cannot tell. The last thing she did for me was to look at the sheets in the dreary little berth in which must be spent my one night between Rotterdam and London, and to say with great indignation to the surprised stewardess. "Call you those sheets clean, in English? Never my lady sleep in such sheets, from Munich to Rotterdam. O, but I think a steamschiff (boat) are place for bad peoples to be punish for sin!"

Then she cried over me a little and went away. I watched her till she had shut the cab door, and was being whirled off to take the early train for Munich. Then I too shed a few tears, saying to myself, "God bless the old darling! I shall never see her like again."

The story of the Fräulein's life I feel a hesitancy about telling. It stands out so in my memory in its quaint, picturesque, eloquent broken English, that to try to reproduce it is like trying to describe one of

Teniers's pictures of peasant life. But nothing, not even the dulness of grammatical speech, can rob it of all its flavor of romance, and no one but myself will know how much it loses in my hands.

PART II.

HER father was a Suabian hunter, and one of the king's rangers. Her mother was a daughter of a subaltern officer. There were ten children, of which my Fräulein and her twin brother were the youngest. They were poor but gay, living a free life in the woods, with venison for dinner every day. When the little Caroline — for now I must give her her name — was three years old her father died; but she never forgot him, remembering to this day, she says, more vividly than almost anything else in her life, how he used to come home in his ranger's uniform, and taking her on one arm and her twin brother on the other, toss them both up in the air, calling her his little "rusty angel," in affectionate jest at her freckled skin.

One year later the mother died, and the ten children, left with very little money, were scattered here and there, in houses of friends and relatives. Caroline was sent to her paternal grandfather, who was a government advocate in Augsburg. The grandmother had written that she would take the handsomest of the six little girls, and the lot fell on Caroline. O, what a picture it was she drew of her arrival, late at night, at the fine house in Augsburg! She was carried, a poor little frozen bundle of baby, into a great parlor, where her grandparents with a small party of friends were playing whist. The servant set her on the piano while they unrolled her wrappings, one after another, for it was a cold winter night.

"Then at last out came I; and they stand me up on the piano, and my grandmother she say, 'Mein Gott!

if this be the handsome, what are the rest?' And one old servant,—and she I hate all my life,—she put both her hands high, and she say, 'Mein Gott, she have red hair and rusty skin!'"

In a few days, however, the little red-haired, rusty-skinned child became the pet of the whole house; and from this time till her grandmother's death Caroline was happy. But before she was six she had become such an unmanageable little hoyden, that her grandparents, in despair, shut her up in a convent school in Augsburg, only allowing her to come home for Saturdays and Sundays and the vacations. In this school she spent seven years, and came out, at thirteen, a full-grown woman, knowing a little of many things, but no one thing well, and too full of animal life to be held with any bonds. That very year came her first lover, asking to marry her.

"My grandfather, he send for me, and I come, like I go always on one foot, jumping like cat for bird; and there sit this man I know not; and my grandfather he point to me, and he say, 'You think to marry that child? Look at her!'" I am sure that the Fräulein was too modest to tell me how beautiful she was as a young girl. But I can easily make the picture for myself. She was above the medium height, and very slender; her cheeks were red, her forehead high and white; her eyes the brightest and wickedest hazel, and her mouth and chin piquant and wilful and tender and strong, altogether. Not often does the world see just such a face as she must have had in her youth.

The next year the grandmother died, and now began dark days for Caroline. Two of her aunts, who had not loved her father, came to keep her grandfather's house. They locked up her piano. They took away the pretty clothes her grandmother had given her. They gave her more and more hard work to do, until in one short year she was like a servant in the house. Then they sent her away to another aunt's house, on pretence of a visit, and kept her there three months; and when she returned, she found that her grandfather, who was now very old and imbecile, had married a new wife.

"Now came for me the worst of all the time. My grandfather's wife, she say, 'You must not stay here, I will not have, you are too fine lady. You can go earn your bread like others.' And I say, 'O, what can I do? I nothing know, where can I go?' And, my lady, I are only fifteen when she tell me to go make living for myself."

The grandfather was too old and feeble to interfere, and moreover had been prejudiced against Caroline by his wife and daughters. So the child went out into the world, with a little bundle of clothes and a few gulden in her pocket. She had about one hundred dollars a year from her father's estate, which luckily was in the hands of a trustee, or the cruel aunts would have robbed her of that. A kind neighbor took her in, and tried to cheer her; but her heart was broken. "All day, my lady, I cry and I cry, till I look so ugly nobody would take such ugly girl to live in house for servant. My face get quite another shape."

At last the good neighbor came home one day in great delight, and told Caroline that the Baroness —— had seen her in church, and liked her face so much that she had asked her name, and now sent to know if she would come and live with her as nurse for her three little children.

"This are like help from Heaven, my lady; and when I go to Baroness, she take me by chin, and she say, 'Would you like to live in my house?' And I cry so, I can no more speak, and I say, 'O, I glad of any house, so I have home.'"

For three years she lived with the Baroness, who proved a kind and wise mistress. The little children were sweet and lovable, and "I think I stay in that house till my time come to be died," said the

Fräulein, with tender wet eyes. But one day came a sharp, authoritative letter from her grandfather, ordering her to return home at once.

"I get great afraid, I think he wish to me kill, and I would not go; but the Baroness say, 'No, he are your grandfather, you must go.' So I go, and my grandfather he look at me with such angry eyes I am sick, I cannot stand up; and he say, 'The Baron love you too much. You are vile, bad girl. You go no more to his house. I will you shut up.'"

Cruel, idle tongues had done poor Caroline this harm. Probably the scandal rose from the careless jest of some thoughtless man or woman, who had observed the beautiful face of the young nursery-maid in the Baron's house. "I should make lie, my lady," said the Fräulein here, "if I say that the Baron speak ever to me one word not like my father. He good man."

After a few wretched weeks in the grandfather's house Caroline found a second home in the family of the Countess —— of Augsburg. Here she lived for seven years as lady's-maid to the old Countess, who loved her much. "But the young Countess, she love me not. She hate me. It are like cat see dog always when we see each other, we so hate; but my old Countess, she say always to me, 'O Caroline, have patient, have patient; for my sake go you not away.'" At last came a day when, for some trifling provocation, the young Countess took Caroline's two ears in her noble hands, and jerked her head violently back and forth, until the girl could hardly see.

"Many time, my lady, I say to her, 'Take your hands away, I will not from any man this bear'; and at last, my lady, I make so," said the Fräulein, hitting out from the shoulder with a great thrust which a prize-fighter might admire, "and she go back against the wall; and the old Count, he come flying and scream, 'You kill my daughter, you shall to prison go.' And he put his hand on me, and I make so again, my lady, that he go back against the other wall. O, I was strong like one hundred men! And my poor old Countess she come with her two hands tight, and she cry, 'O Caroline, Caroline, be not like this; go not away from me.' And I say to her, 'My dear lady, I no more can bear. I go away to-night'; and I go to my room, and in middle of my angry I stop to laugh, to see the old Count like he pinned to the wall where I put him with my one arm, and the young Countess like she pinned to the other wall, where I put her with my other arm."

In an hour Caroline had packed her boxes, and was ready to leave the house, but she found herself a prisoner in her room. The door was firmly locked, and to all her cries she could get no answer. All night long she walked up and down with her bonnet and cloak on. At eight in the morning the bell rang as usual for her to go to the Countess. "Ha!" say I, "the old Count he think I go to my lady, for her I so love. But I open my door, I have heard he come like cat and unlock with key; and I go straight to big door of great hall; and at door stand old Count, and he say, 'What mean you? Go to the Countess.' And I say, 'No, I go no more to Countess, I go to burgomaster. And I look at he so he no more dare move. I think," with a chuckle of delight at the memory, "he no more wish to feel how heavy are my hand, for he are poor little man. I could him kill, like chicken, and so he know very well."

Straight to the burgomaster the excited Caroline went, and told her story. For once a burgomaster was on the side of right; reprimanded the Count severely, and compelled him to give up all Caroline's boxes, and pay her the full sum due of her wages. Now she was, for the first time for many years, thoroughly happy. She had saved money in her seven years' service, and she had become a skilful dressmaker. She hired a little apartment, and sent for an old servant who had been fond of her in her childhood.

Old Monika was only too glad to come and live once more with her young mistress; and as for Caroline, after ten years of serving, to be once more independent, to have an affectionate waiting-woman ready to do her bidding, — "it was like Heaven, my lady. In morning, Monika she bring me my bath, like I lady again; and she say, 'Fräulein, my Fräulein.' And I make my eyes like I sleep, sleep, so that I can hear her say 'my Fräulein' many times, it so me please. Then she be fear that I died; and she come close and take me by shoulder; and then I give jump quick out of bed, and make her great fright and great laugh. But always I eat with my Monika, as if I not lady, for I say, I too have been servant; and I cannot eat by self; I have not hungry; and I love my old Monika very much."

The good Countess sent all her friends to Caroline, and in a short time she had more dressmaking than she could do, even with Monika's help; but she would not employ workwomen. She tried the experiment once, and had a seamstress for three months, but she could not endure the trouble and annoyance of it. "O my lady, I get in such great angry with she, she make so stupid things. I send she away. I think I be died with angry, if she not go."

It was, after all, but a bare living that one woman's hands could earn with a needle in Augsburg, in those days. Caroline and her Monika had only about two hundred dollars a year.

"How could you live on so little money, dear Fräulein?" said I.

"O my lady, in those time all are so cheap. I get pound of meat for nine kreutzers, now it are twenty. I get quart milk for three kreutzers, now it are five. I get nine eggs for four kreutzers, now I must pay two kreutzers for one egg; and in Augsburg then I buy for one kreutzer all vegetable Monika and I eat for two day, and now in my house in Munich I give six kreutzers for what I must give one person at one time."

Even at these low prices they had to live sparingly: one half-pound of meat three times a week; never anything but coffee and bread for breakfast; once a week a glass of wine. But Caroline was happy and content. "Never did I think to ask God for more than I have. I are so glad with my Monika; and I sing at my sew all day."

But fate was spinning a new tint into Caroline's life. In the spring of her third year of dress-making she found herself seized with a sudden ambition to go to Munich and get new fashions.

"It are great journey for me to take alone; and I had not money that Monika go too; I know I need not to go; but I cannot be free night nor day from thinking I will to Munich go, and get fashion for my ladies."

On the fourth day after her arrival in Munich the poor solitary Augsburg dress-maker was taken ill with a terrible fever. In great fright, the lodging-house keeper had her carried to the hospital, and gave herself no further concern about the friendless stranger. There poor Caroline lay in a crowded ward, so delirious with fever that she could not speak intelligently, and yet, by one of those inexplicable mental freaks sometimes seen in such cases, quite aware of all which was passing about her. She heard the doctors pronounce her case hopeless; she knew when they cut off her beautiful hair, but she tried in vain to speak, or to refrain from speaking when the mad raving impulse seized her.

At length one night, the third night, between twelve

and one o'clock, she suddenly opened her eyes, and saw a tall man bending over her bed, with a candle in one hand.

"O my lady, never can I tell what I saw in his face; never, my lady, have you seen so beautiful face. I say to myself, 'O, I think I be died, and this are the Jesu Christ; or if I not be died, this are my darling for all my life.' And he smile and say, 'Are you better?' And I shut my eyes, and I say to myself, 'I will not speak. It are Jesu Christ.'"

This was the young Dr. Anton ——, who had been, from the moment Caroline was brought into the hospital, so untiring a watcher at her bedside, that all his fellow-students persecuted him with raillery.

"But my Anton he say to them, 'I do not know what it are, I think that beautiful girl' (for, my lady, all peoples did call me beautiful; you would not now think, now I am such ugly, thick, old woman), — 'I think that beautiful girl die. But if she not die, she are my wife. You can laugh, all you; but I have no other wife in this world.'"

It was in very few words that my Fräulein told me this part of her story. But we were two women, looking into each other's wet eyes, and I knew all she did not say.

They could not be married, Anton and Caroline; for the paternal government of Bavaria, not liking to have too large pauper families left on its hands, forbids men to marry until they can deposit a certain sum in government trust for the support of their families, if they die. Anton had not a cent in the world: neither had Caroline. For four years they worked and waited, he getting slowly but surely into practice; she, laying by a gulden at a time out of her earnings. Once in four weeks he came to Augsburg to see her, sometimes to stay a day, sometimes only a few hours. "It took so much money for journey, he could not more often come. But he say, 'My liebling, I may die before we can marry; I will make sure to kiss you once in four week.'"

There was, perhaps, a prophetic instinct in Anton's heart. Before the end of the fourth year his health failed, and he was obliged to leave Munich, and go home to his mother's house. For six months Caroline did not see him. Week by week came sadder and sadder letters. Anton was dying of consumption. At last his mother wrote, "If you want to see Anton alive, come."

At sight of Caroline he revived, so much so that the physicians said, if he had no return of hemorrhage, he might possibly live three months; longer than that he could not hold out.

O cruel, paternal government of Bavaria! Here were this man and woman, held apart from each other, even in the valley of the shadow of death, by the humane law providing against pauper children.

The one desire left in Anton's heart was to be moved to Augsburg, and die in Caroline's house. He and his mother were not in sympathy; the family was large and poor; he was in the way. Then Caroline said, "Come."

"O my lady, you think not it was harm. His mother she go on knees to me, and say, 'Take Anton with you.' And I know I can keep him alive many weeks in my house; he will be so glad when he are alone with me, he will not die so soon. No one could speak harm of me, for this man I lead like little child, and lift in my arms, he are so sick."

So Caroline gave up her apartment in Augsburg, hired a little farm-house just out of the city, and took her lover home to die. The farm was just large enough for her to keep two cows and raise a few vegetables. The house had but one good room, and that was fitted up for Anton. Caroline and Monika slept in two little closets which opened from the kitchen. Before daylight Monika went into the city to sell milk and vegetables; while she was gone Caroline took care of the stable and the animals, and worked in the garden. Not one kreutzer's worth of work did they hire. The two women's hands did all.

In the sweet country air and in the sight of Caroline, Anton grew daily stronger, until at the end of three months he could walk a few rods without leaning on her arm, and hope sprang up once more in their hearts.

Then, lured by that illusive dream, which has cost so many dying men and women so dear, they started for Italy to escape the severe winter winds of Augsburg. They went in a little one-horse wagon, journeying a few miles a day, resting at farm-houses, where the brave Caroline took care of her own horse, like a man, and then paid for their lodging by a day's dress-making for the women of the family. In this way they spent two months; but Anton grew feebler instead of better, and when they reached home Caroline lifted him in her arms, and carried him from the wagon to the bed.

"When I lay him down, he look up in my face with such look, and he say, 'Liebling, it are no use. I have spent all my money for nothing. Now I die.'"

The journey, cheaply as they had made it, had used up every kreutzer of the earnings which had been put by towards their marriage. Now they had nothing, except what Caroline could earn, with now and then a little help from Anton's mother. But Caroline's heart never failed her; she thought of but one thing, the keeping Anton alive.

"All day, my lady, it are as if I see Death stand at door; and I look at him in eyes, and I say, 'You go away! I give not Anton to you yet. O Jesu Christ, let me keep my Anton one day the more.'"

And she kept him day by day, until the doctors said his life was a miracle; and Anton himself said to her sometimes, "O liebling, let me go; it is better for you that I die."

At last the day came, but it was nearly at the end of the second year. It was late in the spring. Anton had not left his room for weeks; but one morning he said to her that he thought he would like to sit under the trees once more.

"And, O my lady, the minute he say that, I know he think it are his last day. So I dress him in warm clothes, and I carry him out in my arms, and put him in big chair I make myself out of old died tree; and the sun it shine, shine, O so warm; and I read to him out of book he like. But I see he no more hear, and very quick he say, 'Come close to me'; and I go close, and he put his two hands on my face and say, 'Liebling, I think God be always good to you for your good to me.' And then he point with finger that I take him in house; and Monika and I we have but just get him in bed, when he fall back, and are died in one minute; and, my lady, I can say true, that in the first minute I was glad for my Anton that he have no more pain."

Soon after Anton was buried came Anton's second cousin, Herr Bridmacher, to see Caroline. The Herr Bridmacher owned a great farm of seven hundred acres near Starnberg. By this time all Anton's friends, far and near, had heard of the faithful and beautiful Caroline, who had so well administered the little farm, and made Anton's last months so comfortable. Herr Bridmacher offered her good wages and absolute control of the farm. It was the very life she most liked, and it offered an escape from Augsburg, the very air of which had become insupportable to her. She accepted the offer immediately, and at the end of a week was walking by Herr Bridmacher's side, up the broad road of Brentonrede farm.

"O my lady, my heart he go down in me when I see that farm. The Herr Bridmacher he have been fool. He have the same thing in the same field all his life, till the ground be no more good; and he are so mean, he have on that seven hundred acre only seven servant; he have four coos, three horse, and two pair oxen, and one are lame. And the house, it be shame to see such house; it let water come in in many place; and the floor it go up, and it go down, like the cellar are all of hills. And I say to him, 'It are well for you, Herr Bridmacher, that I not see your fine farm before I come. But I have my word given, and I go not back. I stay.' Then he begin to make great compliment to me, how he think I do all well. But I say, 'O, thank you, I not wish to hear. You think to journey, you have me told. The sooner you go, the better I like. Good night, sir.' So I go to my bed; but all night the wind he blow my windows so I cannot to sleep; but I say to myself, 'Caroline, if only that fool go away, here are splendid farm for you.' So I am quite quiet. And in the morning, Herr Bridmacher he say, 'Good morning, good morning. I start to Italy to-morrow'; and I say, 'I very glad to hear that. You stay two years, I hope.' And when he go down the road I stand at door, and I snap my two hands after he, and I say, 'Long journey to you, my master.'"

With short intervals of interruption and annoyance from Herr Bridmacher, Caroline had the management of Brentonrede farm for eleven years. At end of that time Brentonrede owned seventy-five cows, eight horses, eight pairs of oxen, twenty-four calves, and two hundred chickens. There were twenty-five workpeople, — seventeen men and eight women. The house was in perfect repair, and the place had more than doubled in value. Just before Caroline came to him the poor silly Herr Bridmacher had offered it for sale for sixty thousand gulden (about twenty-five thousand dollars); after she left him he sold it for one hundred and forty thousand gulden.

It would be impossible to reproduce the Fräulein's graphic and picturesque story of her life during this time. She had no neighbors, but she was never lonely. Her whole soul was in her work. At three o'clock every morning she rose, and gave the laborers their first meal at four. Five times a day they were fed, the

Brentonrede people: at four in the morning, bread, soup, and potatoes; at eight, bread and milk, or bread and beer; at eleven, knoedels,* with which they had either meat, pudding, or curds; at four, bread and beer; and at six or eight, bread and soup.

One of her greatest troubles in the outset was the religiousness of her work-people; — the number of Paternosters they insisted on saying every morning in the little chapel on the place.

"O my lady," she said, "I wish you could see that chapel. Such a Mother Goddess never did I see in my life. She look so like fool, that when I go first in I make that I drop something on floor I cannot find, so I put my face close to floor, that they not see me laugh. But I make she all clean; and I make chapel all clean; and then I say to men, 'Very well; if you need pray fourteen Paternosters on week-day, you need pray fourteen Paternosters on Sunday. So many as you pray on week-day, it are my order that you pray on Sunday, if you work at Brentonrede.' Then they grumble, and they tell the priest. They like not to take time that are their own time on Sunday to say fourteen Paternosters; but they like better to say Paternosters in my time than to dig in field. So the priest he put on his big hat, and he come to door, and knock, knock; and I go; and he say, 'Are you the Fräulein of Brentonrede?' And I say, 'Yes, Father, I are she.' And then he begin to say, 'Now, my daughter,' with long face; and then he tell me that he are told I have pigs in the chapel, and that I will not let the people to pray. And I say, 'O no, that are not true.' And I take he to chapel, and show how clean it are; and only I have in corner two big bottle of vitriol, which I have afraid to keep in house, because it are such danger; and I tell him I think Holy Mother God-

---

* Knoedels are dumplings made of flour, chopped herbs, and sometimes a little ham. They are the common food of farmers throughout Germany.

dess will be so good to keep it safe, that it blow not up the house. And he say that are no harm, but why do I not let the people to pray. And I tell him that I say not the people shall not pray. I say they shall pray fourteen Paternoster on Sunday, if they pray fourteen Paternoster on week-day; and since then they pray but one Paternoster on week-day, so that they take not time from their Sunday. And he scratch his head very hard, and know not what to say me to that; and then I give him good bottle wine and a cheese, and I say, 'Now, Father, it cannot be in this world that we believe all what are telled. I do not believe what are telled of you, and do you not believe any more what are telled of me.' And he get red in the face, for he know all peoples say his housekeeper are wife to he; and so he shake my hand, and he go away. And always I hear after that he say, 'The Fräulein of Brentonrede she are good woman; she are good Catholic.' But he know in his heart I laugh at he."

How she gloated over some of her harvest memories, — of wonderful afternoons in which more loads of hay were piled up in Brentonrede barns than had ever been known to be got in in one afternoon before. One particular wheat harvest, I remember, she mentioned. She had seen at noon that a heavy storm was coming up. Whole acres of wheat were lying cut, ready to be made up into sheaves. "Then I call all the men and women, and I say, 'If all the wheat are in before dark, I give you one cask beer, and two cheese, and all bread you can eat, and a dance.' I think not it could be; but I work with them myself, and I tie up with the straw till my hands they bleed, O, so much; but I nothing care. And the wheat it are all in, my lady, before nine o'clock, — twenty-five wagon-loads in one afternoon; and in all the country they tell it for one great story that it was done in Brentonrede."

The Brentonrede farm soon became well known in the whole region about Starnberg. Herr Bridmacher's friends used to make it a stopping-place in their drives; and the Fräulein often entertained parties of them at tea or luncheon. She was very proud of doing the honors of Brentonrede; and to these parties, and to her two years of close intercourse with the invalid Anton, she owed a certain *savoir faire*, which, added to her native gracefulness and quickness of comprehension, would prevent her ever being embarrassed, I think, in any situation.

In the tenth year of her Brentonrede life came a burgomaster from a neighboring town to ask her to marry him. By this time her love for Anton had taken the healthful shape of tender, regretful memory, which made no sorrow in her active, useful life, and set no barrier between her and other men. But her heart was wedded to Brentonrede farm. So, like a true diplomatist, she told Herr Bridmacher of this offer and asked his advice.

"I know very well he not like that I leave farm. He know he cannot make farm by heself. I think he will marry me heself, to keep me for farm. I not love he. O no, my lady, I love no man after my Anton. But I know he go on journey every year, sometimes for two three year, and I think I like very well to be his wife, and stay on farm while he go."

The Herr Bridmacher took the same view of it that Caroline did. Of course he could not have her leave the farm: so he said he would marry her when he came back from Italy, — from a year's journey on which he was about starting. The burgomaster was sent away, and Caroline went contentedly on with her farming for another year. When Herr Bridmacher returned, and their marriage was again discussed, the question of settlements came up, and upon this they fell out. Caroline was firm in her demand that Brentonrede should be settled on her and her children.

"I know very well, my lady, that all his people fine people. They think I am only poor work-girl who can make farm. Never I wish to go as his wife into one of their house. It are only for love of farm that I marry he; if he die, and I not have farm, what I do then?"

But Herr Bridmacher was equally firm. He would settle money on her, but not Brentonrede. Money Caroline would not have, not even if it were enough to buy another farm. It was Brentonrede she loved, and she did not in the least love Herr Bridmacher. "I know all the time he are fool, and like mule, beside," she said; adding with the gravest simplicity, "But I know he have been for ten year the most time away from Brentonrede, and I think when I are his wife he like it not even so much than before."

So Caroline and Herr Bridmacher parted in great anger. With her savings she bought a little house in the suburbs of Munich. But the city air oppressed her. Her occupation was gone. At end of a year she sold the house for two thousand gulden more than she gave for it, and bought another, farther out of the city, with a few acres of ground about it. Here she lived as she had in Augsburg, keeping one servant, three cows, hens and chickens, and working all day in a vegetable and flower garden.

"O my lady, it are like one picture, when I have work there one year. Not one inch in all my place but have a fine green leaf or flower growing on he; all peoples that drive by from Munich, they stop and they look and they look, and I are so proud when I hear them say, 'It are all one woman that do this with her own hands.'"

One afternoon as the Fräulein sat alone in her little sunny parlor, there was a ring at the door.

"I go, and I see, O such nice Englishman! I have he seen before, many times, stands to look in my garden. He are priest I know by his dress, — priest of your church, my lady. Then he say, 'Do you live here alone?' And I say, 'Yes.' And then he try to say more, but he cannot German speak, and I no English understand. So he laugh, and he say, 'I come again with my wife. She can all say in German.'"

The next day he came back with his wife, and the thing they had to say was no more nor less than to tell the Fräulein they were coming to spend the summer in her house. Her face and the face of her garden had been such magnets to them, that their hearts were set on coming to live for six months where they could see both every day.

"I say, 'But I know not how to do for high people. I cannot make that you have comfortable.' But they say, 'We will you show all. We want little.' And so they come. They take my two rooms up stairs; and they sit all day in my garden; and the lady, she grow so fat, and she say she are never so happy in all her life, as in my house; and they are, now these seven years, my best friends in the world."

These best friends of the Fräulein's were an English clergyman and his wife; and her acquaintance with them was one of the crises in her romantic life. In the autumn when it was necessary for them to go back to Munich, they persuaded her to sell her little farm (which was not so profitable as pretty) and take part of a house in the city, and rent apartments. She entered with many misgivings on this untried experiment; but her shrewd, sagacious nature was as successful here as in remodelling Herr Bridmacher's exhausted farm. She has lived in Munich for seven years. Her apartment has never, for one month, stood empty, and she is only waiting for the opportunity to add to it another whole floor. She has nearly paid for her furniture, which is all thoroughly good and satisfactory, and she says, "If I spare (save) very much and spend not on nothings, I think in six year I have enough money to go live as I like in country, and have garden." She yearns for green fields, and the smell of the earth. I am not sure that the English clergyman did well to transplant her within the city walls.

As for Herr Bridmacher, he came to grief, as might have been predicted, soon after parting with Caroline. After several unsuccessful attempts to find some one to fill her place, he sold his farm for one hundred and forty thousand gulden, put most of the money into a commercial speculation and lost it.

The good Caroline, hearing a short time ago that he was seen in Munich looking very shabby and out at elbows, wrote asking him to come to her house.

"I could not bear, my lady, to think that I so comfortable in this nice house by the money he pay me, and he have not money enough to go like gentleman as he always go before; and now I are old woman, I can ask to my house if I like."

But Herr Bridmacher was too proud to come.

"He hate me. I hear from friend that know, that he hate me, O so much! He say I are reason for all his trouble. But I think he are reason heself. Except for he had been one mule, I are in his house to-day, and Brentonrede are worth three hundred thousand gulden, and he have six children to make that he are no more sorry."

Poor Herr Bridmacher! From my heart I pity him, when I think what he has lost. But I have almost more resentment than pity, when I think that, but for his foolish pride and obstinacy, my Fräulein would have been to-day the loving mother of children, and the gracious Lady of Brentonrede.

THE VALLEY OF GASTEIN.

"GASTUNA tantum una,"—"Only one Gastein," —said the old archbishops of Salzburg, hundreds of years ago. "Only one Gastein," echoes to-day on lips and in hearts of all who are so fortunate as to find their way into its enchanted valley.

"From Salzburg to Bad-Gastein, by Hallein and Werfen $70\frac{1}{2}$ English miles, a journey of ten hours with post-horses"; "Route two hundred," in Murray's Guide-Book; that is the skeleton of the story. Even at Murray's best spinning, he only takes six pages to tell it, and probably there have been people who did the whole journey in ten hours. Bodies might; but for souls what a horrible spiritual indigestion must follow quick on the taking at one ten-hours sitting the whole feast of this road!

We did better. People who do just as we did will begin by losing their temper at six o'clock in the morning with the cross chambermaid of the Goldener Schiff in Salzburg, eating a bad breakfast in its dirty dining-room, taking delighted leave of its inexperienced landlord, and galloping out of town at seven to the tune of one of Mozart's old melodies rung on chime-bells. The great Salzburg plain is a goodly sight of a morning; circling meadows for miles, walled at last by mountains which are so far and so green that it is not easy to believe them six or eight thousand feet high; through the meadows the sluggish Salzach River; in the middle of the meadows, and on the river, the shining Salzburg town; in the middle of the town, high up on a rocky crag, the silent Salzburg castle, gray,

THE VALLEY OF GASTEIN.

turreted, and sure to last as long as the world. Those old Archbishops of Salzburg knew how to live. Wherever one comes upon traces of them, one is impressed with their worldly wisdom. The impregnable castle of Salzburg for a stronghold, with the Mönchsberg for pleasure-grounds, a riding-school cut out of solid rock for exercise, Heilbrunn water-works for amusement, and the Baths of Gastein for health and long life, — what more could these jolly old King Coles ask, except the privilege to kill all who disagreed with them? And that little privilege also they enjoyed for some years, enlarging it by every possible ingenuity of cruelty, as many stone dungeons with racks and *oubliettes* still bear witness.

Four hours steadily up, up. Franz does not urge his horses so much as he might. The nigh horse has no conscience, and shirks abominably on the hills. At last I venture to call Franz's attention to the fact, by a few ill-spoken German substantives and adjectives, with never a verb or a particle to hold them together. "Ja, ja," he says, with unruffled complacency; but pointing to the poor off mare, who is straining every muscle in drawing three quarters of the load, "she is a good one; she can pull," touching her up smartly with the whip at the same time. We cross the Salzach, which grows muddy and rough, fighting bravely to bring down all the logs it can; we leave the wonderful Dürrenberg Mountain with its three-galleried salt-mine, and we march steadily out towards the Tannengebirge, which looks more and more threatening every minute. Clouds wheel round its top. We know, though we try not to believe, that storms are making ready: they never look, not they, to see who or what they may drown or hinder. Down the rain pours, and we dash dripping into the basement story of the inn at Golling. It was like an Italian inn; carriages, and horses, and donkeys, and dogs, and cocks, and peasants, and hay, and grain, and dirt, and dampness, all crowded under and among damp arches of whitewashed stone, with only two ways of escape, — the low, broad door through which we had driven in, and the rocky stairs up into the heart of the house. How pitilessly the rain fell! Who of all the gods cared that we wanted that evening to see the waterfall of the Schwarzbach, the finest in all the German Alps, and that if we did not see it then we should never see it, because early the next day we must on to Gastein? Still it rained. Why should one not see a waterfall in a rain? They would not put one another out. This was clearly the thing to be done. Ah, how long the poor damp man, who took me in an einspanner to see that waterfall, will remember the smiling, merciless American, who sat silent, unterrified, and dry, behind the stout leather boot, and went over meadow, through gate, across stream, up gully, in the midst of thunder and lightning and whirling sheets of rain, and never once relented in her purpose of seeing the Schwarzbach! Poor fellow! he shifted from puddle to puddle on his low seat, looking furtively at me to see if I really meant to keep on; at last, in a climax of despair, he stood up, emptied the cushion of water, coiled up the ends of the stout leather reins edgewise into a kind of circular gridiron, sat down doggedly on it, and never looked around again till we reached the end of the road. Here his triumph began; for was not he to stay warm and comfortable by a friend's fire, while I went on foot the rest of the way to the waterfall? This I had not understood before leaving the inn. "Was it very far?"

"O no, not far."

I never saw a Tyrolese man or woman who would say that a place was far off. You might as well expect a goat or a chamois to know distances. "O no, not far, only a little," they say; and you toil and toil and toil, and sit down a dozen times to rest, before you are half-way there. However, if he had said it was ever so far, I should have kept on.

"There was a path?"

"O yes"; and here out skipped Undine to go and show it to me. I did not need her, for there wound the prophetic little brown path very plain among the trees; but it was a delight to see her flitting along before me. Bare-footed, bare-legged, bare-headed, bare-necked, bare-armed, she did not lack so very much of being bare all over; and I do not suppose she would have minded it any more than a squirrel, if she had been. She looked back pityingly at me, seeing how much my civilized gear hindered me from keeping up with her, as she sprang from tree-root to tree-root, and hopped from stone to stone in the water, — for in many places the path was already under water. On the right hand foamed the stream, not broad but deep, and filled with great mossy boulders which twisted and turned it at every step: on the left, fir-trees and larches and still more mossy boulders. Every green thing glistened, and trickled, and dripped; moss shone like silver: and bluebells — ah, I think I alone know just how bluebells manage in wet weather! Nobody else ever saw so many in one half-hour of glorious rain.

Soon I heard the voice of the fall; a sudden turn in the path and I saw it; but I looked for the first few seconds more at Undine. She stood, poised like a bird, on an old tree-stump, pointing to the fall, and gazing at me with an expression of calm superiority. The longer I looked the more inscrutable seemed the waterfall, and the wiser Undine, till I felt as I might in standing by the side of Belzoni before an Egyptian inscription. How well she understood it, this little wild thing as much of kin to it as the bluebells or the pine-trees! But while I looked she was gone, darting up a steep path to the left, and calling me to follow. There was more, then? Yes, more. O wonderful Schwarzbach Fall! It will mean little to people who read, when I say that it shoots out of a cavern in two distinct streams; they blend in one, which falls one hundred and sixty feet between craggy rocks, takes a cautious step or two, wading darkly under a natural bridge of giant rocks and pines, and then leaps off one hundred and seventy feet more in one wide torrent, with veils of silver threads on each side, and a never-ceasing smoke of spray.

Even destiny itself winces a little before a certain sort and amount of determination. Finding me actually face to face with the waterfall, and as thoroughly wet, the storm stayed itself a little, and rent the clouds here and there for me to look off into the grand distances. No sunny day could have given half such delight. This fall is supposed to be an overflow from the Lake Königsee, in Bavaria; but nobody knows; it hides its own secret.

Next morning we kept up a running fight with the rain through the Pass Lueg, past the great gorge Oefen, "not to be missed," said Murray. Neither did we miss it, clambering down and in under umbrellas. It is an uncanny place, where thousands of years ago the Salzach River cut a road for itself through mountains of rock, and never went back to see what it had left. Scooped out into arched and moulded hollows, piled up in bridge above bridge, damming up half the river at a time and then letting it fly, there stand the giant rocks to this day only half conquered. Yellow timbers from the mountains were being whirled through, now drawn under as if in a maelstrom, now shot swift as huge arrows over ledges of slippery dark stone.

In the Pass Lueg was just room for the river and us; and if it had not been for shelves of plank here and there, the river would have had all the road. This pass is called the "Gate of the Pongau." A very hard gate to open it would be to an enemy, for the solid rocky sides of the mountains have been wrought into fortress walls full of embrasures, whose guns one would think must be worked by elf-men in the heart of the mountain, so little foothold seems there for human gunners.

At Werfen, just beyond the pass, we struck the track of the old Salzburg Archbishops again: the great castle of Höhenwerfen, three hundred and fifty feet up in the air, on a wooded crag overhanging the Salzach River, was another of their strongholds, and was used chiefly for a prison, being within easy reach of one of their favorite hunting-lodges, in the Blühnbachthal valley, only a few hours back; so when they were tired of hunting chamois at Blühnbachthal they could ride down to Hohenwerfen and torture a few Protestants. Now, a company of Austrian sportsmen owns the lodge, and the castle of Hohenwerfen is used for barracks of Austrian soldiers.

At Werfen we contracted friendship with a shoemaker, who, with his wife, three children, and three apprentices, lives, sleeps, and sews in one stone chamber, up three flights of stone ladder, a few doors from the inn. I can recommend him as a good man who will put a new heel to an old boot and no questions asked.

Just beyond Werfen we passed a panorama of mill privilege never to be forgotten; eight tiny brown wooden mills, one close above the other, on the side of a hill, and the white stream leaping patiently over wheel after wheel, all the way to the bottom of the hill, like a circus-rider through hoops. What could decide men bringing grain to be ground, whether to go to the top or the bottom mill? It seemed that the eighth miller up, or down, must stand a poor chance of business.

From Werfen to our bedroom at Schwarzach we did not cease to exclaim at the beauty of the fields and roadsides. Everybody's house looked comfortable; everybody's wife was out tying up wheat or pulling flax: everybody else was wearing a high hat and feather and a broad gay belt, and sitting in the sun smoking; though, to be just, we did see here and there an odd-

looking man at work. Hollyhocks ruled the gardens,—
superb stalking creatures, black and claret, and white,
and rose-pink and canary-yellow,—and all as double
as double could be. Crowded along the roadsides, the
forever half-awake bluebells nodded and nodded on
their wonderful necks, which are always just going to
break, but never do. Fields of hemp we saw, and
took it for a privileged weed until we were told better.
Linseed we saw too, in great slippery dark-blue patches, and in the midst of all Franz suddenly reined up in
front of the Schwarzach Inn.

Ah, that Schwarzach landlady! She little dreamed
how droll she looked as she stood pompously courtesy-
ing in her doorway, with her broad-brimmed black felt
hat jammed down over her eyebrows like a thatch.
Her figure was so square and puffy, it looked as if it
had feathers inside, and was made to be sold at a fair,
to stick pins in. At the crease of her waist a huge
bunch of keys bobbed about incessantly, never finding
any spot where they could lie still. Two tables full of
Schwarzach men with beer and pipes, and two lattice-
work cages of hens and cocks, we passed to go up to
the first floor of the inn.

O, the pride of the pincushion landlady in her feath-
er-beds, her linen, her blankets, her crockery! She
had come of the family of a Herr Somebody, though she
did keep an inn and serve beer to peasants. Her family coat of arms hung in my bedroom, opposite a museum in a cupboard with glass doors. The contents of
this museum were only to be explained on the suppo-
sition that they were the aggregate result of a century
of Christmas-tree. Not an article in the protective
tariff of the United States but had been wrought into
some queer shape and put away in this Schwarzach
cupboard; mysteries of wax, glass, china, worsted,
paper, leather, bone. Most distinctly of all I remember
a white wax face stuck on top of an egg-shell painted
red, with a bit of green fringe for neck, and a bit of

THE VALLEY OF GASTEIN. 41

black wood for a leg. This impish thing grinned at me all night.

In this inn is a table round which the leaders of the Protestant peasants met in 1729 and took a solemn oath to leave the country rather than abandon their new faith. If the Schwarzach valley were as cold and dark then, as it was at the sundown we saw it in, I can conceive of heavier sacrifices than to exchange it for any possible spot in Prussia, Würtemberg, or North America, to which, according to the Guide-Book, the thirty thousand Protestants fled.

Next day sunshine and silver tent webs all along the road at eight o'clock in the morning.

A few more miles to the west, through Lend, a smutty little village where men have been melting gold and silver since the year 1538, and then we turned sharply to the south, to climb up through the wild "Klamme" to the valley of Gastein. At the turn we met a royal messenger, the shining river Ache, which said, "Go up the road I have come. I left Gastein an hour ago."

"Less than an hour ago, we should think, O stream, by the rate at which you travel," said we, as we entered the pass and began to mount slowly up.

Four horses now, and Franz is glad if we all walk. What triumph for a road to keep foothold on these precipices! "Chiefly schistous limestone," whatever that may be, Murray says that they are; but they look like giant strata of petrified wood. Small bits of the stone lie in your hand like strips of old drift-wood and crumble between your fingers almost as readily; so that you glance uneasily at the walls of it, to right one thousand feet above your head, and to left one thousand feet more of walls of it, down, down to the boiling river. If some giant were to give a stout pinch to a ton or so of it while you pass, it would be bad.

"Dreadful avalanches here in spring," says Franz.

We are glad it is August, and walk faster. The larches and bluebells and thyme rock away undisturbed, however, and keep the cliffs green and bright and spicy. Here is heath, too, the first we had seen, fairest of lowly blossoms, with tiny pink bells in stiff thick rows fringed with green needle-points of leaves: it crowds the thyme out and makes its purple look dull and coarse.

The Ache seemed to us a most riotous river, all through the Klamme. We never dreamed that we were looking at its sober middle age, and that it had sown its wildest oats far up the Gastein valley.

That is probably one reason it looks so mischievous all through the pass. It knows that people believe it to be doing its best leaping, and it laughs as an old woman who had had mad triumphs in her youth might to hear herself called gay at fifty.

It was through this Klamme that the rich and haughty Dame Weitmoser was riding one day, when she refused to give alms to an old beggar-woman who stood by the roadside.

The beggar-woman cursed her to her face, saying, "You shall yourself live to ask alms."

"Ha, that is impossible; as impossible as that I shall ever see this ring again," replied the wicked Frau Weitmoser, drawing from her finger a diamond ring and throwing it into the Ache. Then hitting the beggar-woman across the face with her riding-whip, she galloped off.

Three days later Herr Weitmoser, sitting at the head of his supper-table, surrounded by a party of friends, cut open a large trout and out flew his wife's diamond ring and rolled across the table towards her. Very pale she turned, but no one knew the reason. From that day Herr Weitmoser's gold-mines began to yield less and less gold, and his riches melted away, until they were as poor as the poor beggar-woman who had been so cruelly treated in the pass. Legends differ as to the close of the story, some killing the haughty, hard-hearted woman off, in season for Herr Weitmoser to marry again and accumulate another fortune; others making her live to repent in her bitter poverty, and, after she had become so kind and benevolent that she shared her little freely with her fellow-poor, giving back to them tenfold their original wealth. At any rate, the Herr Weitmoser is buried at Hof-Gastein; for did we not see the stone effigy of him on a slab in the little church? He lies flat on his back, in puffed sleeves and enormous boots, and two of his gold-miners stand guarding him, one at his head and one at his feet, with lifted hammers in their hands.

At the entrance of this pass, also, is the chapel of Ethelinda, scene of a still wilder story, and, better than all, one which is believed to be strictly true. In the Hof-Gastein church is a picture of its most startling incidents, and there is not a peasant within ten miles of the Klamme but will tell you that on windy nights can still be heard the words "Ethelinda," "Ethelinda," echoing around the chapel walls.

Ethelinda was the wife of another of the rich Weitmosers, who owned the gold-mines in the Radhausberg. Men are alike in all centuries. When Ethelinda died, Ethelinda's husband shed fewer tears than did another of the Weitmosers, Christopher by name, who had loved Ethelinda long and hopelessly. This lover hid himself in the chapel while the funeral rites were being performed. At midnight he went down into the vault where Ethelinda's body had been placed. A terrible thunder-storm made the fearful place still more fearful. By light of the sharp flashes he saw the face of the woman he loved. He bent over to kiss her. As he pressed his lips to hers she sighed, opened her eyes, and said, "Where am I?" But before either of them could comprehend the terror and ecstasy of the moment, Ethelinda exclaimed, "O fly, fly for help! The pains of childbirth are upon me! Hasten, or it will be too late!"

The lover forgets all danger to himself in his anguish

of fear for her, and bursts breathless into the husband's presence with the incredible news that his buried wife is alive, and lying in travail in her coffin, in the chapel. Weitmoser's first impulse is to slay the man whose tale so plainly reveals him as lover of Ethelinda. But he thinks better of it, and, hand in hand, they hurry to the chapel. Angels have been before them, and succored the mother and child. They find Ethelinda kneeling on the altar steps, with her babe in her arms. History wisely forbore to encumber the narrative with any details of how embarrassing it was for them all to live in the same village after this; but in the same little church of Hof-Gastein, where is the picture of Ethelinda in her graveclothes, kneeling on the altar steps holding up her child to the Virgin, are the gravestones of Christopher Weitmoser and his wife and children, from which we can understand that time had the same excellent knack then, as now, of curing that sort of wound.

The Gastein valley reveals itself cautiously by instalments, being in three plateaus. Coming out on the first, and seeing a little hamlet brooding over green meadows before us, we exclaimed, "Gastein, O Gastein!"

"No, indeed," said Franz, contemptuously, "only Dorf Gastein."

We wondered and were silent. Miles farther on, another sharp ascent and another valley. "Surely this is Gastein?"

"No, no, only Hof-Gastein." We wondered still more, but were glad, because Hof-Gastein is white and dusty and glaring. The houses elbow each other and are hideous, and the Ache takes a nap in the marshy meadows.

Steadily we climbed on; one mile, two miles, three miles, up hill. Snow mountains came into view. The Ache began to caper and tumble. Cold air blew in our faces; this was the noon weather of Gastein. Pink heath bordered the road; bushes of it, mats of it; it seemed a sin to scatter so much of anything so lovely. Dark fir woods stretched and met over our heads; gleams of houses came through.

"Yes, *this* is Gastein," said Franz, with proud emphasis, which meant, "Now you will see what it is to mistake any other place for Gastein."

Sure enough, wise old proverb: "There is but one Gastein."

For, knows the world any other green and snow-circled village which holds a waterfall three hundred feet high in its centre? One hesitates at first whether to say the waterfall is in the town, or the town in the waterfall, so inextricably mixed up are they; so noisy is the waterfall and so still is the town. Some of the houses hang over the waterfall; some of the threads of the waterfall wriggle into the gardens. The longer you stay the more you feel that the waterfall is somehow at the bottom of everything. From one side to other of this valley an arrow might easily fly. Both walls are green almost to the very top with pastures and fir woods, and dotted with little brown houses, which look as if birds had taken to building walled nests on the ground and roofing them over. To the west the wall is an unbroken line. Behind it the sun drops early in the afternoon like a plummet. Sunset in Gastein is no affair of the almanac. Every point has its own calendar. Long after Gastein — or Bad-Gastein, as we ought to begin to call it — is in shadow, Hof-Gastein, in the open meadow three miles below, is yellow with the sun. To the east and south are more mountains and higher, but not in range with each other, — the Stühle, the Radhausberg, Ankogel, and Gamskarkogel, all between six and twelve thousand feet high. Thus the view from the west side of the valley has far more beauty and variety. There are now on this side only a few houses, but ultimately it must be Gastein's West End.

The geologists, who know, say that where now are the valleys of Gastein and Böckstein were once two great lakes, which the earth in a spasm of thirst some day gulped down at a swallow; all but the water of the perverse river Ache, which would not be swallowed. When the cold water went in, some of the pent-up hot water jumped at the chance of getting out: hence the famous hot springs, great marvel and blessing of Gastein.

There are eighteen of these hot springs, some trickling slowly from the rocks, some bubbling out in the very midst of the cold water of the cascade. They make the best of their loopholes of escape, coming into town at the rate of one hundred and thirty-two thousand cubic feet every twenty-four hours. The water is perfectly colorless and tasteless; yet the list of sulphates and chlorides, etc., of which it is made, is a long one, numbering nine in all. The recipe is an old one, and probably good, though it sounds formidable.

The legend of its discovery is, that in the year 680 three hunters, following a wounded stag, found him bathing his wounds in one of these hot springs, whose vapor attracted their attention. A little later the Romans, seeking after gold and silver, penetrated to the valley and found living there two holy men named Primus and Felicianus. This was in the days of Rupert, the first of the Salzburg Archbishops. Primus and Felicianus were carried prisoners to Rome and thrown to the lions in the Coliseum. But they still live as the Patron Saints of Gastein. All good Catholics coming to be cured of disease, — and most who come are good Catholics, — invoke the prayers of Saints Primus and Felicianus, and, when they go away, leave grateful record in the chronicles of Gastein, beginning: "To God and the Saints Primus and Felicianus be thanks."

The Salzburg Archbishops kept possession of the valley until late in the seventeenth century. Then it went through half a century of political and religious warfares, passing from the Archbishops to other rulers, then to Bavaria, and finally to Austria, which still holds it. There is an Austrian commandant at St. Johann, an Austrian judge at Hof-Gastein, and at Bad-Gastein an Austrian bath inspector and government commissioner.

But still the church holds sway. There is a Roman Catholic curate in every village, a magnificent Catholic church going up in the very centre of Bad-Gastein, and nobody can stay two days in the town without being visited by the sweet-voiced Sisters of Charity in black, who ask, and are sure to get, alms for the poor in the name of Primus and Felicianus.

Life in Gastein begins bewilderingly for the newly arrived. How it began with us I would not dare to tell. It would be foolish to throw away one's reputation for veracity on the single stake of an utterly incredible statement as to the number of beds one had slept in in forty-eight hours. But not the most experienced and cautious traveller in the world can be sure of escaping an experience like ours. He will have telegraphed beforehand for rooms, having read in his Murray that Wildbad-Gastein in August is so crowded with the nobility of Russia, Germany, and Austria that it is not safe to go there without this precaution. As he steps out of his carriage in front of Straubinger's Hotel, Gustav, the pompous head-waiter, will wave him back, and explain with much flourish that there is not so much as one square inch of unoccupied room under Straubinger's roof, but that he can have for one day a room in the great stone Schloss opposite. At end of that day Lord A—— is coming to take the apartment for a month. By that time Count B—— will have vacated another, Gustav does not remember exactly where, but he can have it for a few hours; and then when the Prince, or Duke, or Herr, who has claims on that at a fixed minute, arrives, he can move to another which will be sure to be vacant; or if it is not, he can go to sleep at Böckstein, four miles farther up the valley, or at Hof-Gastein, three miles farther down.

There can be nothing on earth like the problem of lodging at Bad-Gastein in August, except jumping for life from cake to cake of ice in the Polar Sea. It is very exciting and amusing for a time, if the cakes are not too far apart. In the mean time, you eat your breakfast on the cake where you have slept, your dinner on the road to the next one, and your tea when you get there. Very good are the breakfasts and teas in all these lodging-houses, served by smiling, white-aproned housekeepers, who kiss your hand in token of allegiance, and bring you roses and forget-me-nots on your name day, if they happen to find out what it is. Good butter, milk, raspberries, strawberries, blueberries, figs, tomatoes, grapes, pears, plums, eggs, — all these you can have for the asking; bread which is white and fine, and which they think delicious who have not communed with Liebig and learned to ask for the good, nutritious bran. But with the milk and the fruit, and now and then a resolute pull at the native black bread, anise-seed and all, one can breakfast and tea happily. But when you ask for dinner, the face of nature changes. The thing called dinner you can eat at a *table d'hôte* in the hotels, or in a *café*, or you can have it sent to you at your lodgings, in a slippery tower of small white china tubs, which, when they are ranged round you on your table, make you think of a buttery washing-day. What may be in these tubs, Heaven forbid that I should try to describe. Who lives to dine would better not go to Gastein; in fact, who cannot get along without dining would better stay away. He who is wise will fight clear of the hotels and *cafés*, make interest with his landlady to give him a sort of picnic lunch at noonday, and postpone ideas of dinner till he returns to that paradise among hotels, the Europa at Salzburg.

These hearty, strong, tireless Germans, who climb a mountain or two of a morning for summer pleasure, find it nowise unsatisfactory to stop anywhere on the road, and eat anything for dinner. They do it as naturally as goats nibble a living from one rock to-day and another to-morrow. They are better off than we in being so much less wedded to routine; but it is a freedom not easy to acquire. For the average American to sleep in one house, breakfast in a second, dine in a third, tea in a fourth, and sleep again in a fifth, seems to turn life into a perpetual passover, not to be endured many weeks at a time.

Having made sure of a breakfast, and that Lord A, B, or C will not require your apartment before noon, you go out to look Gastein in the face, hear the sound and feel the heat of its wonderful waters.

Water to right, water to left, cold water, warm water, hot water, water trickling from rocks, water running from spouts, water boiling out of sight and sending up steam, and in and around and above and beyond everything the great waterfall thundering down its three hundred feet, deafening you with noise however far you go, and drenching you with spray if you come near.

"O, which water is for what disease?" we exclaim, curious to taste of all, afraid to taste of any, remembering Hahnemann, whom we revere.

"Go to Dr. Pröll," says everybody. "He is the man to tell you all about Gastein. He knows it thoroughly."

Indeed he does. He may be said to have Gastein by heart.

Between nine and eleven in the mornings there is a chance of finding Dr. Pröll at his tiny, odd, three-roomed office, which is composed of equal parts of bare rock and vapor-bath. At all other hours of the day they who wish to see him must watch and waylay him as sportsmen do game. Each man you ask will have seen him just the minute before, running rapidly up or down some hill, but you will be wise not to attempt overtaking him.

Dr. Pröll is a man whom it belongs to Victor Hugo to describe. Words less subtile than his cannot draw the lines of a nature at once so electric, so simple, so pure, so wise, so enthusiastic, so gentle, so childlike, so strong. Reverently I ask his pardon for saying, even at this distance, this much.

On the table in the room where Dr. Pröll receives his patients stands a dingy little apparatus at sight of which one idly wonders, — a magnetic needle swinging by pink floss silk under a low oval clock-case of glass, a small electrical battery, and a red glass vessel half full of water. These are the silent but eloquent witnesses which tell the secret of the naiad of Gastein. The doctor's blue eyes sparkle with eagerness as he immerses the battery in the water from the hot spring, and, connecting the wires with the electrometer, watches to see the needle move. He has done this perhaps thousands of times, but the thousandth time and the first are alike to all true lovers of science, — to all true lovers in the world, for that matter.

"You see? you see?" he exclaims.

Yes, we see that the needle swings fifty degrees. The temperature of the water was 14° Réaumur. Then he puts the battery into distilled water of the same temperature; the needle swings but twenty degrees, into common well-water, same temperature, and it swings but fifteen.

"Now I will to you show that the Gastein water is the only thing in this world over which time has no power," says Dr. Pröll, filling the red glass vessel from another bottle. "This is hot spring water, one year old. It would be the same if it were one hundred years old. Look!"

Yes, the needle swings fifty degrees.

"And now remains the most wonderful experiment

of all. I will show you how a very little of this magical water can electrify other water, just as one electric soul can electrify hundreds of commoner natures."

We smile at this. It is not possible in the first moment to be lifted quite to the heights of Dr. Pröll's enthusiasm. But wait! Here is the battery in common boiled water, temperature 26° Réaumur. The needle moves sluggishly, barely ten degrees.

"You see? you see? we will repeat; all experiments should be twice."

Yes, the needle moves barely ten degrees.

"Now we will turn in an equal quantity of hot spring water two years old, temperature the same. Look! look!" exclaims the doctor, clasping his hands in the delight of the true experimenter.

Sure enough. The heavy boiled water is electrified into new life. The needle swings forty degrees!

"And this is why I say that the water of Gastein is the water for souls," continues the doctor, lifting out the battery with unconscious lovingness in his touch; "And this is why I say in my book on Gastein, that these baths are the baths of eternal youth; and this is why an old physician, more than a hundred years ago, wrote a little poem, in which he makes the naiad of Gastein say to the invalids,

> "If I cannot please all
> And cannot bring health to all,
> That is common to me and God.
> Where there lingers in the blood
> The poison of sin and passion in the soul,
> There can enter neither God nor I."

One is a little sobered by all this. It is nearer to the air of miracles than we commonly come. Under the impressive silent pointing of this magnetic needle-finger, we listened with grave faith to the account of the effect of these waters on wilted flowers. This is a curious experiment, often tried. Flowers which are to all appearance dead, if they are left for three days in this warm water hold up their heads, regain shape, color, fragrance, and live for several days more. No wonder that old madman Paracelsus thought he had discovered in the Gastein waters the elixir of life. No wonder that to-day the sweet wild paths of Gastein are crowded with old men seeking to be made young, or, at least, to be saved from growing older.

"It is a strange thing, though," says dear, true-hearted Dr. Pröll, — "it is a strange thing, but in all these twenty years never has one woman come to me to be made young. Every year come many men, praying that they may not grow old; but never yet one woman."

Ah, we thought, perhaps the women are less honest than the men, and do not tell their motives.

But there is not time to grow very superstitious over these tales of magic, for there is so much else to be seen. In the rear room of the office is the hot-vapor bath; through a hole in the floor up comes the hot steam, heated no human being can tell how far down in the heart of the earth; night and day the fires go; for twelve hundred years the bath has been standing ready to steam people. Over the hole in the floor is a mysterious wooden structure, looking like a combination of pillory and threshing-machine. In five minutes, the doctor has shown, by a series of slippings and fittings and joinings, how, for every possible disease, every mentionable part of the body can be separately steamed, inch by inch, till one is cooked well. He wound up with imploring me to put my ear to the end of a long, narrow, wooden pipe which he screwed on the apparatus. "This is sure cure for deafness," he said.

I leaped. I should think it might be. In that second I had heard scouring through my brain all sorts of noises from spheres unknown. The ear-trumpet, which Hood's old woman bought, and, "the very next day, heard from her husband at Botany Bay," was nothing to it. The doctor could not understand why I should shrink so from listening to this wild rush of scalding steam from the earth's middle. He would have been shocked to know that, to my inexperience, it seemed nothing less than a speaking-tube from the infernal regions.

But we went nearer yet to the central fires. Up, up a winding path, shaded and made sweet like all Gastein's paths by fir-trees, mosses and heath, and bluebells; and there, sunk in the solid rock, was a polished iron gate. A peasant-woman keeps the key of this, and gets a little daily bread by opening it for strangers. She brought suits of stout twilled cloth for us to wear; but we declined them, having learned in the salt-mines of Hallein that, the inside of the earth being much cleaner than the outside, it is all nonsense to take such precautions about going in. A poor sick man who was painfully sitting still on a bench near the gate, seeing our preparations, came up and asked to join our party. I fancied that he had a desire to get a little nearer to the head-quarters of cure, and reassure himself by a sight of the miraculous spring. The peasant-woman went on before, carrying a small lantern, which twinkled like a very little good deed in the worst of worlds. The passage was very narrow and low. Overhead were stalactites of yellow and white; the walls dripped ceaselessly; the path was stony and wet. Hotter and hotter it grew as we went on. How much farther could we afford to go, at such geometrical ratio of heat? we were just beginning to ask, when the woman turned and, setting down her lantern, pointed to the spring. It was a very small stream, running out of the rock above her head fast enough to fill a cup in a very few seconds, and almost boiling hot. We all put our fingers solemnly in and solemnly put them to our lips; the woman nodded and said, "Good, good"; crossing herself, I suppose in the name of the good Saints Primus and Felicianus, she led the way out. I felt like crossing myself too. High-temperature underground places are singularly uncanny, and give one respect for the old mythology's calculation of the meridian of Tartarus.

For rainy days — and those are, must we own it? seventeen out of every thirty in Gastein — there is a most curious provision in the shape of a long glass gallery, four hundred and fifty feet long and twelve wide. Here the noble invalidism and untitled health and curiosity may walk, read, smoke, eat, trade, and sleep too, for aught I know. It is the oddest of places; so many hundred feet of conservatory, with all sorts of human plants leaning against its sides, in tilted chairs; I never grew weary of walking through it, or flattening my nose against its panes just behind the aristocratic shoulders of his Highness the Grand Chamberlain of ——, as he sat reading some court journal or other. A little room at the end holds a piano and two tables covered with a species of literature which was new to me, but which all Gastein seemed to feed and subsist on, that is, the lists of all the visitors at all the baths and watering-places in Europe. Pamphlet after pamphlet, they arrived every few days, corrected and annotated with care, the silliest and most meaningless census which could be imagined. But eager women came early to secure first reading of them, and other women with eyes fixed on the fortunate possessor of the valuable news sat waiting for their turn to come. This room is exclusively for women; opening out of it, in continuation of satire on their probable requirements, is a confectioner's shop; next comes the general reading-room, where are all the continental journals of importance; next a long, empty room for promenading, where your only hindrance will be the appealing looks from venders of fancy wares, who have their glass cases in a row on one side; then comes the covered walk, also four fifths glass, on the bridge over the waterfall; and then comes the Straubinger Platz, the smallest, busiest, noisiest, most pompous little Platz in the world; one side hotel, three sides lodging-house, and all sides waterfall; lodgers and loungers incessantly walking to and fro, or sitting on benches taking coffee, and staring listlessly at other lodgers and loungers; booths of fruit; booths of photographs; booths of flowers; booths of shoes; booths of inconceivable odds and ends, which nobody thought of wanting before they came in, but which everybody will buy before they go out, and will wish they had not when they come to pack; here, every day, come bare-kneed hunters, bringing warm, dead chamois slung on their shoulders; black and yellow Eilwagens drive up with postilions in salmon and blue, wearing big brass horns at their sides; Madame the Countess ——, dressed with blue silk trimmed with point lace, sits under a white fringed sunshade, on a chair in front of Straubinger's Hotel; and Madame the Frau —— sits, barefooted, bareheaded, opposite her, selling strawberries at eight kreutzers a tumblerful, and knitting away for dear life on a woollen stocking; all this and much more in a little square which can be crossed in ten steps. It is like a play; once seated, you sit on and on, unconsciously waiting for the curtain to fall: on your right hand is the orchestra, ten pieces, who play wild Tyrolese airs very well, and add much to the dramatic effect of things. Sunset is the curtain for this theatre, and dinner the only *enter' acte*. The instant the sun drops, the players scatter, the booths fold up; Madame the Countess sweeps off into the hotel; Madame the Frau rolls up her knitting, cautiously mixes together her fresh and her old strawberries, and starts off brave and strong to mount to her chamber in the air, miles up on some hill.

This play grows wearying to watch sooner than one would suppose. After a few days, one finds that all the climbing roads and paths lead to better things. There are the Schiller-Höhe, the Café Vergissmeinnicht, the Kaiser Friedrichs Laube (where the Emperor Frederick III. took baths four centuries ago); the Pyrker-Höhe, named after the patriarch of Erlau, the poet Pyrker; the Rudolfs-Höhe, the Windischgrätz-Höhe, and many more *cafés* or summer-houses on shining heights, all of which give new views of the wonderful Gastein valley, and at all of which whoever is German eats and drinks. The lure of a table, a chair, and a beer-mug seems a small reward to hold out, when for every additional mile that is walked a new world opens to the eye, but the Germans see better through smoke and beer-colored glasses.

Strong adventurous people, who can walk and climb without reckoning distances by aching muscles, have unending delights set before them for every day in Gastein.

In the Kölshachthal are four thousand chamois. Every summer come royal hunting parties to Höf-Gastein, and they who follow them may see chamois flying for their lives; poor things, so helpless in spite of all their marvellous speed and spring.

Then there is the lofty plateau of Nassfeld, the old "Wet Field" mentioned in Roman history. From this can be seen a great amphitheatre of glaciers and the passage by the Malnitzer-Tauern into Carinthia: this dangerous pass has an ineffable charm, from the fact that it is one of the only two ways out of the smiling Gastein valley. Once in, should any chance destroy the road in that wild Klamme through which the fierce Ache goes and you came, you have no possible way of escape, except on foot or on horseback, by the Malnitzer-Tauern.

After the Nassfeld come the old gold-mines in the Radhausberg, where the old Weitmosers made and lost their fortunes, and every stone has its legend: the Böckhardt Mountain, with a poisoned lake in which no fish can swim, near which no bird can fly and no flower can grow; the valley Anlaufthal, on one side of which rises the royal hill Ankogel, eleven thousand feet high, and called the Eldorado of mineralogists; and last, because greatest, the snow-topped mountain Gamskarkogel, The Righi of Austria, which looks down upon more than one hundred glaciers.

All this and more for well people. As for sick people their tale is soon told, either here or elsewhere. Hood's definition of medicine was exhaustive. In Gastein, however, little is done with spoons; people go into their medicine, instead of its going into them. Nobody takes but one bath a day; the stronger invalids take it in the morning before breakfast, and are allowed to go their ways for the rest of the day. The weaker ones take it at ten o'clock in the forenoon, lie in bed for an hour after it, then eat dinner, then are commanded to dawdle gently about out of doors until one hour before sunset, after which they are, upon no excuse whatever, to leave the house. There are they who drink mineral waters from Böckstein, drink whey, drink goats' milk, eat grapes, eat figs, all for cure. They all look tired of being ill; and they all give a semi-professional and inquisitive stare at each new-comer, as if they were thinking, "Ha, he looks as if he had it worse than I!" Poor souls. It seems a considerable price to pay for the rush-candle, to keep it burning under such difficulties and restrictions.

In a little pamphlet written by Dr. Pröll upon Gastein are some explicit directions as to the proper course to be pursued by all invalids who hope to be cured by the Gastein waters. Reading them over, one smiles, quietly, wondering if careful following out of such directions would not be of itself sufficient cure for most ailments.

"Before arriving at Gastein, visit all such places, cities, mountains, mines, as you would wish to see.

"Also close up all your most annoying or engrossing business affairs."

Among the "leading conditions of success in the use of the baths," he enumerates,

"A cheerful, amiable, and contented disposition," and

"Implicit obedience to the physician"; and adds that, after the treatment, there must be, during a period of from three to twelve weeks,

"Mental tranquillity.

"No business nor bodily fatigue.

"No long walks nor climbings.

"No remedials, internal nor external; a tepid bath once a week, but no other bath!"

But from the days of the Archbishops until now, it seems to have been held especially incumbent on all persons coming to these baths for help to come with quiet souls and pure consciences. The first volume of the "Chronicles of Gastein" is black and battered and yellow as an old monkish missal. More than half of the writing is entirely illegible; but clear and distinct on its first page stands out the motto, written there in 1681, and copied, I believe from the bath of some Roman Emperor, —

> "Curarum vacuus hunc adeas locum
> Ut morborum vacuum abire queas
> Non enim curatur qui curat."

Which good advice freely translated, would be something like this, "Whoever comes here to be cured must leave his cares at home; for if he worries he will never get well."

These "Chronicles of Gastein" are a never-failing source of amusement. There are fifteen volumes of them, written by the invalids themselves, from 1680 until now. The records are written in old Latin, old German, old French, all more or less illegible, so that there is endless interest in groping among them on the thousandth chance of finding something that can be deciphered. The books are carefully kept at the *curé's* house, and the volume for 1869 is quite a grand affair, having a mysterious locked brass box in one of the covers. This is to receive the contributions of charitable people who are not sick, and of sick people who are superstitious and wish to propitiate the good Saints Primus and Felicianus.

The box has the following inscription: —

" For the support of the school, and of the poor of both churches of the holy Primus and Felicianus, and the holy Nicholas church at

WILDBAD-GASTEIN.

In order that the Almighty God may bless, by the prayers of those holy patrons of the Bath, the noble gift of the health-giving spring to all the patients."

There are many most curious entries in these chronicles, and no one can look through them without being impressed by the singular unanimity of testimony, during two hundred years, to the efficacy of the waters. Here and there, however, a discontented soul has written out his grumblings; as, for instance, one Count Maximilian Joseph, Chamberlain of the King of Bavaria, who wrote on the 4th of July, 1747, in very cramped and crabbed old French: " Reader, greeting ! May God preserve you from the *four* elements of this country which are all equally wonderful, even the ennui"; and an unknown grumbler of the English nation, one hundred and five years later, who was too courteous or too politic to sign his name to this couplet, —

"Drenched with fountain, bath, and rain,
God knows if I 've been drenched in vain."

In 1732 Ludovic Frierfund wrote: " The fourth of July I began to use these baths. Now I am so much better, I believe I shall regain my health." (15th July.)

A few days later the grateful Baroness Anna Sophia, of Gera, writes: " To God and the two patron saints

Primus and Felicianus shall be the greatest thanks that I have used for the second time these blessed baths."

In 1752 the Countess Anna Maria Barbara Christiana, of Rönigs, declared: "I have finished this cure with the aid of God, and the Holy Mother, and the two saints Primus and Felicianus, and depart in full health on the 17th of July."

In 1830 Babette Brandhuber, may her soul rest in peace! left on one of the pages of the chronicle a little German verse, of which this is almost a literal translation: —

"O holy spring and friendly vale,
  I came here full of pain!
My full heart writes this grateful tale,
  I leave thee well again."

I am sorry to say that there have been in Gastein two or three Americans and English less poetically gifted than Babette, who have filled several pages of this volume with rhymes for which one blushes.

The two best things I found were a little record of one "Ruf, a money-changer of Munich," who, probably in a half-defiant display of his unpoetical calling, left only that signature to this couplet: —

"TO THE NAIAD OF GASTEIN.

"A kiss from woman's lips brings luck:
I kissed thee and am well."

And the following French verses. The author's name seems to have been purposely written so that no human being can decipher it, though the date is so recent. But the handwriting is evidently that of a woman: —

"AUX BAIGNEURS.

"Savez-vous qu'et est à Gastein
  Ou vous baignez pleins d'espérance?
Mes chers amis, j'en suis certain
  C'est la fontaine de jouvence.

"Dans ses eaux jettez une fleur,
　Rose depuis long temps flétrie;
Bientôt fraicheur, parfum, couleur
　A la rose rendront la vie.

"Ainsi puis qu'on peut y gagner
　De quoi prolonger l'existence;
Amis, venez souvent baigner
　A la fontaine de jouvence."
　　　　　　(20th July, 1820.)

Half a century ago! Youth and hope are over for her by this time; though perhaps youth and hope are just beginning for her by this time, — the true youth, the immortal hope; but whether she be to-day old on earth or young in heaven, I fancy her all the same, cherishing in her heart the memory of the rare, beautiful, blessed, dear Gastein valley.

Gastuna tantum una !

THE AMPEZZO PASS AND THE HOUSE OF THE STAR OF GOLD.

OUR month's voyage of Venice had come to an end. We had said so many times to each other in the mornings, "We must go," that the meaningless declaration had come to be received with bursts of laughter, and nobody dared say it any more. Nevertheless it was true: people who meant to summer in the Tyrol must not spend the whole of June in Venice. Silent, sad, beautiful Venice, how did our eyes cling to thy spires, as looking backward from the railway carriage we saw them slowly go down in the pale water. That one can leave Venice by rail seems the most incredible thing in life. At the first turn of the wheels and snort of the engine we began to doubt whether the city had been real; the first sight of green land was bewildering; and when at the first station we saw wheeled carriages waiting for people, we were struck dumb. What a gigantic and agile creature did the horse appear! and what a marvel of beautiful solidity the level earth, brown under foot, and full of locust hedges and pink-blossomed trees! It is no small proof of the subtile spell of that wonderful city of water and stone, slowly sinking at anchor, that one month's life on its bosom is enough to make all other living seem unnatural.

We even felt dull misgivings about the Tyrol, and the dolomite mountains of the grand Ampezzo Pass through which we were to pass to reach it. Nevertheless, "Ampezzo Pass" was so stamped upon our whole bearing, that, as soon as we stepped out of the carriage at Conegliano, we were taken possession of by screaming vetturini, each man of whom possessed the very best carriage and the very best horses, and was himself the very best guide in Conegliano! O the persistence, the superhuman persistence, of an Italian with a hope of money! Into the inn, into our very bedchamber, followed the man who spoke loudest and fastest.

Sixty francs a day! O that was very little. The ladies would not find any other man to go for so small a price. And his horses! If we could but see his horses!

How energetic grew our Italian! We would not give sixty francs a day, and we wished to be alone. The dilemma became embarrassing. Women, even if they be American, even if they be three in number, cannot put a man out of a room by main force; but at last moral force prevailed, and he went surlily away. We took counsel; it was nearly dark; we wished to begin our journey early the next morning; no doubt this vetturino would inform his fellows, and they would combine and agree; but sixty franks a day was a most exorbitant price for a carriage and two horses; we would not pay it; we could go by rail to Inspruck, and give up the Ampezzo Pass. Sadly the two who knew the least Italian set forth on errand of research among other vetturini. There is surprising advantage sometimes in conducting such bargains in a language which you do not understand. Armed with a few simple phrases stating time, sum, distance, and obstinately reiterating them, ignorance will sometimes conquer by virtue of its very incapacity.

We had barely crossed the threshold of the inn, when the same fierce-mouthed man sprang upon us.

"Go away. We do not want you. We will not take you."

Go away, indeed! as well dismiss our shadow! Bowing, gesticulating, falling back, and then overtaking, all the while talking like a macaw, he kept on all sides of us, that man of Conegliano. At last he surrendered. That is, he said meekly, "What will the ladies give?"

The moment he said that, we knew the day was ours. Now came my hour of success. I glibly said my lesson, "Forty francs a day. No more!"

A voluble reply ten minutes long, with heart-rending gestures.

"I do not understand Italian. Forty francs a day. No more."

Fifteen minutes more of volubility, appealing grimace, and gesture.

"I do not understand one word! Forty francs a day. No more!"

Our man fell. He would go for forty francs a day, this father of a family who had assured us with streaming eyes that his children would die of hunger if he went for less than sixty!

Once having accepted our terms, he was abjectly our servant.

"Show us your horses!" Meekly he led the way to his stables. With as knowing look as we could assume we scrutinized the lean black horse and dingy white horse which were walked up and down before us.

"O, they can trot. Yes, yes, Signora!" and lashing them with the halter's end he ran them up and down the hill at a good pace.

Triumphantly we led our conquered vassal back to the hotel; the story of our victory was received incredulously by the friend whom we had left behind; and who, speaking Italian as fluently as she speaks English, had vainly met the wordy extortioner on his own ground with his own weapons. The contract was signed; supper and bed and night passed, and at seven o'clock next morning, sunniest of Saturdays, we were off. Giacomo, the driver, looked like a Barnstable fisherman: thin, wiry, light blue eyes, pale brown hair, and scanty red whiskers. "O, how came you over here?" thought we as he jumped up and took the reins.

The whole country seemed on the broad laugh. So bright, so green were flower and leaf and field; waving locust hedges, full of morning-glories; and everywhere wide stretches of vineyards, in which the vines were looped across from tree to tree, looking like an array of one-legged dancers.

Lunch at Santa Croce, a town which has a lake, and beech-woods and glimpses of the far-off dolomite peaks. In the distance we could see a misty fringe of solid green, high up in the air. It was the top of the great beech forest, from which the Venice arsenal gets wood for its oars and masts and gun-carriages. Ninety miles in circuit is this government forest, full of game, and with an isolated plateau in its centre, where the keepers and officials live. This would not be of especial moment to know, except that it is said that Titian used to go there to learn how trees grow, and that he spent three months in this neighborhood drawing the background for his " Flight into Egypt."

After lunch I walked on in advance of the carriage. A man and woman who were working in a vineyard on the right sent their little baby to beg of me. I do not know why I remember that baby as I do no other child in all Italy. She was literally a baby, certainly not more than two years old; she was beautiful, yet not more beautiful than scores of Italian babies; but she was shy as a wild thrush; she absolutely could not take a step towards me if she looked at me. So she clasped her two little inches of hands tight over her eyes, and crept on, in the middle of the dusty road, more and more slowly, till at last she stood still, two yards off; then taking one sly peep at me through her fingers, she instantly shut them down again tighter than ever and stood there, kicking up little clouds of dust with her bare toes, the most irresistible blind beggar I ever saw.

It is of no consequence to anybody that the name of the town where we slept that night was Longarone. If only journeys could be told and the names of towns left out, how marvellously improved stories of travel would be. But whoever sleeps at Longarone will remember it always, the dark, frightened, poverty-stricken looking little town which huddles in such bare hollows of mountain and rock. The dismal inn, also, they will never forget: rooms so huge that lights cannot light them; two stalking high beds in every bedroom; and on the mouldy walls of the great dining-room ghastly pictures of Bible characters in giant size, — the Queen of Sheba leading up to Solomon, on his throne, a procession of black boys loaded down with pumpkin-shaped jewels; Samson with his head in the lap of Delilah, who brandishes aloft at least two pounds of coarse black hair; and Pharaoh's daughter receiving Moses in a knife-tray, while his mother stands in full sight knee-deep in water on the opposite side of the river.

The Ampezzo road, just beyond Longarone, enters the country of Cadore, the country of Titian. No wonder they were strong in fight, the Cadorini, and loyal of soul. To be born in such mountain fastnesses, to climb such precipices, to breathe such air, and to see such flowers, at once, could not fail to make souls both strong and sweet.

A strange hopelessness almost holds me back from the attempt to speak of that day's journey through the Ampezzo Pass: they who have not seen it will not believe; they who have seen it will smile that one should try to put such shapes in words. Possibly geologists can tell what a dolomite mountain is; how and why it is so seamed, so jagged, so wrought into castle and battlement and obelisk and cathedral-front; beautiful and terrible and graceful and grotesque; by turns, all at once; in sunlight, in shadow, at noon, at night; shifting and changing tint with every breath of wind or cloud on its surfaces: but to common men's eyes, these dolomite ranges are as unlike all other mountain forms as is Cellini's carven work to market-place pottery.

They seem like supernatural architecture gleaming out of supernatural realms in upper air. There are spires and minarets and bell-towers and turrets and colonnades and wrought walls; that they are ten, twelve, thirteen thousand feet away, that no human foot can scale them, no living earthly thing abide among them, only makes their distinct semblance of palace and church and city the more uncanny. And when, as often happens, a sudden wreath of cloud or fantastic growth of moss changes some scarred and lined rock into giant likeness of human face, it becomes still harder not to believe that they are tenanted by beings not of flesh and blood. One such face we saw, which never took its eyes off us for miles. Even sharp turns in the road made no change in it, except to draw the gray hood of fir closer round its cheeks and to make it look more and more weird.

These startling and fantastic mountain shapes hedged us, walled us, seemed to marshal themselves to oppose us, all the way from Longarone to Tai Cadore. In spite of ourselves we were overawed. If the sun had not shone gayly and the peasants had not whistled and sung, I think we might have been afraid. But every little village was astir with work, and babies were everywhere; we met low two-wheeled wagons filled with hay, slowly pulled along by donkeys, while the driver slept on his back; wagons loaded heavily with beech and pine boards, and drawn by oxen which looked like gigantic maltese kittens with horns. The meadows were green with a greenness so shining that it seemed to blaze; whole fields were solid mosaics of color, with red and blue and yellow and white flowers.

Little chapels were perched up on apparently inaccessible heights, above every village. "Why do they put the chapels so high up, Giacomo?" said I. "It must be very hard to climb to them."

"Ah, Signora, the air is holier there," replied the Barnstable fisherman.

At Perarollo, the river Boita, and the river Piave, and the huge dolomite Antelao, eleven thousand feet high, all join hands to close up the Ampezzo Pass. This is perhaps the most picturesque spot of the road. The rivers force the mountains back a little, and the sun pours in; high up on all sides are small plateaus of green pasture; the village is built into every niche of foothold it can find, and is full of pretty summer-houses of brown and yellow wood. On each river are lumber-mills, and the glistening logs are rolling and drifting down on both sides.

Three times this wonderful Ampezzo road winds across the front of the Antelao before it can venture to turn it; it seems to cling to the mountain's side like an elastic ladder of stone, a perfect miracle of engineering. We were hours climbing slowly back and forth on that dolomite wall, tacking, like a ship in contrary winds. From the first tier of the road we looked up to the other two, hanging above our heads; from the upper, we looked down into Perarollo, and could see no trace of the road by which we had come.

At last we fairly rounded the mountain, and, turning back again into the valley of the Boita, saw the village of Tai Cadore shining before us. In an hour we had reached the little inn. But a guest had arrived before us, sudden, unannounced. His unwelcome presence filled every room. As Giacomo, with a ludicrous affectation of effort, reined in his only too willing horses, a man came running out of the house with significant gestures exclaiming, "Do not stop, do not stop; the padrone lies dying." He was the padrone's son, and his eyes were red from crying. A crowd of peasants

THE AMPEZZO PASS. 69

stood about the door and in the hall; the little dingy windows of the room on the left hand of the door were darkened by heads rising one above the other, but all motionless. No doubt it was in that very room that the poor landlord lay, drawing his last breaths with unnecessary difficulty in the close air made still closer by such crowding in of friends and neighbors. I was struck by the oneness of the look which death's presence brings on faces of simple-hearted, solitary people all the world over. These men of Cadore were earlier on the spot than it is the custom in Maine or New Hampshire for neighbors to gather; but I have seen at many a New England funeral just such a silent, eager circle of men standing around the door through which the dead must be borne, and looking and listening with a weird sort of alert solemnity which seems not wholly sorry for the occasion.

It was a most opportune moment for us, however, which this good soul had selected for his dying. Nothing for the reluctant Giacomo and the nerveless horses to do but to take us a mile and a half off the route for dinner and rest, at Pieve di Cadore. Pieve di Cadore! the very place we had had at heart ever since we left Venice, and which we had had many misgivings about being able to see, while Giacomo rested his horses at Tai. At Pieve di Cadore "Il divino Tiziano" was born in 1477; at Pieve di Cadore he lived till he was ten years old; to Pieve di Cadore he returned year after year, for love of his kindred, men, and mountains. There, after the death of his wife, in 1530, he took refuge with his three motherless little children; and during this visit he painted, on a banner for the village church, a picture of three little children giving flowers to a Madonna seated on a throne.

There, in 1560, he came again, old, but not bent, and bearing the titles of Count of the Empire and Knight of the Golden Spur.

There also he would have fled, in 1576, when the

plague was sweeping Venice; but brave and strong to the last, he delayed going until an edict had been issued forbidding the departure of any citizen from Venice. So in Venice he died, ninety-nine years old, alone, forsaken even by his servants; and the pestilence which had taken his life thwarted his purpose even after his death, for none dared carry his body — as he had willed, and left order for its burial — to Pieve di Cadore.

They buried it in haste in the church of the Frari, in Venice, dropping into the grave the knightly insignia which the emperor had given to the painter; and for nearly half a century no stone marked the spot where the insignia lay turning to dust, and the dust lay turning into insignia of those mysterious things "which shall be."

"No one ever goes to the inn at Pieve di Cadore," said the displeased Giacomo, with a shrug.

"Why then is it an inn?" said we with sharp logical retort, inwardly blessing the conjunction of our star with the dying landlord's at Tai, and not caring whether we could dine or not, in an inn on a street where the little boy Tiziano Vecellio had played.

But the inn was an inn, and the dinner not so bad that I remember it. I shall never forget, though, how it was cooked; in big iron pots, swung from derricks of cranes, above a big bonfire, built on a big stone platform, raised up in a sort of bay-window chimney, filling one whole side of the kitchen; benches to right of the bonfire, benches to left of the bonfire; benches and bonfire all in the chimney bay-window; and people sitting on the benches, I among them, with feet at the bonfire; and all the while the great iron pots boiling and steaming and bobbing their covers, among and above our feet; the landlady reaching over and among our shoulders, and sticking in ladles and pokers here and there. If she had knocked off my hat, at any minute, it would have seemed the most natural thing in the world; merely taking off my cover and the beef's at once, lest we should boil to pieces.

She told us with pride how a deaf and dumb English artist had stayed with her for two months, had walked all over the Cadore country, and had carried away a box full of the most beautiful pictures which he had painted. "Poor gentleman, there was not much else he could do, since he could neither speak nor hear." "He was the sweetest gentleman." "Never made any trouble." "Lived on polenta chiefly." "All the children knew him and used to follow him when he went off to paint." And so she ran on, adding adjective after adjective in the sweet Italian superlatives, which are so silver smooth in their endings that there seems far less of exaggeration in them than in the harsher measures of more and most in other tongues. It was plain that the poor lonely deaf-mute had won for himself warm place in the village heart. His speechless language was a universal one; and perhaps, after all, he stood less helpless among the people than we did with our stammer of poor Italian.

After dinner we followed a thread of path down sharp terraces, and behind houses, into a meadow which one must cross to reach the ruins of the Castle of Cadore. The Castle was a castle so late as 1809. Now it is a ruin, and the ugly village church, they say, was built out of its stones. But it is far better as it is, — a great gateway tower, high battlements, several lengths of crumbling wall, and a high square tower in the middle. From its heights must be magnificent view of the valleys of the Piave and the Boita, and the grand mountain masses of dolomite in all directions. But we did not see this view; we climbed no hill; we asked for no castle; we knelt in the meadow among the flowers. The path was so narrow that two could not pass, unless one stepped out; but to step out was like stepping into spicy sea. No foot could fall there without crushing more flowers than it would be easy to count, and the mere brushing by of garments stirred fragrance heavy like incense. We were speechless; we could not believe; the mosaic fields of bloom we had seen on our way were dull and scanty. Then we said, "O, no doubt the legend is true, that Titian, when he was only eleven years old, painted with juices of flowers a picture of the Madonna; this is the field where he picked the flowers; and these are the same reds and blues and yellows which he used." Up and down in the meadow we went, picking flowers in the sort of frantic haste with which in dreams or in fairy stories men snatch enchanted gold in caves or palaces of wizards. If the meadow had melted away of a sudden, and left us empty-handed in a dusty place, I think it would have been less startling than it grew to be, to see each slope and hollow lying minute after minute unaltered, undiminished in color, while we filled our hands over and over again with flowers whose shapes and whose tints were all new to us. By the reckoning of clocks we were not in that meadow more than twenty minutes; but we carried out of it thirty-two different kinds of flowers which no one of us had ever seen before. Besides these there were dozens more, which we did not pick, because we knew them, — clovers, and gentians, and ladies'-tresses, and buttercups, and columbines, and bellworts, and meadow-rue, and shepherd's-purse. We never saw such spot again. It is part of my creed that there is no other such spot in the world, and I call it Titian's Meadow.

It is but a few moments' walk from this meadow to the house where he was born. It is a poor little cottage, low and black and smoky; an old woman, who looked as if she might be a hundred or a thousand years old, was hobbling and mumbling about in the kitchen, over just such a stone platform of cooking-stove as we had left in the inn. She was used to receiving visitors in the name of Titian, and had a glib string of improbable story at her tongue's end. The huge rafters overhead were burned and smoked into blacks and yellows and browns, which were stronger witness to centuries than any words could give; and an old stone fountain in front of the house, presided over by a nameless, featureless stone saint, plashed away into an eight-sided stone basin; a very dirty little boy was sailing a chip in it; probably he looked not unlike another little boy who sailed chips in it four hundred years ago, and whose name now gives honor to the cottage walls in this inscription: "Within these humble walls Tiziano Vecelli began his celebrated life."

Titian is more honored by this inscription than by the full-length painting of him, which stretches up and down on the bell-tower of the Pretura. Anything uglier than the Pretura is seldom seen, and the ambitious Cadorini have made bad matters worse by stuccoing the building from top to bottom and painting it in imitation of old stone. But they carefully refrained from disturbing the picture of Titian, and there it still stands in giant hideousness; a man apparently twelve feet high, and weighing five or six hundred, swathed from neck to ankles in a stiff robe of bright blue, which has so little semblance of fold or fulness that it looks less like a robe than like a huge blue sarcophagus into which the unhappy painter had sunk up to his ears; his left hand points to the "Casa Tiziano"; and at his side, on a table covered with a flagrantly gaudy cloth, lie his palette and brushes; behind the whole, a straight wall of sky, ten shades bluer than the blue robe, and if possible more unnatural. The continued existence of this picture is proof that spirits do not revisit this earth; or at any rate cannot make use of physical machinery to accomplish material ends in this atmosphere. Wherever Titian is to-day, he has not forgotten his beloved Cadore, and he would not let this colossal abomination look down into that piazza another night, if he could help himself.

From the Pretura to the church through the Sunday crowds of smiling people; women with short, dark blue gowns and white or gray handkerchiefs tied in the Albanian fashion over their heads; men with higher hats, symptom of the nearing Tyrol; children rosy and fat and merry, — comforting contrast to the pallid little ones of Venice. No soul, old or young, but looked at us with straight, curious, friendly gaze; they are off the common routes of travel, the Cadorini, and are all the friendlier and nicer for it. The old sexton knew very well, however, as soon as we crossed the threshold of the church, what we would see; and it was with great pride that he drew the curtain from the group of family portraits under name of Madonna and Saints, which hangs in the chapel of the Vecellio family, and which Titian painted.

There seems odd mixture of reverence for earth and irreverence for heaven in the way the masters painted portraits of wives and nephews for Madonnas and Saints. In this picture, "San Tiziano" the patron saint of the Vecelli kneels on the right hand of the Madonna. He is, however, only Titian's nephew Marco, and the Madonna is Titian's wife; while Titian's uncle Francesco figures, by help of a cross on his shoulder, as St. Andrew, and in one corner Titian himself appears as a sober acolyte. A more comfortable and domestic looking family group was never photographed under name of Smith or Jones. Except that the little baby curled up in the mother's lap is naked, there seems nothing unnatural (or supernatural) about their all happening to be there together just at that minute.

There is another of Titian's pictures here, said to have been painted when he was only twenty years old. This also is of a Madonna and Saints; there were a few other pictures which the sexton pressed us to see, a Pordenone, he said, and a Palma Vecchio; but we liked the open air of the market-place and the sight of the mountains better. Stands and wagons of fruit and silk handkerchiefs and chickens and earthen pipkins filled the corners. Cadore is a rough country, and gives small reward to them that farm it, but it has always been famous for fruits. Even in the thirteenth century there came to be a proverb,

"Cadore and Feltre for apples and pears,
Serravalle for swords."

The clouds began to gather and wheel among the crags of the dolomite mountains. They were ten thousand feet up in air, to be sure, and miles away to north and west and south; but they meant rain, — rain close upon us, violent, pelting, driving rain. These were such sudden gatherings and massings of clouds as Titian had watched and studied and carried away in memory, and reproduced, when, living on the serene, soft, gliding level of Venice, he threw into so many of his pictures marvellous backgrounds of sharp, abrupt mountain outlines with clouds circling round their summits. Doubtless Venetian critics who had not been in Cadore found these mountain backgrounds unnatural and impossible. Certainly a faithful drawing of the weird and fantastic dolomites would seem simply grotesque caricature to one who had never seen them. Even a photograph would seem incredible.

The peaks of Marmarolo and Duranno disappeared; great sheets of mist came driving down, blotting out even the castle; blotting out also every trace of content and good-humor upon Giacomo's face. This small addition to his prescribed route had been too much for his philosophy, and our delays had finally piled the last feather on the camel's back of his patience. Perhaps, however, we were unjust; perhaps he knew even better than we did the feebleness of the spectral horses which drew us slowly out of Pieve di Cadore in that streaming rain; it was an uncanny atmosphere; all shapes seemed lost; and then, again, all shapes seemed to loom and quiver and dance; the black horse looked white, and the white horse did not seem to be there, though we heard his languid footfalls.

"Shut up the carriage, Giacomo," said we. "It is of no use to keep it open in such a blinding storm."

Quickly and silently he roofed us over with the ill-smelling leather flap; and as silent as he, and almost as sullenly,—shall I confess?—we took the stifling afternoon's journey to Cortina d' Ampezzo. We seemed driving in the teeth of sudden winter; the rain changed to sleet and the wind howled; the jagged peaks of dolomite thrust themselves here and there out of the clouds as if they were being hurled at us by invisible giants. It was nearly eight o'clock when we drove into the little piazza of Cortina d' Ampezzo. Suddenly we halt. In the stormy twilight a woman has run across the road, and almost taken our horses by the head. "Are these the American ladies? Then they are to come to our inn. Their friends are awaiting them there."

This was one of the sisters Barbaria, who keep the "House of the Star of Gold"; and lest by any ill chance we might go to the rival inn, she had been watching the Cadore road all the afternoon.

O, how beamed the pleasant English faces which smiled our welcome in that low doorway! and how crackled the fire in the kitchen where two sisters Barbaria, with high-crowned black hats on their heads, were washing dishes; one sister Barbaria was picking feathers off tiny birds; another sister Barbaria was piling up our bags and bundles on her brawny arms; another sister Barbaria was asking what we would have for supper; and a fifth sister Barbaria was standing in the hall looking on: five sisters Barbaria! and they have kept the "Albergo Stella d' Oro" for many years, without any help from man.

Presently appeared a sixth sister Barbaria, but she was a fine lady of quite other style. She was Barbaria no longer, having married a young German engineer, a clever fellow who had had charge of that part of the Ampezzo road between Cortina d' Ampezzo and Cadore; and, staying at the "Star of Gold," had found a wife among his landladies. This sister wore a silk gown and a show of jewelry, had been with her husband to Rome and Venice, and was now summering at Cortina, like any other lady of means. But she was far less interesting than her guileless sisters, who had never been out of the village in which they were born, and who shared all the work of the inn, even the hardest and most menial, with a sisterly good-will and good-cheer which were beautiful to see.

The two who wore black hats like common peasants, and who drudged all day in the low basement kitchen and outhouses, seemed as happy and loving as the others, who were much better dressed, and who cared for the rooms, waited at table, kept accounts, etc.

One of these was a woman who would have been an artist if she had not been an innkeeper and lived in Cortina. It was pathetic to see how this poor soul had found outlet for her artistic impulse in works of worsted and crochet cotton. The "best room" of the "Star of Gold" was decorated with her handiwork, — full long curtains of knit lace at the windows and over the bed; a counterpane of the same lace; a full draping for the toilet-table; and crocheted covers for all the chairs. The patterns were all singularly graceful and pretty. Lifting the chair covers, we found, to our astonishment, that the chair bottoms were all most elaborately worked in gay worsteds on cloth. Then we said to one of the sisters, "How pretty these things are! Did you make them?"

Her plain old face lit up with pleasure. "O no; my sister Anita made them all. She does most beautiful work, Sister Anita. She shall show you." And running out, she called Anita, who came shyly but with pleasure; poor, brown, withered, simple old maiden woman, whose one joy had been to fashion these gay flowers. She brought in her hand pieces of black and brown broadcloth, enough for half a dozen chairs and two crickets, most elaborately embroidered.

The patterns were stiff, and the colors not always good.

"We have to take what we can get, here in this poor place," said Sister Anita; sometimes I think, if I could go myself to Brixen, I could surely find prettier patterns, but I must send always. *Are* there not prettier patterns?" she asked with pathetic eagerness. Could any human heart have been flinty enough not to equivocate in reply to this question of this poor hungry soul? Then when she found that we were so interested in her work, and admired it so heartily, she darted away and returned presently with great wreaths and bunches of worsted flowers, — lilies and poppies and gentians and pinks, and long ivy vines, made upon wires, and really beautiful. These were to decorate the house with on festa day; she had many drawers full of them; had enough to decorate the whole house, " till it looked like garden!" And no one had ever taught her to make them; she had picked the flowers in the field, she said, and set them up in a glass before her, and copied them as nearly as she could. "Why do you not make up these chairs and crickets?" we thoughtlessly asked; "they are too pretty to be laid away in a drawer."

Anita replied that she was too poor; it would take much money. But Anita did not tell the truth. I saw in her cheek another story, written in red, as indeed it might well be, — the story which had in it a hope deferred, perhaps lost forever. Poor Anita, she is old and ugly. I am afraid the embroidered chairs will never grace a wedding-feast.

Next morning we looked out on snow; everywhere fine feathery dust of snow; thin rims of ice in the stone fountain before the inn, and solid masses of white on the sides of the mountains. But the first hour of sun melted it all off the meadows, and left the flowers brighter than ever, glistening as after a heavy dew. Tiny white lilies not two inches long nor more than eight inches from the ground, and low gentians of a blue like the blue of lapis-lazuli, — these were growing everywhere; we filled our hands with them within five minutes' walk of the inn. Later in the day the German engineer brought in a bouquet which he had gathered farther up on the hills, of such flowers as we had seen at Pieve di Cadore; twenty-four different kinds in that bouquet, all colors, all shapes, all fragrances!

There is one shoemaker in Cortina d' Ampezzo. His shop is in an upper chamber, about eight feet square. There I found him sitting on a low seat, with a leathern apron, and spectacles way down his nose, holding a shoe wrong side up between his knees, and sewing away like any old man in Lynn. I sat down gravely in front of him, held out a morocco bow in one hand and a tattered American boot in the other, and asked if he could sew the bow on the boot. He was a German, but the apparition of my boot was too much for even his phlegm, he turned it over and over and over. A boot that buttoned he had never seen; I showed him my button-hook; his amazement deepened; he buttoned and unbuttoned the boot with it, grunting out thicker and thicker, "Jas, jas," at every turn of the instrument. Finally he set about the sewing on of the bow. The door opened; more men of Cortina came in; they had seen me go up; they scented adventure; one, two, three; the room grew very hot; the button-hook was passed about; the three men turned it up and down, and looked at me. I could not understand a dozen words they said. It was very embarrassing. The time came to put on my boot; the shoemaker leaned forward to see how I did it; the three men of Cortina crowded around and stooped down to see how I did it; a sense of the ludicrous helplessness of my situation so overcame me that I broke out into a genuine laugh, which, improper as it might have been, seemed to put me quite at my ease again, and I displayed to the good souls the mechanism of button-hook, button, and button-hole as complacently as if I had been a vender of the patent. Then they all four accompanied me to the door, and bade me good morning with the reverence due to the owner of such mysterious boots. But I resolved not to take off my boots again in Tyrolese shoe-shops!

How bitterly we regretted the ignorant haste in which we had, at Conegliano, pledged ourselves to ask but one day's rest at Cortina d' Ampezzo. We would gladly have stayed with the sisters Barbaria a week; we comforted ourselves by air castles of another summer in which we would come again and stay a month, bringing with us them whom we most loved. Hopefully the elder sister made it clear to us that she would welcome us as guests for a month at seven francs a day. A month, face to face with those wonderful pink and yellow and gray and white and salmon-colored mountains of dolomite! A month of those flowers! Thirty times as many as we had picked that day; and dear soft brown eyes which we knew, to light up with joy at sight of all we could bring! What a dream it was; on what shore does it stand now, pale in its death, but transfigured in its resurrection among other sweet things which we dare to call lost, when they have only gone before!

The dining-room windows of the "Star of Gold" are filled with geraniums; not "plants," not "bushes," as we commonly see, but trees, — trees tall, branching, sturdy, and bearing flowers as apple-trees bear apples; blossoms scarlet and rose-pink, and marvellous white with purple and crimson markings. Lavishly the elder sister gathers them for departing guests; and we drove off in the early afternoon, each of us with a big bunch in our lap.

We were not yet at the summit of the Pass. Hours

more of slow climbing among larches and pines and rocks and flowers; at last the larches disappeared, then the pines; nothing was left but stunted firs. On a dark icy plateau at the very top of the Pass we came suddenly upon a great field of blue forget-me-nots; just beyond that, a silent lake which must be unfathomable, to look so black; and then we began to go slowly down, down the other side; soft wooded slopes, and valleys of grain, and a look of thrift. We felt almost like dodging, as if we were pelted with pebbles, when the German gutturals first began to fly in the air. We forgot the German for "chicken," and fell back on "Kut-kut-ka-da-kut," which is language for "chicken" all the world over. We shuddered at sight of the huge effigies of the dead Christ, at corners of the roads; we found the men surly, and women and men alike hideous, and hideously alike; we no longer thought the horses too slow; we grudged each mile that they took us farther from Italy. Each of us had left half her heart in Venice, and the other half in the "House of the Star of Gold," with the sisters Barbaria.

A MAY-DAY IN ALBANO.

WE went Maying on donkeys, and we found more flowers than could have been picked in a month. What a May-day for people who had all their lives before gone Maying in india-rubbers, and an east-wind, on the Atlantic coast of America; had been glad and grateful over a few saxifrages and houstonias, and knelt in ecstasy if they found a shivering clump of dog-tooth violets.

Our donkey man looked so like a New Englander that I have an uncomfortable curiosity about him: slim, thin, red-haired, freckled, blue-eyed, hollow-chested, I believe he had run away in his youth from Barnstable, and drifted to the shores of the Alban Lake. I watched him in vain to discover any signs of his understanding our conversation, but I am sure I heard him say "gee" to the donkeys.

The donkey boy, too, had New England eyes, honest dark blue gray, with perpetual laugh in them. It was for his eyes I took him along, he being as superfluous as a fifth leg to the donkey. But when he danced up and down with bare feet on the stones in front of the hotel door, and twisted and untwisted his dirty little fingers in agony of fear lest I should say no, all the while looking up into my face with a hopeful imploring smile, so like one I shall never see again, I loved him, and engaged him then and there always to walk by my donkey's nose so long as I rode donkeys in Albano. I had no sooner done this than, presto, my boy disappeared; and all I could see in his stead was a sort of human pin-wheel, with ten dangerous toes for spokes, flying round and round by my side. What a pleased Italian boy, aged eleven, can do in the way of revolving somersets passes belief, even while you are looking at it. But in a moment he came down right end up, and, with the air of a mature protector, took my donkey by the rope, and off we went.

I never find myself forming part of a donkey, with a donkey man in rear, without being reminded of all the pictures I have seen of the " Flight into Egypt," and being impressed anew with a sense of the terrible time that Holy Family must have had trying to make haste on such kind of animal: of all beasts, to escape from a hostile monarch on ! And one never pities Joseph any more for having to go on foot; except for the name of the thing, walking must always be easier.

If I say that we climbed up a steep hill to the Capuchin church and convent, and then bore off to the right along the shores of the Alban Lake, and resolved to climb on till we reached the Convent of Palazzuola, which is half-way up the side of Monte Cavo, it does not mean anything to people who do not know the Alban Lake and Monte Cavo. Yet how else can I tell where we had our Maying? The donkey path from Albano up to Palazzuola — and there is no other way of going up — zigzags along the side of the hill, which is the south shore of the Alban Lake. Almost to the last it is thickly wooded; looking at this south shore, from a distance, those who have been through the path can trace its line faintly marked among the tree-tops, like a fine thread indenting them; but strangers to it would never dream that it was there. The path is narrow ; only wide enough for two donkeys to pass, if both behave well.

On the left hand you look down into the mystic lake, which is always dark and troubled, no matter how blue the sky; never did I see a smile or a placid look of rest on the Alban Lake. Doubtless it is still linked with fates and oracles we do not know. On the right hand the hill stretches up, sometimes sharply in cliffs, sometimes in gentle slopes with moist hollows full of ivies and ferns; everywhere are flowers in clusters, beds, thickets. It seemed paltry to think of putting a few into a basket, hopeless to try to call the roll of their names. First come the vetches — scrambling in and out, hooking on to everything without discrimination; surely a vetch is the most easily contented of plants; it will hold by a grass stalk, or an ilex trunk, or lie flat on the roadside, and blossom away as fast as it can in each place. Yellow, and white, and crimson, and scarlet, and purple, and pink, and pale green; — seven different vetches we brought home. Periwinkle, matted and tangled, with flowers one inch and a half in diameter (by measurement); violets in territories, and of all shades of blue; Solomon's-seals of three different kinds; dark blue bee-larkspur whose stems were two feet high; white honeysuckle wreathing down from tall trees; feathery eupatoriums; great arums, not growing like ours, on a slender stalk, but looking like a huge cornucopia made out of yellow corn-husks, with one end set in the ground; red catchfly and white; tiny pinks not bigger than heads of pins; clovers of new sorts and sizes; one of a delicate yellow, a pink one in small flat heads, and another growing in plumes or tassels two inches long, crimson at base and shading up to white at top. One could not fancy this munched in mouthfuls even by sacred cattle; it should be eaten, head by head, like asparagus, nibbled slowly down to the luscious color at the stem.

The holly was in blossom and the white thorn, and huge bushes of yellow broom swung out across our path at every turn; we thought they must light it up at night. Here and there were communities of crimson cyclamens, that most bewildering of all Italy's flowers. "Mad violets" the Italians call them, and there is a pertinence in the name; they hang their heads and look down as if no violet could be more shy, but all the while their petals turn back like the ears of a vicious horse, and their whole expression is of the most fascinating mixture of modesty and mischief. Always with the cyclamens we found the forget-me-nots, nodding above them in fringing canopies of blue; also the little flower that the Italians call forget-me-not, which is the tiniest of things, shaped like our forget-me-not, but of a pale purple color. Dandelions there were too, and buttercups, warming our hearts to see; we would not admit that they were any more golden than under the colder sun where we had first picked them. Upon the chickweed, however, we looked in speechless wonder: chickweed it was, and no mistake, — but if the canary-birds in America could only see it! One bud would be a breakfast. One bud, do I say? I can fancy a thrifty Dicky eating out a ragged hole in one side, like a robin from a cherry, and leaving the rest for next day. The flowers are as wonderful as the buds, whitening the ground and the hedges everywhere with their shining white stars, as large as silver quarters of dollars used to be.

Now I come with shamefacedness to speak of the flowers whose names I did not know. What brutish people we are, even those of us who think we love Nature well, to live our lives out so ignorant of her good old families! We are quite sure to know the names and generations of hundreds of insignificant men and women, merely because they go to our church, or live in our street; and we should feel ourselves much humiliated if we were not on what is called "speaking terms" with the best people wherever we go. But we are not ashamed to spend summer after summer face to face with flowers and trees and stones, and never so much as know them by name. I wonder they treat us so well as they do, provide us with food and beauty so often, poison us so seldom. It must be only out of the pity they feel, being diviner than we.

The flowers which I did not know were many more

than those which I knew, and most of them I cannot describe. There was a blue flower like a liverwort, only larger and lighter, and with a finely notched green leaf; there was a tiny bell-shaped flower, yellow, growing by twos and threes, and nodding perpetually; there was a trumpet-shaped flower the size of a thimble, which had scarlet and blue and purple all blended together in fine lines and shadings; there was another trumpet-shaped flower, quite small, which had its blue and purple and scarlet in separate trumpets but on one stem; there was a tiny blue flower, shaped like a verbena, but set at top of a cluster of shut buds whose hairy calyxes were of a brilliant claret-red; there was a yellow flower, tube-shaped, slender, long, white at the brim and brown at the base, and set by twos, in shelter of the joining of its leaves to the stalk; there was a fine feathery white flower, in branching heads, like our wild parsley, but larger petalled, and a white, star-shaped flower which ran riot everywhere; and besides these, were so many others which I have no colors to paint, that at night of this wonderful May-day, when we numbered its flowers, there were fifty-two kinds.

As we came out of the woods upon the craggy precipices near the convent, we found the rocks covered with purple and pink thyme. The smell of it, crushed under the donkey's hoofs, was delicious. Somebody was homesick enough to say that it was like going across a New England kitchen, the day before Thanksgiving, and spilling the sweet marjoram.

The door of the cloister was wide open. Two monks were standing just outside, absorbed in watching an artist who was making a sketch of the old fountain. The temptation was too strong for one member of our party; when nobody looked, she sprang in and walked on, determined to have one look over the parapet down into the lake. She found herself under old ilex-trees, among dark box hedges, and the stone parapet many rods ahead. A monk, weeding among the cabbages, lifted his head, turned pale at sight of her, and looked instantly down at his weeding again, doubtless crossing himself, and praying to be kept from temptation. She saw other monks hurrying to and fro at end of the garden, evidently consulting what was to be done. She knew no one of them would dare to come and speak to a woman, so she pushed on for the parapet, and reached it. Presently a workman, not a monk, came running breathlessly, " Signorina, Signorina, it is not permitted to enter here."

"I do not understand Italian," said she, smiling and bowing, and turning away and looking over the parapet. Down, down, hundreds of feet below, lay the lake, black, troubled, unfathomed. A pebble could have been swung by a string from this parapet far out into the lake. It was a sight not to be forgotten. The workman gesticulated with increased alarm and horror: "O dearest Signorina, indeed it is impossible for you to remain here. The holy fathers," — at this moment the donkey man came hurrying in for dear life, with most obsequious and deprecating gestures and words, beckoning the young lady out, and explaining that it was all a mistake, that the Signorina was Inglese and did not understand a word of Italian, for which gratuitous lie I hope he may be forgiven. I am sure he enjoyed the joke; at any rate, we did, and I shall always be glad that one woman has been inside the closed cloister of Palazzuola, and looked from its wall down into the lake.

We climbed round the convent on a narrow rocky path overhanging the lake, to see an old tomb "supposed to be that of Cncius Cornelius Scipio Hispallus." We saw no reason to doubt its being his. Then we climbed still farther up, into a field where there was the most wonderful massing of flowers we had yet seen: the whole field was literally a tangle of many-colored vetches, clovers, chickweed, and buttercups.

We stumbled and caught our feet in the vetches, as one does in blackberry-vines; but if we had fallen we should have fallen into the snowy arms of the white narcissus, with which the whole field glistened like a silver tent under the sun. Never have I seen any flower show so solemnly beautiful, unless it might have been a great morning opening I once saw of giant pond-lilies, in a pond on Block Island. But here there were, in addition to the glittering white disks, purple and pink and yellow orchids, looking, as orchids always do, like imprisoned spirits just about to escape.

As we came down the mountain the sunset lights kindled the whole Campagna into a flaming sea. The Mediterranean beyond seemed, by some strange optical effect, to be turned up around the horizon, like a golden rim holding the misty sea. The lake looked darker and darker at every step of our descent. Mt. Soracte stood clear cut against the northern sky, and between us and it went up the smoke of that enchantress, Rome, the great dome of St. Peter's looming and fading and looming and fading again through the yellow mist, like a gigantic bubble, as the power of the faith it represents has loomed, and faded, and loomed, through all the ages.

AN AFTERNOON IN MEMORIAM, IN SALZBURG.

PARACELSUS, ST. RUPERT, AND MOZART.

THESE were the names on our list, the guide-book, and not we, being responsible for the odd succession.

Poor Paracelsus! it has always seemed that the world dealt hardly by him. Undoubtedly he believed that there was an Elixir of Life which could be put in a bottle, and a philosopher's stone, at touch of which all things would turn into gold. We have all been searching after these very things all our days, and without half so much philanthropy about it as he had; for we try, by secret ways, after only just so much elixir as will keep our own poor little body fresh, and enough gold to provide it with clothes and pleasures. But he spoke openly of his researches, and meant to sell his elixir to the whole world, and to hire out his philosopher's stone by the day. Three hundred and twenty-eight years ago he died in Salzburg, and is buried in the churchyard of San Sebastian. The house he died in is still pointed out, but that had no interest to us, while the grave drew us strongly. What unconscious tribute we pay to the doctrine of the resurrection by the love and honor in which we hold graves, century after century! Surely in our hearts we believe that each such spot becomes forever unlike all other ground: by whatever process the dear flesh crumbles, returns to dust, and is changed into the leaf, flower, and seed that perish, in our hearts we believe that the grave remains a grave, and that at least this much is sure;

that the happy, soaring, growing spirit, which has gone on in the worlds, will never forget where the tiny spot is on this one in which its human body was laid.

In the time of the cholera, old men and women of Salzburg went in crowds to pray over the grave of Paracelsus, hoping to secure his protection against the disease; such immortal force is there to an earnestly believed idea. Paracelsus, even dead, and three hundred years dead, still finds believers in his Elixir of Life. Doubtless, also, this praying saved many people from cholera; faith being the best Elixir of Life yet discovered.

We had no chance to benefit by any efficacy which may still linger in his tombstone, for find it we could not, though we walked patiently round and round, and over and over the San Sebastian graveyard. Sacristans are always out of the way when you wish them in, and *vice versa*. There were several sorrowful people there, planting flowers on a grave, and a lifeless old man saying his beads before a shrine, but no sacristan, and nobody who had ever heard of Paracelsus. Probably we saw the stone and walked over it fifty times, for there were many so sunken and old that we could make nothing of the letters on them, and over the oldest and most illegible we spent most time and emotion. The graveyard is so full of stones and crosses, and boxes of earth with little gardens in them, that it looks like some sort of sepulchral shop. The crowding in these German churchyards has something positively blasphemous about it, and is noways redeemed by the setting of flowers and hanging of wreaths. The whole expression is of jostle and jam, suggests all sorts of irreverent conjectures, and robs the words "God's Acre" of all meaning. When God has so many acres, it is a sin to so crowd graves.

Around three sides of the San Sebastian churchyard are cloister-like galleries, fenced off by iron railings, and divided into compartments for families. Each enclosure was filled with plants in pots, running ivies, and crosses, usually one large and ugly stone in each compartment, and on the crosses most hideous wreaths and pictures; paper wreaths of rusty black and dingy white, looking more like sea-weed than anything else, twists of old limp crape, old evergreen wreaths darkbrown with age, and common penny pictures with tattered artificial flowers round them. But the final horror was in a sort of grotto near the gate. Behind an iron railing in this grotto were shelves holding rows of ghastly skulls, carefully arranged, piled one above another, and labelled with their names. Whether these were skulls which had been crowded out of their graves by the increase of population in the San Sebastian churchyard, I have no right to say; but this seemed the most probable solution of their being where they were. A mumbling old woman stood by one side, and peered in between the rails, her head shaking with palsy, and her poor skinny hands clutching a rosary. "We are all alike in death, alike in death," muttered she, half to herself and half to us. We walked faster to get away from her. She sounded and felt like an ill omen.

Next on our list came the Church of St. Peter's; with enthusiasm somewhat damped as to graveyards, we drove there. Here, as before, crowded graves, hideous stones, faded wreaths, and no sacristan. We saw in the church a monument to Michael Haydn, brother of the composer, too ugly to be described. We saw St. Rupert's cell, which is a hole in a rock, and St. Rupert's tomb, and then we went on, with still damper enthusiasm, to look up Mozart. This is always the way, I find, in a day of sight-seeing of the historical or memorial order. In the morning, heroes are heroes, and their graves are shrines. By noon, they are nobodies, and you don't care where they are buried; or, at least, you don't believe they are buried where people say they are.

But all our weary indifference vanished the moment we crossed the threshold of the chamber in which Salzburg keeps the relics of her Mozart. We were met by a little sturdy red-faced man, all smiles, from whose lips it would not have surprised us to hear, "Och, an' it's mesilf that's afther bein' glad to say yees: an' ye'll plaze to walk in, shure." Really, it is impossible to accustom one's self to this perpetual recurrence of Cork in South Germany; it sounds as oddly to hear these red-headed, red-faced, freckled fellows speaking German, as it would to hear a squad of laborers on the Erie railroad speaking Latin. However, nothing but German could this little man speak, and an avalanche there was of that, so enthusiastic and warm was he in displaying his cherished relics.

Nothing daunted by our ignorance of his language, he went on and on, pouring out information, till, partly by dint of his reiterations, and partly by the mesmeric effect of his determination that we should understand, we really did comprehend much that he said.

On the walls were portraits of Mozart at different ages, beginning with him at six years old, in the court dress which he wore when he played before Maria Theresa. In this he is a round-cheeked, stupid, obstinate-looking little boy, just such as play in the dirt in every road in Germany to-day.

A large and not very good oil-painting shows him as a young man playing a duet with his sister, to the severe critic their father, who sits by listening with his violin resting on his arm. Above them hangs the picture of their mother, a portrait within a portrait, far the most striking face in the group. If the portraits be good, it is easy to see that however much mechanical facility Mozart may have inherited from his father, the Chapel-Master, his fine quality of genius came from his mother.

Constance Weber, with her hair in indescribable snarl, hangs between Mozart's mother and sister. If she

IN SALZBURG.

habitually wore her hair in that fashion, Mozart's marriage is inexplicable. Farther on she appears again, subdued into the meekest of old ladies, with light curls and a close cap, the Frau Nissen. Her "2d Mann," as the good little Irishman wrote it down for us, was one Nissen, a Danish consul, and a very commonplace-looking Nissen he was, if one may judge from his picture, which looked strangely out of place in the room devoted to relics of Mozart.

In the middle of the room stood Mozart's piano, a small one of only five octaves, but shaped like the grand pianos of to-day. Tinkle, tinkle, went the keys under the little man's red puffy fingers. We did not dare ask him to let it alone, but with each note that he struck it became harder than ever to fancy Mozart's ever having been seated before it. No wonder that Beethoven said disrespectful things of pianos, if this be a specimen of the best their day afforded. What would he and Mozart say to an Erard or Chickering of 1869! Against the wall stood a still more old-fashioned thing with still more pathetic tinkle to its keys, a little old spinet, on which, if we understood correctly, Mozart composed his Requiem. This, too, we wished to see locked forever; how much more touching memorial of a great musician would be his instrument forever locked, never to be played on by mortal hand, than set wide open in a museum to be thrummed by masters and misses in the same mood in which they would carve their names on the legs, if it were permitted.

My letter will be too long, if I tell in detail of all the interesting relics in this room; manuscript music, composed and written by Mozart at the age of eight; old exercise books from which he had practised; four large volumes of manuscript letters; one short note which can be bought for the small sum of two hundred francs; an old frayed and faded satin letter-case, which was embroidered for him by one of his wife's sisters, and which he always carried in his pocket; a seal and a ring which he always wore; these were tossing about loose in a common wooden box, and with them a garnet cross which had belonged to his sister. We said hard things of the Frau Nissen for not having made sure that these treasures were kept sacred from public view.

We bought a bad photograph of the fat little boy in court dress, wrote our names in a big book, where all the musical and many of the unmusical celebrities of the world had written theirs before us, and then we bade good by to the pleasant and voluble German Irishman. On the way home we looked at the bronze statue of Mozart in the centre of the Michael Platz. It is stiff and unmeaning. Then we drove past two houses, in one of which he was born, and in the other lived; but by this time we were tired again, and were seized with sudden doubts as to the truth of the inscriptions on their walls. At any rate, whoever has or has not been born, lived, and died in them, they look exactly like four fifths of the dreary, pale-colored houses in Salzsburg.

THE RETURNED VETERANS' FEST IN SALZBURG.

"' Ah, that I do not know,' quoth he;
'But 't was a famous victory.'"

THE Austrians must have the same happy faculty of being pleased about victories which the old man in the memorable Waterloo ballad had. Seeing them yesterday (June 27, 1869), one would have supposed that the Austrian eagle never slunk out of Italy, and that every one of these veterans had won his title to the name, by helping on a series of glorious successes. On some of the banners there were even names of places where they had memorable defeats, and the wind seemed to take particular pains to keep those banners spread out at full size; but I dare say few people knew the difference: the beer was good, and the bands played the tunes of conquerors.

All the way from Innspruck to Salzburg we had caught glimpses in the little towns of pine arches, green mottoes, and a general expression of "fest"; the Veterans were in our very train, many of them, and we saw them kissing each other, but did not know who they were, nor understand what it all meant, till at Salzburg, in the hall of the Europa, we read the pink placard giving the programme for the Festival the next day.

They begin things early in this country: "Music at six" was first on the list. Sure enough, at six o'clock, there it was, band after band, and a procession of Veterans (all under fifty years of age), marching past our windows. Each man had a bunch of green leaves in his hat, and one involuntarily thought of St. Patrick's Day in New York. At ten o'clock there was to be a

High Mass in one of the churches: armed with a phrase-book and a dictionary, we set out to take part in the proceedings. O the delusion of a phrase-book! Lives there a man who ever found in one the thing he wished to say? Who does not throw it down in a rage a hundred times a month, and resolve never to look in it again? And then in cooler moments, when you have no immediate need of them, the sentences sound so sensible, so probable, that you go back again to your old belief that they must be of use, will certainly come in play to-morrow. As for pocket dictionaries, they are almost as vexing as the phrase-books. If you have knowledge enough to get much good out of one, you have knowledge enough to do without one, and might as well have something else in your pocket. But the blessed language of signs! For that one's respect increases daily; during this one short month in Germany, I have come to doubt whether to be a mute is so terrible a thing as we suppose. Taking into account that they are usually born also deaf, and thereby escape so much dreadful discord of cannon, pianos, and bad English, it is by no means clear which way should swing the balance of their loss and gain.

The great element of probability of our success this day was the certainty that the driver of our *einspanner* undoubtedly wanted to see the same things that we wanted to see; on this it was safe to count. By help of this we saw the Festival, and never once opened our phrase-book or dictionary.

Firstly, the square in which stood the church in which the mass was to be. It was hung with flags, and every window was festooned with long wreaths of green, fastened by rosettes of black and yellow. Unwillingly enough we confessed to each other that, setting patriotism aside, the effect of the hated Austrian colors was finer than that of blue and red. The crowd was great, but quiet and grave to an inexplicable degree. It seems to me, thus far, even truer of the

Germans than of the Americans, that they take their pleasure solemnly. The other day I saw forty or fifty peasants at a wedding dance in a little inn, and, though I watched them for half an hour, not a laugh did I see, except on one or two of the youngest faces, and they were laughing at us. The rest whirled slowly round, with a stolid, uninterested expression which could not be outdone in the Ocean House in Newport. Several of the men had the comfort of cigars in their mouths, which the Newport men can't have. It seems something of a feat to waltz and smoke at the same time.

It was said that more than six thousand Veterans had come to this Festival. I think there were almost as many more of the peasants, who had come in from the country to look at them. It was hard to move in the streets. Country people always seem to have more than the usual allowance of elbow; and when to the world-wide country elbow is added the German woman's hip, the estimate of standing room for each person must be made big. The men were gayer than the women; truer to nature in that, I suppose, than we, since in fish, flesh, and fowl we see always the male with brightest colors. But it strikes civilized eyes oddly to see men with huge shining silver buttons on the fronts of their coats, two and three rows, bright bows of green or red at the knee, and in their hats feathers and flowers and ribbons; while women are wearing plain short black petticoats, and on their heads either sombre black hats, high - crowned, broad-brimmed, and without ornament, except a couple of gold tassels, or else, still worse, a thick black silk kerchief bound tight over the whole head, low on the forehead, down· nearly to the eyebrows, and twisted in some mysterious knot at the back, so as to leave one long ear-like flap hanging down on each side. Anything uglier could not be invented. It made young, good-looking faces hideous; and on old and plain ones the effect was uncanny. Many of the women wore round their necks broad necklaces of twenty or thirty rows of small silver beads, clasped tight in front by a great buckle of colored stones and gilt. These seemed, however, to be worn less for ornament than to prevent or conceal the frightful goitre with which four fifths of them were disfigured. One's first sight of a goitre swelling is something never to be forgotten.

Mingling in picturesquely with the peasants from the country, and the common people of Salzburg, were to be seen here and there showy Austrian officers, English heads of families, with the families behind in waterproof, commercial travellers of all nations, nobilities in fine carriages, and American women, — to be known from all the rest by their quick peering faces, and their being sure to get in everywhere. Really, I think that the day after Babel could not have seen on that memorable plain more sorts of men than made up the crowd in this square yesterday.

At last, by much help from many people, we got into the church and a seat. A High Mass is always an ordeal of endurance; but this one was made endurable by intervals of Mozart's music, and by the Veterans' faces. They filled the seats, and stood in double rows down the central aisle. Had I seen them in New York I should have said, "From where did all these Irishmen come?" And those that did not look like Irishmen looked like Yankees. Dark hair and eyes were the exception; red hair and freckles were common; and almost universal was the hard, keen, overworked look which we know so well in America. The more intelligent the face, the surer it was to have this expression. The poorer peasants looked calmer and stupid. Next me sat a barefooted boy, with a heavy, unawakened face. He wore in his hat a gray feather and an Edelweiss. When I made signs to him that I wanted the Edelweiss, and took it out of his hat, and put fifteen kreutzers in his hand in exchange for it, he looked blankly at the money and at me, as if he had not common belief in his senses. But his mother kissed my hand in gratitude.

At the end of the mass the organ and band struck up one of Wagner's best marches, and we and the Veterans poured out. The Veterans had the best of it though, and got so firmly wedged in the square, ahead of us, that before we could fight our way through to our carriage, we were as tired as ever they were on the fields of Lombardy.

The banners and flags were all stacked on one side of the square, and made a fine show of color beyond the swaying mass of the Veterans' black hats, with the green leaves and feathers in them. From a window on the right, orators began to speak most eloquently, I believe; but I only know that they all gesticulated wildly with white-gloved hands, and waited, like all stump speakers, at the places where they expected the Veterans to throw up their hats and cheer.

In the afternoon the performances were to consist of music, cakes, and ale on the Mönchsberg. This sounded simple and virtuous; but how little we dreamed what it meant till we saw it. Why the Mönchsberg — Monk's Hill — is so called I do not know, unless it be because it is a continuation of the high rocky ridge on which the great castle of Salzburg stands; and in that the archbishops of Salzburg lived, held court, and defied their enemies for centuries. It is a wonderful wall of rock, so steep that it can only be ascended by flights of stairs; so broad that its top spreads out into fields and valleys and groves, as it were, a second story of country, hundreds of feet up in the air. At its narrowest point it has been tunnelled, and the tunnel is four hundred and fifteen feet long. It was built by an Archbishop Sigismond, a hundred years ago, and will keep him in memory so long as the world stands. A clumsy stone head of him stands over the entrance to the tunnel, and looks down into the road, with the superfluous boast, " Te Saxa coquuunter."

They tell you that from bottom to top of the Mönchsberg it is only two hundred and eighty steps. "O," you say gayly, "that is nothing," and spring up. If they had mentioned also that the staircase is for the most part steep as a ladder, and intersected by long stretches of path almost as hard to climb as the ladder, one could better reckon the cost of going up. Also, both staircase and path are very narrow, and when, as yesterday, throngs of people are coming down, it adds sensibly to the fatigue of going up to be obliged to swing on a pivot once in two minutes, to let big German women, big German soldiers with pipes, children by dozens, and men with beer casks go by. We swung off in this way and let so many hundreds pass us, that we almost thought the Festival must be coming to an end. But how we laughed at our want of comprehension of what a German out-door Fest could be, when we first caught sight of the broad, crowded plateau, and realized that the hundreds we had met were only two or three people who had to go home early. I do not know how many acres full of men and women there were. I only know that the space they filled was so large that at the farthest end of it the gay colors of the banners could scarcely be distinguished, and two full bands and an orator could be going on at once and not jangle with each other; and yet from the higher ground the whole could be seen, one great sea of good-fellowship. On the outer edges of the crowd, under trees, were rows of booths; beer, brown-bread, and snaky sausages for the mass; white bread, cakes, and candies for the few; the whole hillside was settee; greener-cushioned never mortals had; but it was too much stuffed with stone, and in spite of the picturesqueness and jollity of the scene, bones would ache, especially if they were withheld by superfluous scruples from doing among Germans exactly as Germans did, and lying down at full length every now and then to rest.

The family groups sitting here were pleasant to see; father, mother, six or eight children, all drinking beer, even the baby that could not speak plain, all nibbling at the ends of sticks of sausage, all good-natured but not talkative.

They do more thinking than their share, this German nation; the world is the better for it, no doubt, but if they could only borrow a laugh from Italy, it would do them good.

Next to us on the hillside sat a young German, evidently a mechanic of some sort, who had brought his sister and sweetheart to the Fest. They had one huge glass mug of beer between them, and I observed that the man drank first and oftenest; for the rest, their feast was of white bread and sausage; and they munched and looked at each other, and looked at each other and munched, and not a dozen times did they open their mouths to speak during the two hours and a half that we sat by their side, yet they looked the picture of content.

The Veterans, though there were six thousand of them on the ground, were lost in the crowd. Now and then half a dozen of them would be seen sitting and smoking together, but they formed no distinguishable feature of the occasion which bore their name. Just as we were unwillingly beginning to think of the stairs which lay between us and our carriage, a sudden stir among the people, and much taking off of hats, announced the arrival of dignitaries.

There they were, at our very elbow, and no instinct had told us, — the Archduke, and several ladies and officers of the court. By some magic chairs appeared, and in a few minutes the group were seated in the centre of a hollow square of staring faces. I never supposed that divinity hedging a king could be so undignified and droll as was the fat pompous little man who went up and down before and behind, and pushed the people back if they crowded up too close. Even at risk of getting a wave from his official hand, we walked several times quite close to the backs of the sublime people, and took our fill of looking at court clothes. White muslin over blue silk, Valenciennes lace, and fine white straw hats with blue crape streamers for the women, very dainty and pretty, but just such as any woman may buy in New York at Virefolet's or Baillard's; but for the officers — ah, are there elsewhere in the world such colors as the cherry scarlet gray blue, pomegranate red, and deep sea green which these Austrian officers wear? And then the fit of them! It is profane to suppose they are cut and made. It is the coats that come first; and the men are melted over night and poured in in the morning.

The Archduke has light blue eyes, and a weak cruel face; I was glad he was only the Emperor's brother; I could fancy his doing deadly harm with power. The women were beautiful, the first beautiful women I have seen in Germany. Full into the face of the youngest and most beautiful of them, the handsomest of the officers puffed clouds on clouds of tobacco-smoke as he stood talking with her. This universal smoking in Germany is enough to cure one of all fancy for the practice; cars, dining-rooms, all made insufferable by it; and women sitting by and breathing it all in, hour after hour, as if it were the wholesomest, most delicious air.

We lingered till sunset; then, though nobody appeared to be going away, we found the stairways just as crowded as before with ups and downs; until midnight, they told us the Fest would last.

This morning at six o'clock, music again, and more Veterans, but such different-looking Veterans from those of yesterday! Slowly they dragged along to the railway-station to take the early train; the green leaves in their hats drooping and wilted, and their whole atmosphere bearing that unmistakable expression, common, the whole world over, to "next morning."

A MORNING IN THE ETRUSCAN MUSEUM IN THE VATICAN.

CRETE had a Labyrinth, and Rome has a Vatican. I wish I knew how many times the Labyrinth could be contained in the Vatican, and if it would not seem a place for plain sailing in comparison. When you read in Murray that the Vatican has four thousand rooms, it conveys no precise idea to your mind; when you look at the huge, irregular pile itself, which appears to have no particular beginning and never to leave off, and to make St. Peter's look trig and tidy beside it, even then you do not comprehend; when you are told that for many years the little chapel of San Lorenzo, with its solemn frescos by Fra Angelico, was lost in this labyrinth, — utterly lost out of the memory of man, and was accidentally discovered by a German artist, who had to climb in through a window, — even then you are not fully alive to it. Not until you have entered, and toiled and wandered for hours, trying to find some gallery or chapel to which you have been a dozen times, and which you proudly assured your confiding friend you could " go straight to," do you begin to realize what the Vatican is like. If you could only " bark" your way, as you do in other wildernesses, there would be some hope; but, if you ever do turn the same corner twice, you never know it, and the more you try to remember just how you went the last time, the less likely you will be to go that way. There are in the guide-books plans of the Vatican. They are of use, if carefully studied at home; but once take them out on the ground, after you are already a little confused, and you are hopelessly lost. Your bewilderment is instantly heightened by a sense of conspicuous humiliation, which is unbearable. Twos and threes, and sixes, and sevens of all nations come immediately in sight, walking toward and past you, — heartless Levites, who know the road. Never have I found the Samaritan of the Vatican; no, though I have sat begging by the way. But I have always comforted myself by believing that the Levites also got lost before they had gone far; in fact, I myself have sometimes come upon them, later, standing stock-still and helpless, while I, in my turn, passed by on the other side.

It was on one of the rawest of the raw days for which winter in sunny Italy is not, but ought to be, famous, that we saw the Etruscan Museum. We had walked round and round it, and over it, and under it, till we had almost ceased to believe in it, before we found the door. Once in, we should have known, even without the inscription over the entrance, that we were in the right place. On three sides of the small vestibule lay life-size figures of terra-cotta; a man, crowned with a wreath of laurel, and two women, wearing necklaces, bracelets, and rings. They were a good-deal chipped and knocked, these old Etrurians, and one of the women must have been a sad fright in her day, if her portrait were a good one; but, true or false, high or low, there they lay, three citizens of Etruria, in solid shapes of stone, as big as they were when alive, and more famous than they ever dreamed of being. On the walls were fastened several horses' heads, taken from the entrance to somebody's tomb. Among the Etrurians, it seems, the horse was an emblem of the passage of the soul to the other world; from which it is fair to infer that break-neck riding and driving are not modern inventions. In the middle of the vestibule was a great scaldino, filled with red-hot coals; and the two custodi of the museum stood over it, blue and shivering, trying to warm their hands. Of all flimsy pretences, the scaldino is the flimsiest and most pretentious. Why a huge kettle of coals, which glow red to the eye, and breathe hot and choking to the lungs, cannot keep you warm five minutes, is unexplainable; but it does not. You rub your hands over them with a vigor which would warm you anywhere, and you might as well spare yourself the unwholesome stifle of the scorched air.

When the custodi saw us take from under our cloaks a big green bound book, and walk off independently into the first chamber on the right, they roused a little from their torpidity, and followed us to see what manner of people those might be who needed none of their help. Ah! we were luckier people than they knew, for the book was "Dennis's Cities and Cemeteries of Etruria." Dennis's description of this museum is so accurate as to seem marvellous when we are told that it was written entirely from memory, — the Pontifical Government, for some reasons best known to itself, not allowing any memoranda to be made in the rooms.

The first chamber is filled with cinerary urns, or ash-chests. Undertaking must have been a more cheerful trade in those days than in these, and have offered openings for fine artistic talent; in fact, these carved ash-chests looked so little like things belonging to burial, that it was hard to believe that they had not been meant originally for some other purpose. There was an endless variety of them, — square chests, oblong chests, round chests, oval chests, big chests, little chests, high and low and wide and narrow chests, — carved figures on all the lids and on the sides, some of them mythological signs, some of them allegorical representations of the last journey of the inhabitants of the chest, in which the soul, looking in nowise unlike the body, is seen, wrapped in a toga, sitting upright astride a horse, which is led by a frisky little demon. On shelves above the chests were heads of the same terra-cotta, portraits of the dead. There had been handles to the lids. Some of the heads of little children were very sweet and lifelike; one, especially, looked so like a baby I know, that I started, and wondered in my heart if really just such another darling had laughed and played on earth two thousand years ago. At the end of the chamber was a large chest, in which had been buried the ashes of a husband and wife, who were perhaps fortunate enough to be "not divided" in their death, as their full-length figures are carved on the lid, lying fondly clasped in each other's arms.

In the centre of the next room stood a huge sarcophagus, of great interest as an antiquity, carved and carved and carved again with scenes from the stories of Clytemnestra, and Orestes, and the Theban Brothers, and from thence all the way back to the brothers Cain and Abel, one would think. There are minds which take a species of anatomical, statistical, archæological interest in this sort of thing; and will tell you, down to the last joint of Agamemnon's little finger, what it all means. But I confess I listen to their accounts with a fatiguing mixture of reverence and incredulity. On shelves in the corner of this room were some little stone huts, not more than ten inches high, which interested me far more than the great historical sarcophagus. They were two ash-chests of the very oldest forms, made to imitate the shape of the low, round huts of skins, stretched over cross-poles, in which the Latins lived. They made you think of beehives. Ashes and bits of burnt bone were in them still. They were found, with many other rare things, in a big jar, hid away in one of the Alban Hills; and the people whose dust they held died before Rome was a city.

After one more room of terra-cottas, urns, statues, and bass-reliefs, you come to the rooms of vases. There are four of these rooms, and the vases are arranged on pedestals and shelves. The first thing you do is to resolve that you will learn the names of the different shapes. In a few minutes you persuade yourself that you know, and will remember, which is an amphora, a pelice, a calpis, and a patera. For that one day you will; but in a week all that you will know will be that the amphora, and the calpis, and the pelice are all beautiful kinds of jars, and that the pateræ and pelices are the shapes which lucky people who have them use for card-receivers.

The rarest and most beautiful vases are on single pedestals, in the centre of the rooms. Mythological and historical scenes are painted on all of them. One of these has a picture of Ajax and Achilles playing at the game of "Morra," which is played all over Italy to-day. As I write, some handsome Albanese men are playing it under my window, and shouting out the numbers so loudly that I cannot, do what I will, help keeping run of their game. It looks stupid enough to one not born to it. Two men thrust out their right hands at each other, shutting up some fingers and opening others. Each man calls out on the instant what he thinks the whole number of extended fingers. If both are right or both are wrong, nothing is counted; but if one only is right, it counts one for him. Nobody would suppose that a mistake could ever be made in calling the number; but it is played with lightning quickness, and there could not be so much excitement in it if blunders were not frequent. On this vase Ajax calls out "Four!" and Achilles "Three!" (the words, printed in Greek letters, coming out of their mouths,) and both the heroes look as intent as if they were planning a battle.

Some of the scenes are very comic, and belong to all time. For instance, a short-legged fat man, looking up hopelessly at his lady-love, sitting in a high window, and a kind friend appearing in the distance, bringing a ladder to his assistance. This was none the funnier when it was meant to show Jupiter serenading Alcmena, and Mercury running to help him up, than it would be as a passage from the life of our Mr. Falstaff. On another vase is a picture of a tall boy, with a hoop in one hand and a cock in the other. His whole expression shows that he has stolen the cock, and is trying to make off slyly with it, — which is a hard thing to manage, as he has no clothes on. Striding along behind him comes a man, either the owner of the cock or the boy's teacher, with a long switch in his hand, from which there is plainly no escape for the young thief.

In the last vase-room are many curious goblets, — some with great eyes painted on them; some with " Hail, drink ! " which seems a good and friendly motto to set on the rim of glasses in a hospitable house. But now we have reached the ninth room, fullest of wonders. To begin with, what is this? A small iron bedstead? Exactly that. And I dare say generations of single Etrurians slept on it. Finally, it came to be the bier-bedstead for the last long sleep of somebody; and in his tomb at Cervetri it was found. Monsignore Regolini and General Galassi discovered this tomb; and it has ever since been known by their names. Antiquaries believe it to be three thousand years old; so it is possible to please one's self with the fancy that the great warrior or priest who was buried in it died of having eaten too much peacock at the first supper given to Æneas after his arrival in Italy. He must have been the best-dressed man at supper, if he wore the magnificent gold ornaments in which he was buried. Here they are, outshining all the other gold and silver array in the large glass case in the centre of the room, — a broad gold breastplate, embossed with twelve bands of figures, sphinxes, goats, panthers, deer, and winged demons; another ornament for the head, made of two large oval plates, fastened together by a broad band, embossed in the same way, with smaller plates and fringes to hang down behind, bracelets several inches broad, ear-rings several inches long, all matching the breastplate. No worker in gold to-day can equal the shaping and chasing of these ornaments. In an inner room of this same tomb were found also other bracelets, armlets, wreaths, chains, ear-rings, and brooches, — all of the same exquisite workmanship; and it is supposed that some woman of high rank, possibly a priestess, was buried there. One wonders whether it were honesty or superstition which kept tombs so safe in Etruria, and involuntarily fancies the fate of such treasures if buried in public cemeteries to-day.

It is hard to leave this room; but at the end of a day we should not have seen all. On the walls hang rusty metal mirrors, fans, candelabras, shields dented in many fights, visors, axes, javelins, cuirasses, spears, and all shapes and sizes of armor. On shelves are innumerable and inexplicable tools and instruments, — forks, and pins, and ladles, and strainers, and pails, and jugs; in cases by the windows are pounds and pounds of odds and ends, — coins, and weights, and clasps, and little metal bulls, and fishes, and cats, and daggers, and chains, and bits of bone, looking for all the world as if they had been emptied out of some boy-giant's pocket. Here is a curious stone bottle, — an ink-bottle, they say, — on which some idle scholar scratched off a bit of his primer, "Ba, Be, Bi, Bo, Bu," in old Pelasgic letters. Going to school must have been as stupid then as now. Here is a pair of clogs; yes, real Etruscan clogs, bronze, filled in with light wood. No. 4½ at least, and much worn by some enterprising woman who went out in all weathers in Veii. Here is the brazier by which she dried her feet when she came home, and the shovel and tongs and poker lying across the top, just as she kept them. The tongs are on wheels and end in snakes' heads, the shovel-handle is a swan's neck, and the poker or rake finishes off with a human hand.

Near these is an oval silver casket, most exquisitely carved, found in a tomb at Vulci. The handle is made of two swans, one bearing a boy and the other a girl, holding on by their arms round the swans' necks. In this were found a little hand-mirror, two broken bone combs (O unneat woman of Vulci), two hair-pins, an ear-pick, and two small pots of rouge.

Three things more, and we have finished our glance at this room, — a Roman war-chariot, found on the Appian Way, and looking triumphant still; a great arm and dolphin's tail, of bronze, cast up by the sea at Civita Vecchia.

The next room is hung with paintings, exact copies of the painted walls of the tombs of Tarquinii and Veii; and the next and last is the "Chamber of the Tomb," a long, narrow, low, dark room, fitted up in imitation of the common Etruscan tombs, — stone couches on three sides, bronze and pottery hanging on the walls and standing about, — an exact reproduction, they say, of a real tomb. But it gives you no thrill, probably makes you smile, and remember things you have seen in panoramas. The real presences have been in the other rooms.

We went out through the Gallery of Inscriptions, which is one of the solemn places. On the left hand the tombstones of the early Christians, on the right those of their enemies. It is touching to read these records of the first triumphs of Christianity's first faith over the grave. "A sweet soul, who sleeps in peace," is an inscription constantly recurring. Among the Pagan inscriptions are no such comforting words; only grief and gloom.

In the court-yard the Pope's gay guards were flaunting up and down like enchanted tiger-lilies, making ready for his Holiness to take such modest airing in a close red coach as befits the representative of Jesus Christ; the beggars buzzed up round our ears; the scorching sirocco blew in our faces; and in a few moments we had bridged the gap of twenty centuries, and taken up again our own little thread of to-day.

ALBANO DAYS.

THERE are but seven in a week. That is their only fault. How clever those gentlemanly fellows, Pompey and Domitian, were, to put their villas on this hill; and as for the cruelties said to have been committed in Domitian's amphitheatre, a few rods from our hotel, we have decided that there is some mistake about that. In Rome one can believe in all tales of old tortures — and new ones too, for that matter. Even when the larks sing loudest in the Coliseum the stones cry out louder; the air reeks with sirocco vapors, and seems not yet purged from the odor of blood. But in the pure, sun-flooded air of this hill, which must always have been full of marvellous delights, it is impossible to believe that bad men ever did bad deeds. Whatever they might have been in Rome, they were virtuous as soon as they got here. I cannot fancy Domitian's ever doing anything worse than having a few larks killed for supper; and I am sure he spent most of his afternoons lying on purple thyme on the shores of the Alban Lake (as we lay yesterday), perhaps slyly reading the good sayings of the poor Epictetus whom he had banished. We read yesterday what Epictetus said "concerning those who seek preferment in Rome"; and, as we looked over at the hot, smoky domes and spires, it seemed hard to believe that any one going thither, even if he were "met by a billet from Cæsar," could choose to stay.

Albano is 1,250 feet above the sea, says Murray. That may be true, say we; but we know it is much more than that above Rome. Have we not been looking

longingly at it for months, set high on the side of the
Alban Hills? From every height in Rome to which
we wearily climbed we saw it, triumphant with banners
of clouds, and crowned with green of forests, saying as
plainly as tower could say, "Come up here, and I will
do you good." When the watchmen in the old Sara-
cen towers saw the pirate-ships coming over the Mediterranean, they sounded the alarm, and all the people
in the plains fled into the mountains for safety. To-day
the towers are in ruins, and no corsairs sail from Africa
across the sea; but the sirocco, a more deadly foe, comes
in their stead, hotter and hotter with each day of May,
and wise souls escape to high places.

Of all those within easy reach of Rome, Albano is
best. It is only an hour off by the cars. And even at
the railroad station you are met by beauty and good
cheer — a garden full of roses, and white thorne, and
wall-flowers, and ranunculus; and a station-master
who, if he treats you as well as he treated us, will
give you a big bunch of all, and look hurt and angry
when you offer to pay him. From this garden to the
village of Albano, two miles and a half, over a good
road, up, up, up! the air grows purer minute by minute; the Campagna behind sinks and stretches and
fades, and becomes only another sea, purpler and more
restless-looking than the broad band of the Mediterranean into which it melts. On each side are vineyards,
looking now like miniature military encampments, with
play-guns of cane stacked by fives and threes, and little
soldiers in green going in and out and playing leap-frog
among them, so fantastic are the baby-vines in their first
creeping. Olives, gray and solemn, sharing none of the
life and joy, most pathetic of trees. The first man who
saw an olive-tree must have known that there had been
Gethsemane. Never else could such pathos have been
put into mere color; they could never have been so
gray before that night. Still up and up! It is a long
two and a half miles. The bells tinkle slowly at the

horse's head. The driver's neck bends suspiciously to one side; he is half asleep. You would not be sorry if the horse and he dozed off together, and you stood still for an hour to look. On the right hand is a valley garden, an old lake-bed, set full of vines and fig-trees and fruit-trees in full flower, and wheat, and all the numberless and exquisite-leaved "greens" which Italy boils, eats, and manages to grow fat on. We find them beautiful everywhere but on the dinner-table. High on the crater-like side of this garden is the tower of Ariccia, looking like a gray bird which had just lit on its way up to Monte Cavo. Between Ariccia and Albano is a sharp ravine; and the sensible Pius IX., some twenty years ago, built a fine stone viaduct across it, toward the cost of which we pay half a franc each time we drive over. But only blind men could grudge the money. From every point it is a most beautiful feature in the landscape, with its three tiers of arches; and from its top you look down two hundred feet into the valley garden on one side, and two hundred feet into the tops of a forest of trees on the other. You follow the valley garden till it loses itself in the Campagna; the Campagna, till it loses itself in the Mediterranean, which glistens in the sun twelve miles off; and you hear coming up from the forest the voices of thrushes and nightingales and cuckoos and larks, till you believe that there must be a bird-fancier's shop in one of the old gray houses joining the bridge. To stand on this bridge for an hour is to see Italian country-life in drama. The donkeys, the men, and the women of Albano and Ariccia and Gensano act their little parts, and are gone. We stayed late at this play last night. The wardrobes were poor, but the acting was nature itself; such pantomime, such chorus! Priests in black, looking always like a sort of ecclesiastical crow, such silly solemnity in their faces, so much slow flap to their petticoats and the brims of their hats; barefooted monks, rolled up in cloaks of faded brown — they also have their similitude,

H

and look as the olive-trees might if they gathered their rusty skirts around them and hobbled out for a walk; workmen, going home from the fields, with odd hoes and pickaxes over their shoulders; women, with the same hoes and pickaxes, going home from the same work in the same fields, and carrying also, firm-set on their heads, bundles, loads of wood, little wine-barrels or water-jars, or anything else which it can happen to an Albanese woman to need to carry. No one gives herself any more trouble about her barrel, or jar, or load of wood, than if it were a second head, which she had worn all her life. They talked and laughed as if it were morning instead of night. They were not tired. Watch them at what they call work, and you will see why. As the sun sank lower the crowd of laborers thinned; the farmers, one degree better off, came riding on donkeys. Two men and a boy on one donkey; four large bundles of wood and one woman on one donkey; four large casks of wine, a bundle of hay, two chairs, some iron utensils, and two small children on one donkey. O the comic tragedy of donkey! the hopeless arch of their eyebrows, the abjectness of their tails, and the vicious twist of their ankles! Nobody can watch them long without becoming wretched. Israelites, coolies, and negroes, — all they have died of misfortunes; but the donkey is the Wandering Jew of misery among animals, and Italy, I think, must be his Ghetto.

Before we reached the hotel we had come upon another drama, in the street, — a lottery drawing; prize, two hens. If it had been two thousand scudi, there could not have been much more excitement. Fifty chances had been sold. The street held its breath, while a storekeeper dropped the counters one by one into a box, held by a rosy boy, mischievous enough, but too young to cheat. Then the boy put in his little brown fingers, and drew out one: "Thirty!" Then the street broke out into chatter for an instant, guessing and betting what would come next; then held its breath stiller than ever. "Thirty-one!" "Thirty-one!" No "Thirty-one" answered. "Thirty-one" was sick at home, or had married a wife, and could not come; and the street grudged him his two hens all the more that he was not on hand to carry them off. The hens screamed and scuffled; the storekeeper crammed them back into a coop on his window; and the street went back to its work, i. e. to sitting about, smoking, and knitting, and selling saddles and fish and shoes and salad and handkerchiefs and donkeys and calico and wine all along its doorsteps, never by any chance being under roof, so long as there is daylight.

We took our sunsetting at the Villa Doria. It is a princely thing of the rich Romans to throw their beautiful villas open to the public. Could it be safely done in America? I fear our people are not gentle enough, and have too much money to spend on cake and peanuts. Here no harm comes of it. In the Villa Doria are ilex-trees which are a kingdom in themselves. It would not seem unnatural to make obeisance to them. They stand in groups, making long vistas, high arches, locking and interlocking their branches, their trunks looking as old as the masses of ruins among them; and the ruins belonged to Pompey's walls. At sunset the sun slants under and through these ilexes; the purple and wine-colored bands of the Campagna and sky beyond seem to narrow closer and closer round the hill, and flocks of birds wheel and sing. In the Villa Barberini, higher up, is a great field of stone-pines, stately as a council of gods. No wonder that Theodore Parker, when he saw a stone-pine, asked that one be set on his grave. No tree grows which has such bearing of a solemn purpose. Such morning and evening as this make a day in Albano. Words give but glimpse and no color. For other days there are other villas, and fields, and ruins, tombs of Pompey and of Aruns, Lake Nemy and its village, Gensano, and Marino, and

Rocca di Papa, all within easy reach and always in sight. There are four lovely winding avenues of trees, called Gallerie, where you drive for miles under arches of gray ilex as grand as stone, and where the oldest trees are propped by pillars to save their strength and keep them alive. There is Monte Cavo, the highest of the Alban Hills, one thousand feet above Albano, where there used to be a temple, and Julius Cæsar went up to be crowned one day. To think that an English cardinal dared to pull down the ruined temple, and build a convent and church in its stead!

Some of the roads are very smooth and good, others are rough and narrow. For these you must take donkeys, and go perhaps two miles an hour; but, going so slowly, you will have great reward in learning the faces of the wayside flowers and getting into fellowship with the lizards. Fifty different kinds of flowers I counted in one afternoon, all growing wild by the road; and the other day, on the road to Marino, I made acquaintance with two lizards, who were finer than Solomon in all his glory, and had a villa with a better view than the Barberini.

A SUNDAY MORNING IN VENICE.

"SCOTCH PRESBYTERIAN CHURCH!" There were the words, in white letters on a blue ground. We rubbed our eyes and sprang up in our gondola. Yes, we were in a gondola, and we were on the Grand Canal in Venice. But there were the words, and no mistake; white on blue, so plain that he who rowed might read. "Scotch Presbyterian Church!" We had seen, unmoved, the palaces of Doges, Titians, Marco Polos, Lord Byrons, and Dictator Ruskins; we had looked the Lion of St. Marks in the eye, and the statue of St. Theodore out of countenance; but for this we were not prepared. A Presbyterian meeting-house on the Grand Canal! The resolute little sign held our eyes with a fascination amounting almost to an uncanny spell; the distant hand-organ seemed droning off into a sleepy Dundee; our good Luigi's features seemed changing into something more stern than their wont; the measured sweep of his oar took on a solemn significance; and when the legless beggar who haunts the Grand Canal rowed up by our side, we should not have been surprised if, instead of his usual whine of "qualche cosa," he had struck up "Life is the time to serve the Lord." "Scotch Presbyterian Church!" The letters defied perspective, and looked bigger and bigger as we glided away.

"Luigi, is there really a church there?"

"O yes, yes, Signora; every Sunday."

"Very well. Next Sunday we will go to it."

Luigi looked glad. The Sunday before, when we

went out to take our evening row, he asked with timid interest if we had been to mass in the morning. On hearing that we had not, his face clouded; and I think that after that his gentle soul had been troubled by misgivings as to our future. But now he was reassured. If we could not be good Catholics, it was something that we had a worship of our own. Perhaps, after all, we should not be left forever in purgatory. There was real liberality in the approbation, softened perhaps by pity, with which he smiled on us, as we stepped out of our gondola at the picturesque low stone door, over which was the sign "Scotch Presbyterian Church."

We were too early by an hour. Even Scotch Presbyterianism had so far accommodated itself to the air of Venice as to postpone the hour of morning service till half past eleven. The door was shut. What should we do? By way of making the antithesis of things sharper yet, we might hear a Roman Catholic mass first.

"Luigi, we will go to St. Mark's." Luigi looked gladder still. Surely his "forestiere" were in the right path to-day. His oar dipped fast, and in a few minutes we had slipped into the little sombre canal which creeps under the Bridge of Sighs, and were walking off, in the sunshine of Luigi's patronizing smile, through the court-yard of the Doge's Palace, into the great solemn shadows of St. Mark's. It was crowded,—the first time I had seen it so; but even the stir and hum of so many living men and women did not seem to give it a breath of the atmosphere of to-day. Each man seemed, as soon as he entered and knelt down, to be transformed, as by a magician's touch, into an enchanted figure which had been praying there for centuries. The priests moved to and fro; the incense films rose, and floated, and faded; invisible bells tinkled sharply. It was only a common, low mass, but it seemed like the worship of some old spell-bound race doomed to kneel, and pray, and swing censers till some predestined deliverer should come, possibly the next hour, possibly not for a thousand years, to set them free. Perhaps it is strange that the worship of the Roman Catholic Church should ever seem like anything less than this. Surely her millions are spellbound, waiting the deliverer who will one day come. Involuntarily I looked up at the giant apostles and saints frescoed in blue and crimson and gold high overhead; and I half thought that they stirred, as if the hour was near. No; it was only a misty sunbeam stealing around pillar after pillar, and lighting up their stone faces with quivering colors of life. After the mass was over, a fair, gentle-faced priest pattered out from some dark recess behind the high altar, and, standing in front of the railing, read bans of matrimony for many men and women.

They were really alive then, and they married and were given in marriage, these weird Venetians who made up the spectacle at which I had been looking. I saw also that a young girl nudged her neighbor and smiled scornfully as one name was read. Ah, they had also envies and scandals! From these, too, must come a deliverer. The incense will not help them, nor the naming of saints, nor the keeping of days; only the Lord himself from heaven. As I walked slowly out among the kneeling figures, I thought of Paul in the Athenian temples, and what glorious thrills must have warmed his blood when he called out his watchword of Christ in the midst of their altars.

When we again reached the room of the "Scotch Presbyterian Church" the minister was reading the first hymn. The room was small, with three chintz-curtained windows opening into a green and sunny garden. I much suspect the desk of having been only a temporary arrangement of chairs and tables, with a dark tapestry flung over them. Every seat was filled; there were, perhaps, forty men and women, earnest-looking, plain people, English and Americans.

We sat down just outside, in a small anteroom, of which one door opened wide into the sunny garden and the other on the Grand Canal. In the garden, on my right, birds sang riotously; on the canal I could see gondolas and great black barges constantly going up and down. Before me stood the young minister, reading, with his odd Scotch accent, that good verse of the Bible, which says that we must bear one another's burdens. As he read it, it sounded "Bayre ye one anoother's buddens"; but the doctrine was none the worse for the brogue. Just as I had fairly delivered myself up to the enjoyment of the whole scene, I was touched on the shoulder, and an elderly man, having somewhat the bearing of a Western congressman, said: "Ma'am, are these the American services?"

There was an emphasis on the word "American" which suggested that he had the Fourth of July — stars, stripes, fireworks, eagle, and all — in his pockets. I strangled a wicked impulse to reply, even under the minister's very face, that I did not know what "American services" were, and answered: "I only know the sign above the door is Scotch Presbyterian Church."

In a loud, resentful whisper he rejoined: "I was informed that the American services were held at the house of the American Consul." All this time his family stood waiting in the rear — mother, two young misses, a boy fifteen, and a dear, sturdy little baby-boy, possibly three years old. I replied again, as gravely as I could: "There is no American Consul in Venice at present. The English Church service is held in the house of the English clergyman." He turned away and strode out, the family procession following. No worshipping under foreign flags would this patriotic family do. The American service or none! The earnest young minister went on with his Bible-reading, and I had almost forgotten the interruption, when lo! a stir at the door, and there they were again, — the

A SUNDAY MORNING IN VENICE.

discomfited patriots returning crestfallen, after I know not how much research and consultation, — ready at last to make the best of Scotch "services," since American could not be found.

The mother had, I thought, a sweet and gentle face; and, as she took the baby in her lap, I prepared myself for an hour of delight in watching them. Alas, what a mistaken hope! The baby was restless. Who would not be, for that matter, with the tempting garden and singing-birds on one hand, and the fairy spectacle of the boats and the water on the other? Moreover, the mercury stood at eighty degrees, or higher: only by help of much fanning did the grown-up people keep still. What was a baby to do? Of course he tried to slip down and run out; and of course, before long, he began to fret and whimper. At last she rose, took him by the hand, and walked into the garden. My heart gave a bound of joy. "O," thought I, "kind, sensible mother! She will sit in the garden with him, and let him play."

"O mamma! me be good, me be good!" came down the garden-alley in those unmistakable tones of terror which are never heard from the lips of any children except those whose nerves have had the shock and the pain of blows. All the sunlight seemed in that instant to die out of the fair green place. But I said to myself, "Poor darling. He will escape one whipping at least. She will never dare to whip him here." Mistaken again. In less than a minute there came from the distance that sharp, quick scream which means but one thing; once, twice, three times, — then all was still. In a few minutes more they returned; the poor baby subdued into a sort of hysterical silence, worse to see than violent crying, his cheeks crimson, and his eyes full of tears. I buried my face in my hands, and tried to take comfort in remembering how many friendly diseases there are which carry little children to heaven. The words of the sermon sounded to me like inarticulate murmur; now and then came the refrain, "Bear ye one another's burdens." How I wished I could bear that baby's! For perhaps one half-hour he sat perfectly still; but, at the age of three, memory is short and animal life is strong. He had a splendid physique, full of nervous overflow; it was simply a physical impossibility for him to sit still long. He began again to make struggles and impatient sounds. Again she took him up, this time with impatience and irritation in her manner, and led him into the sunny garden. Louder and more piteous came the cry, "O mamma! me be good, me be good!" and the poor, sturdy little legs held back with all their force as she dragged him down the walk. I could hear no more. I fled through the opposite door, and sprang into our gondola so quickly that Luigi came running up with alarm and inquiry on his rugged face. In my excitement and indignation I found even Italian language enough to tell him what had driven me from the church. "Ah, it was very terrible. No wonder the signora could not bear it. Now he (Luigi) had four children, one little girl only a year old; and never, no, never, did he strike them. He always talked with them; never a blow, — O no!"

Ah, polite and courteous Luigi! Six months' observation of the ways of Italian fathers and mothers made it hard for me to believe that his children led lives of such exceptional peace. The Italians never entirely "grow up" themselves; and they are with their children much as children are with kittens — affectionate and cruel by turns. But it was at that moment an unspeakable comfort to me to hear Luigi tell his sympathizing lie.

When the services were ended, I watched with morbid eagerness to see the baby once more. As the gondola of the patriotic family rowed away, I saw the poor little fellow's flushed face lying, weary and listless, on his father's shoulder. All day it haunted me.

I could not shake off the fear, so well do I know that type of parent, that he had, after he reached the hotel, a third whipping, — such a one as is called in fiendish satire "a good whipping." Poor baby! Three whippings and a Scotch Presbyterian service in one forenoon; and he is only three years old, and has at least eight or nine years more to live under the lash. Poor baby!

VENICE, ITALY, June 1.

THE CONVENT OF SAN LAZZARO IN VENICE.

THE longer one stays in Venice the more of a magnet the Lido becomes, and the surer one is to row thither daily. Its low line looks one minute like a mirage, the next like firm and pleasant land; one day it is gone, and the next morning back in its place again; and all the while you know that, shifting and shadowy as it seems, it is really the one solid bit of genuine earth which Venice owns — her life-preserver, so to speak, without which she would not keep her head above water through a single storm. The Adriatic pounds away at the outer edge of it, macadamizing the beach in pink and white with broken shells, but it gains no ground. The quieter sea on the inner side is at work just as industriously, engineering for the harbor defence, sifting and piling the sand which hidden currents bring, night and day, from the feet of the Alps. They come so overloaded that they spill by the way; and, in consequence, there is no straight road to any island in all the Lagoons. Suddenly, without any warning, you find yourself running aground on sand-banks, and have to row many an extra mile to get round them; and, what is more surprising still, at sunset are to be seen men walking about in all directions, apparently on the water. There is no miracle in it, however. These Peters sink only half-way to their knees; and are buoyed up by no greater faith than that they will on the morrow sell at a good price, to Venetian fishermen, the poor sidling crabs which they are scooping up by handfuls on the sand-banks.

THE CONVENT OF SAN LAZZARO. 125

But when one sails Lido-ward, no marvels of men walking on water, no hindrance of unexpected mud countries to be coasted, no glories of color in the sky, — no, not even when a day is setting, — can long withhold his eyes from the Convent of San Lazzaro. Loveliest of all lovely islands in the Lagoons, it seems, in some lights, to be floating, and rising, and sinking on the smooth water, like a great red lily, with gray battlement calyx folding about it, and a fringe of green beneath. Then one stray petal flutters off in the wind; that is the fiery flag of the Sublime Porte, with its pale waning crescent. The dwellers on San Lazzaro are subjects of the Sultan. Then a soft bell-note swings out from the slender bell-tower on the left; it is the hour for vespers. The dwellers on San Lazzaro say prayers after the fashion of the Latins.

But neither the Sultan's yoke nor the rule of the Latin Church casts any shadow of burden or weariness over the faces of the monks of San Lazzaro. Such peaceful contentedness I have never seen, except in a child's eyes, as beamed in the smile of the brother who welcomed us, and introduced us to the Egyptian mummy who (should one say who, or which, of a mummy?) occupies the place of state in one of the three fine library-rooms which are shown to strangers. He took us a little by surprise, — the mummy. We had not looked for him in an Armenian convent. But, with the exception of his features, he was handsome; and the bead coverlid in which he was tucked up, and the painted box he journeyed in, were very fine. One could not help wondering, in looking at him, what his next transition would be, and if he did not get out of his glass case at night and study Armenian by starlight. Nowhere could he do it better than in these libraries, whose windows look out over rose and fig trees to the sea, and whose shelves are loaded with the rarest Armenian manuscripts.

Some of the illuminated copies of the Bible are very

rare and beautiful. One of the most beautiful of all, though not the oldest, was written and illuminated by one man, probably the work of his whole lifetime; but his name is not even known. Another one, very old and rare, once belonged to an Armenian queen; and the monk showed to us with great reverence a paragraph in it which was written by her own hand. They have their share of devotion to royalty, even these simple-hearted monks; for on the table in the first library-room, where the visitors are requested to write their names, we found a separate book for the names of kings and queens and nobilities. In it we saw the somewhat cramped signatures of poor Maximilian and Carlotta. Lord Byron's autograph occupied a still more distinguished place, being framed by itself and hung in the window. It was written both in English and in Armenian; so he made that much progress during the months that he lived and studied at San Lazzaro. The table at which he wrote is shown, and the monks appear to regard his having lived with them as an honor. This struck us as a singular inversion of the true order of things; Lord Byron seeming to us the person honored by the arrangement.

We saw the refectory and the kitchen, both as spotlessly neat as if they belonged to an establishment of Shakers. A huge black cat in the kitchen had become so thoroughly imbued with the monkish view of women that he sputtered savagely at sight of our party. "Poor Pussy," in the gentlest of feminine voices, produced no effect on him, except to set his back still higher in the air.

In the printing-room six lay-brothers were busily at work running off the sheets of a translation of Æschylus into Armenian. In the cool stone stables twenty-seven Swiss cows were eating their fresh clover, mowed that morning on the Lido. In the mouth of a great artesian well, under a thatched straw roof, were floating twelve pails of rich cream and milk, ready to be sold

THE CONVENT OF SAN LAZZARO. 127

that evening to the Hotel Danielli, in Venice. In the pleasant, airy school-room, eighteen Armenian boys were studying away, — and hating it, I suppose, like boys of any other nation. In chambers here and there, which we might not see, were learned fathers, studying, translating, writing, and planning, all for the instruction of the Armenian people. In one chamber, most sacred of all, of which our guide spoke in lowered tones, was an old lay-brother, one hundred and two years old, — not dying, but yet not quite living; too feeble to walk; waiting with his eyes fixed on the Celestial Mountains, and listening for the feet of the messenger with the token. In the walled gardens were all manner of pleasant things growing, — figs and beans, pomegranates and artichokes, peas, wheat, and maize, and oleanders, roses, lemons, and oranges. Under the schoolroom windows was the garden of the pupils, in which each boy has his own bed. Good boys have flower-seeds or roots given them as rewards. One lucky fellow had twenty-one kinds of pansy in his garden.

Round all this peaceful, beautiful life stretched the stone-walls, — not like walls, but sheltering arms. Outside the soft water seemed also to be circling and sheltering; and no sound, unless of a passing oar, interrupted the quiet. We longed to stay for the rest of our lives, and drink cream, and translate good books for the benefit of the Armenian nation; and only wished that we had been wicked men and written poetry, so that we could make a precedent of Lord Byron's having been taken to board there. When we said as much, or nearly as much, to the gentle, smiling brother who had guided us over the convent, he warmed up, in kindly response, and begged me to come again the next Sunday and attend the service in the chapel.

This we did, and it was the crowning pleasure of our glimpses of San Lazzaro. In our first visit we had been mere strangers, to whom were civilly afforded the ordinary facilities for seeing the place. In our second we were invited guests, and now the gracious courtesy of Eastern hospitality surrounded us. While we were sitting in the library, and looking again at the words which the Armenian queen had written thousands of years ago, there entered noiselessly a venerable man, who also might have come, it seemed to me, from quite as far back as her day, and who brought in his hands such refreshments as, I make no doubt, she set before strangers in her court; rose-leaves steeped in syrup till the syrup had become rose and the rose was transparent as syrup, of this one teaspoonful for each guest; the teaspoons resting on tiny glass plates, which took a soft, red tint from the pulpy rose-leaves. In the centre of the tray, a dish of sweets for which I have no name; small square cakes, which might have been honey arrested and made solid by some magic means, and almond meats set thick in the luscious juice. This was all, except glasses of cool-filtered rain-water, almost as great a rarity as the magic honey-cakes and the rose-leaf syrup. "Oh! where were these delicious sweets made?" said we. "By Armenian ladies in Constantinople. They send them to us every year," replied the monk. "And you, what do you send to them in turn?" said I, — "figs and pomegranates from your garden?" "O no; nothing but letters," laughed the monk, with a shrug of his shoulders which could not have been as worldly wise and cynical as it looked.

The Armenian liturgy is one of the most solemn in the world. We had read carefully the English translation of it, so that we were not wholly at loss in listening to the sonorous ring of it in the Armenian tongue. The boys chanted with sharp inflections and unusual intervals, which gave to the whole a wild and not unmusical cadence. But it was impossible not to be diverted from the service by the faces of the brothers. Without an exception, they were at once scholarly and

THE CONVENT OF SAN LAZZARO. 129

childlike, — rare faces, which one would note and admire and trust anywhere, the very realization of the apostolic injunction to be wise as serpents and harmless as doves.

After the services were ended, we went into the little bookstore room, and looked over the specimens of their printing, and translation, and photography. They have done the Emperor Napoleon the honor to translate his history of Cæsar. By its side lay a translation of Paradise Lost, handsomely bound, and dedicated to Queen Victoria. We bought several pamphlets: one a brief history of their society, from which I suppose I ought to have half filled my letter, and told all about its being founded in Constantinople, in 1700, by Mechitar, a learned Armenian; and thence moved to Modon, in the Morea, in 1702; then broken up by the war between the Venetians and Turks in 1715, and moved to the island of San Lazzaro in 1717, where it has been thriving and prospering ever since, and is now rich, owning lands in Padua and Rome, and bankstock in Venice, not to mention the twenty-seven Swiss cows. It is doing a great work in the gratuitous education of Armenian youth, the translation of standard books into the Armenian language, and the distribution of them throughout Asia. I bought also an odd little book, a collection of popular Armenian songs, translated into English, from which I copy one. We see that the things of the earth speak the same words to poets under all suns.

THE YOUNG MAN AND THE WATER.

Down from yon distant mountain
The water flows through the village. Ha,
A dark boy came forth,
And washing his hands and face,
Washing, yes, washing,
And turning to the water, asked: "Ha,
Water, from what mountain dost thou come,
O my cool and sweet water, Ha?"

"I came from that mountain
Where the old and the new snow lie one on the other."
"Water, to what river dost thou go,
O my cool and sweet water, Ha?"
"I go to that river
Where the bunches of violets abound, Ha!"
"Water, to what vineyard dost thou go,
O my cool and sweet water, Ha?"
"I go to that vineyard
Where the vine-dresser is within, Ha!"
"Water, what plant dost thou water,
O my cool and sweet water, Ha?"
"I water that plant
Whose roots give food to the lamb;
The roots give food to the lamb,
Where there are the apple-tree and the anemone."
"Water, to what garden dost thou go,
O my cool and sweet water, Ha?"
"I go into that garden
Where there is the sweet song of the nightingale, Ha!"
"Water, into what fountain dost thou go,
O my cool and sweet little water?"
"I go to that fountain
Where thy lover comes and drinks;
I go to meet her and kiss her chin,
And satiate myself with her love."

Just as we were ready to leave, our friendly host — for not knowing whose name we shall never forgive ourselves — came running in from the garden with a large bouquet of roses, and verbenas, and orange blossoms, and said, in his pleasant broken English, "Again you will come?" "Yes," I said; "again I will come, if there be a next summer."

ENCYCLICALS OF A TRAVELLER.

NICE, Monday, November 23, 1868.

DEAR PEOPLE: Nineteen days since I sailed away, and this is the first minute when I could look far enough ahead to venture to try to tell what I had seen. It has been a whirl and a maze. On the whole I like it, though I would rather not be out of breath. But that I can't help till I get to Rome; so if my letter has the sound of one who has just run up hill, and cannot wait a moment before beginning to tell his news, you will be patient, and put in your own colons and commas where I leave mine out, which will be all along.

Of the voyage you don't care to hear. The smooth ones are pretty rough, I think, and the rough ones must be unspeakably awful. This was a smooth one, they said, and also they said that I was not at all seasick. I suppose they must know, and so I give you their version of it. Every day we sat on deck; the waves were high, emerald at top, and broke into foam-falls to right and left; the flocks of gulls followed us all the way, and I almost found out the secret of their flying, I watched them so constantly. We ate a great deal oftener and a great deal more at each time than we ought; we had hot-water jugs at our feet at night; and the stewards and stewardesses said to us twice a day that it was a most beautiful voyage, and fine weather as "''eart could wish"; and so we came to Liverpool. I did not get the storm I hoped for, and of which the third mate said to me, two days out, "We'll horder one hup for your hespecial be'oof, mem."

Now that it is over, I am rather sorry I was not lashed to a mast in a gale.

When I saw the mail put ashore at Queenstown, it began to dawn on me what a big place the world must be. Eighty-seven huge bags of mail, half of them too large for a man to stagger under; and when they were piled up on the deck of the tug, they made a small hill. Even little Belgium had three big bags.

As we were going into the Liverpool harbor, we met the Russia coming out, and waved our handkerchiefs out of good-fellowship to anything or anybody bound for America. In London I found out that Professor and Mrs. B. had sailed in the Russia; so if I had only known, my signal would have had great meaning.

Liverpool looked very old and musty, as if it had been finished centuries ago and put away: solid beyond anything I ever saw; such piers, such posts, such foundations! Great Normandy horses, with shaggy pantalettes of hair around their hoofs, seemed to be stalking about in all directions, drawing tons of things on drays, with wheels too broad to roll. To the Washington Hotel we were to go for dinner. Washington himself, eleven feet high, done on glass, with a stained border of allegory gone mad, confronted us as soon as we entered the door. I suppose it is intended as a delicate bait for Americans, this enormous transparency. There may be souls so patriotic as to thrill at sight of so much Father to their country. We were profanely irreverent, and never stopped laughing at it while we stayed. It was only by accident that I discovered, in time to secure the afternoon train to London, that my ticket, which I supposed all right for Paris, must be changed at an establishment in Water Street, Liverpool, for something else; so P. and I jumped into a hansom, and drove at such a pace to find the man and the spot! P. had always been afraid to get into a hansom, from a vague instinct that it was not the thing to do it; but, emboldened by my vagabond indifference, she yielded to her long-suppressed desire, and off we dashed. Do you want to know what a hansom is like? I'll tell you exactly, and I think myself that it is not just the thing for " dames seules" to drive about in, but I'm very glad we did it. It is a Franklin fireplace, with cupboard doors in front, swung between low wheels, with a high-chair fastened to it behind. In this sits the driver with his coat-tails flying and his elbows out, far above your head, and drives by reins which, to your bewildered eyes, appear to go nowhere and communicate with nothing. You jump in; the cupboard doors fly together, and away you go at a rate which would make Broadway stare. If I drew pictures for Young Folks, I'd draw a hansom in shape of a larkspur-blossom, with a wasp for a horse, and a cricket rearing itself up behind to drive. Well, we did it all, got our luggage weighed, and bribed a guard at the railroad station with a shilling, and he took care of us as if we had been his grandmothers. He was such a gorgeous creature in uniform, that it seemed to me very audacious to offer him a shilling. I should as soon have thought of giving thirty-seven and a half cents to General Scott; but, dear me, how he appreciated it! A burly old Englishman came up, and made as if he would get into the carriage with us; unblushingly our champion told him the seats were all taken, and hustled him off to another car. Then he came back, and without a smile, said as deliberately as if he were recounting the most praiseworthy action, " I've got 'im into another car, but I donno as 'ee'll stay there."

Before we knew it, we had glided out of the station; they have such a marvellous way of beginning with their engines, noise being the one thing forbidden. Only three stops we made between Liverpool and London and we were only five hours on the road. It was so soon dark that I had but glimpses of the fields and houses. The houses were odd-looking; so much more color than ours; gray, with red and white bricks in borders up and down the sides. The fields were as green as if it had been September, smooth and tilled and ditched to the last possible point of cultivation. Even in those two hours of daylight, I ached to see a *tangle* in something, or a rough corner. The railway station in London was as quiet as possible. I am perfectly bewildered to conceive how they manage to have such quiet. There must be as many trunks and as many people, but nobody screams and nobody bangs; no cabman comes near you; you find your luggage all in a pile by itself, sorted out as exactly and alphabetically as if it were clean clothes from the wash; and there you are, the whole thing over. I should think that when a foreigner is first confronted by a mob of New York hackmen with their whips, he would be positively frightened. But I shall never get through at this rate. I must lay down the rule in the outset not to say what I *think*.

At nine o'clock we were going up the steps of Batt's Hotel, 41 Dover Street, Piccadilly. We had telegraphed for rooms, so we were met and welcomed, which is always pleasant; and by such a stylish-looking dame, in a black silk gown, with a gold chain! Another eminently respectable dignitary lit our fires; she wore a Honiton lace cap. A third, also in a lace cap, lugged up our bags. If a preponderance of our own sex could make us reputably established, we were on the pinnacle of propriety. O, how blessed it seemed to have the floor quiet under our feet, and no wriggling or twisting screw in the cellar, no plash of water on our bedroom walls! The first house in which one sleeps after a sea-voyage must seem like a Paradise, I am sure. Nothing will seem to *me* again so home-like as those smutty bedrooms and that dingy parlor. Great blazing fires of cannel coal in every room, and the air filled with the smoke of them! They are "too fillin' at the price," cosey as they look at first. All day you wipe your face, and at night you start back from it in the glass. The streets are smoky, the bread is smoky, the pillow-cases are smoky. I wonder the word "white" does n't die out of the language. We saw no sun till we came away; — it was always just before light!

We had our dinner and breakfast in state in our own sitting-room, and a waiter in such a dress-coat, with such a white lace necktie, and such gold studs of the size of a pea! He was too fine to be reproved for never remembering the kind of bread we ordered. Sunday morning P. and I took a cab, and drove three miles to South Place Chapel, Finsbury, to hear my old friend Mr. Conway preach. Strangely enough, it chanced that he gave that day an account of the meeting of the Free Religious Associations, which met in Boston last May. It was like overtaking a tidal wave, to have journeyed to this little English chapel in time to hear those grand words of John Weiss and Robert Collyer, echoing on this shore!

In the evening we went to hear Spurgeon. This was a great disappointment. The Tabernacle was worth going to see, — eight thousand people with intent upturned faces, — but when at least six thousand of those eight are *coughing* incessantly, and only *one man* to out-tale the coughing, the result is uncommonly unpleasant. It is a scramble to get a seat, but a worse scramble to get out. We did not stay. We tried to look as if we were faint, but I fear we got quite too red, what with the elbowing and the disgust. Spurgeon may be eloquent sometimes; he certainly was not eloquent that night. He was simply a great, strong, coarse, earnest man, who said commonplace things with huge emphasis of fist and voice. He called the scribes "spiritual mosquitoes," and said that when Christ asked them certain questions, he "had 'em there." This is all I remember of what he said, except that his prayer lasted twenty minutes.

Monday was a day never to be forgotten. From

ten until five P. and I drove about that great city, peering into book-shops on Paternoster Row (no Christina Rossetti could I find in twelve shops, — had to go to her publishers); getting water-proof cloaks, and walking through Westminster Abbey, all in a breath; palaces; Houses of Parliament; dinner at Blanchard's; *mob* and *orator* in some great square, — how they did scream and toss their hats, and the police ordered one brougham to move along; the famous Mrs. Brown's millinery shop, where hats went by dozens and guineas by scores; Regent Street; Trafalgar Square; all in a smoke, and all so cold, so raw, we shivered like Boston people in March; home after dark to dinner; and that was my day in London.

Tuesday, the train to Folkestone, — ten till one, — woods all yellow and brown, — hedges black and filmy-looking as we whirled by. Folkestone, picturesque old town, built up and up, high gray stone houses; on the wharf, a motley crowd, as the newspaper-writers say, — English, Scotch, Irish, Yankee, and French, — and the hideous green Channel leering triumphantly out at us all from under a fog. It was rather ugly. A drizzle, almost a rain; people scrambling for floor-room to lie down in the cabin; before we had been out ten minutes, sailors coming up from below with *stacks* of unpleasant crockery bowls, which they put down here and there by twos and threes in everybody's reach! How could the stomach of any but a blind man resist that? We clung to a settee on deck; pitying men who sailed the boat took off their coats and covered us up; and it only lasted two hours; then we were at Boulogne. This was France. Drolly enough, the Frenchiest-looking thing I saw on the hill was a little dog, which behaved so comically about his barking and running and stricking up his tail, I fancied he would have looked foreign to me if I had seen him in America. His every hair seemed electric.

We walked to the railroad station, and a jabbering

French boy carried our bags. Behind us and before us clattered the fishermen's wives, with their wooden shoes, down at the heels and slipping off at every step. I thought horses were coming directly upon me, and jumped to one side; three of these women ran by laughing! We lunched in a buffet, where the big cook was all in white, — white paper cap, white linen apron, — things astonishingly good to eat and hard to pronounce. Then more railway, five hours of it, and we were in Paris. Here the same astonishing quiet, but a tedious waiting till the luggage was sorted. Presently a tall man, with "Interpreter" on his hat-band, appeared. Even N., with all her excellent knowledge of French, was glad to see him. Only one little trunk, of all our *eight* packages, was opened by the Custom House officer, and he politely looked another way while he lifted the lid. Several ornamented and caparisoned creatures helped us off, and we rattled away, luggage and all, long before some of the parties who had *men* to look after them, had got out. "9 Rue Castiglione, — whatever time by night or day you arrive, come straight there," S. C. had written to me. So there we went, and at the head of the eighth (I *think*) flight of stairs, there she stood waiting to welcome me! P. and N. drove on to the Hotel Windsor, where their rooms had been engaged by telegraph, — and this was the beginning of Paris! I began to scent the world, the flesh, and the devil before I had been in the house five minutes. I found my friends up to ears in clothes, and whereas I had been harassed with thinking they were waiting for me all this time, no, they were not ready to set off for Rome yet! More "things" were yet to come home, and we could not possibly get off till Thursday night. Well, thus it moved on again to Friday morning; and those two days in Paris cost me, I won't say what, because it was so very little *intrinsically*. Only I and my own conscience know how much more it was than I ought to have spent. Paris is just what I thought it was, — New York grown up, graduated and with a diploma! I do not care if I never see it again; certainly I did not see much of it then. It was absolutely necessary to rest all day Wednesday. Thursday I looked at the outside of some of the lions, and the inside of some of the stores. It is evident that people ought never to buy anything in Paris without a Paris *resident* to go with them and show them how. None of the things that we have bought are cheap. I had great fun out of not speaking French, — for in the midst of all the humiliation of it, it is funny. The conversation with my chambermaid — I talking English and French, and she French! — somehow by dint of fingering a good deal, we made out. The ignorance of the English language among these people is really melancholy. But it is a consolation sometimes to tell them face to face what they can't understand! The woman who brought home my hoop said, eying my humble attire with ill-concealed contempt, "Madame will need some other things, will she not?" "Heaven forbid!" said I, shaking my head, and adding "Non, non," — P. sitting by convulsed with laughter at the woman's stare. French women who have things to sell never stop trying to make you buy. She kept on — I dare say she did really pity me for having to wear such clothes, — "Madame would certainly like a ruffled petticoat *pour le voyage*." "Get thee behind me, Satan!" I said, bowing and smiling, and pressing her towards the door. I think she crossed herself when she got outside! So did I too! What becomes of conscientious convictions on the subject of dress, what becomes of exact calculations as to the proper expenditure of a limited income, in the Paris air, I don't know. I should like to see the woman who could go through Paris, and not buy a gown. O the shape of the things! their dainty last touch! and they pile up their temptations so! You must have gloves; of course it is simple duty to go to the glove store and buy them. Ah, what do you see just under your elbow ! — neckties, — just a few, — blue, with point lace and seed pearls, — just the ravishing thing for some brown-haired darling in America — and it would almost go in a letter, — and it is only twelve francs ! How you pat yourself on the head if you get out of the shop without buying it —

GENOA, Friday Evening, November 27.

Right into the middle of that last sentence, my dears, broke the decision that we must set out for Genoa in an hour. We had waited all day Monday for sunshine, and half of Tuesday, and it was foolish to wait longer. I have always heard Nice called a "garden." It is the moistest, coldest, muddiest garden I ever saw, and has the worst fireplaces! The flowers, to be sure, are like a carnival in every direction, — roses of all colors, oranges, aloes, all the flowers I ever saw in a conservatory, all blossoming at once, apparently, in and out of season, — but how they stand the cold fog, I can't imagine. They did n't seem to shiver. I suppose, now, I shall never tell you how we rode from eleven o'clock, Friday morning, till *five Saturday*, P. M., to get from Paris to Nice, and did n't die of it; nor about the American Consul, Judge A., who came to see us Sunday evening, and told us volumes of gossip about the old dethroned kings, and unprincipled princesses and Russian countesses who pull each other's ears in Nice; all about the poor Prince of Monaco, who sold his soul to the Devil to pay his tailor and keep his little handful of kingdom, making it the legalized gambling-ground for all Europe. (Afterward, we looked down on it from the high hills on the Cornice Road; it looked like a tidy enough little peninsula, with no elbow-room for either saints or sinners.) Monday morning the kind Judge came again and walked us about to have one glimpse of the Public Gardens and the fine Promenade Anglais. This lies along the shore of the sea, and all fashionable people walk there in fine clothes every afternoon. It is a concentrated Bellevue Avenue, dear Newporters, and all the Nice people (not the nicest, I suppose) go away and let their houses just as you do. Every other villa has its sign up, "*à louer*," and it seemed positively odd not to see "apply to Alfred Smith" below it. I can't tell you about all this, nor about these three last days on the Cornice Road, because the latter is too long, and I have no time here to write. The last three days have been to the eye what the full orchestra is to the ear. Even from divinest music one must rest. I looked away from the sea, the olives, the crags, the snow-covered hills, and studied the little roadside flowers till I could look up again. Sweet-alyssum grows like grass all along the road from Nice here.

Now I shall warm myself before a fire in a *cave* under a marble mantel-piece and go to bed. I don't think I should have any more realization of being lodged in an old palace, if I knew what particular Guelph or Ghibelline had toasted his feet on this very slab, than I have now. Such a fresco is over my head, — such a distance as my walls reach up! I go about in the dark with a candle like an old woman in a great dark barn with a lantern. I get up on a chair to step into my bed. There is a tapestry-hanging which conceals a door; the door is just behind my bed, — it won't lock, and has already been opened once by mistake. If this is n't splendor, what is! We are so gay with it all, we don't know what to do with ourselves, and we are unpacking our pin-cushions and slippers as if we meant to stay a week, instead of two days. Tomorrow, palaces, churches, jewelry! Monday we move on towards Rome, — just how we don't know, but as fast as we can.

Nobody knows half so well as I do how stupid this letter is. But when you come to try at it yourselves, you 'll find that it is harder than you think. There is so much too much to say.

ROME, Monday, December 14, 1868.

DEAR SOULS: Now we are at housekeeping, and this is my house-warming letter. Did n't we have a time of it to get a house at all? O, how easy it looked at first! Every other house has up its sign, "Camere Mobiliate": we were not at all ambitious; all we demanded was to have sun in all our rooms, three bedrooms, and a fire in each bedroom. What could be simpler? How our spirits went down, down, as we climbed up staircase after staircase, and found dark rooms, no stoves, or else a kitchen where the *Padrona* must have the privilege of coming to cook "just a little trifle two or three times a day"; or else a rent of one hundred and forty dollars a month. Ah, at the end of the first day we were very meek people, and at the end of the second we were abject! There can't be many things in this world so bewildering as looking after lodgings in Rome. In the first place, the door into which you enter, at the beginning, looks like the very dirty and neglected entrance to some old warehouse on a wharf, in a city where there has not been any business for a hundred years. You stand there a minute, and say, " O dear!" (especially if you have already been up five or six hundred steps that morning,) "I do wish they would tell on their cards how *many* rooms there are!" Perhaps we shall find somebody on the third floor who can tell us. Not a bit of it; up flight after flight you crawl; on each floor is one great grim iron door, with a ring and a chain hanging outside. You have no business to pull the ring on any floor but the floor with which your business is; and if you did, they

would n't know anything about any floor but their
own. Each floor is its own *house*, as much as if it
were six miles off from any other floor. When you
get up to the one hundred and seventh stair you would
be so glad to sit down, but you can't. They don't put
either chairs or benches in these grim passages;
and the stairs are all stone. You can't sit on them,
not if you are half dead; so you lean up against the
wall and get your black cloak all white and cobwebbed,
while you wait for the mysterious chain and ring,
which you have pulled, to bring forth an answer.
Then the great door creaks and opens, and you get
breath enough to ask if they have furnished rooms to
let, and if there are *three* bedrooms, with sun and fire.
After a little while you learn that it makes no difference whether they have or have not; they always
say, "Sì, sì, signora." Before you learn this you go in
quite gayly, and think you are all right. Then you see
one great bedroom with two beds, and one little one, on
neither of which the sun has apparently ever shone;
a fine parlor, with stands of artificial roses under high
glass cases, no end of china teacups sitting around;
usually about twenty frightful pictures on the walls;
in the dining-room there is a great display of glass and
china on the table; and the *Padrone*, if he is at home,
and the *Padrona*, and the one or two or three daughters, all down at the heel, and down at the neck, and
huddled up somehow with pins and strings in the middle, and looking like rag-men and rag-women, begin
to talk, all at once, with their tongues and their shoulders and their fingers; and they tell you that the sun
shines at some impossible hour of the day, at some impossible angle, into all three rooms; and that two beds
in one bedroom are exactly the same thing as two
bedrooms with a bed in each; and that their linen and
their silver and their furniture are "so much, so much,"
and "so fine, so fine"; and they smile and show white
teeth, and their eyes are such a lovely brown-black,

that you are in some danger of believing them; and then if you say that you must have a "free kitchen," which means simply that they are not to have the use of your tea and sugar and bread, they shrug their shoulders, and look at each other, with such an expression of injury, that you feel like an awful sneak *yourself*,—just as if you had stolen all your life; and for all that, you know that you are the honest one, and *they* steal, and you know the rooms won't do at all, and you edge along to the door; and then the faces of the Padrone and the Padrona and the daughters all grow black, and the white teeth go down their throats apparently, they disappear so absolutely and forever; and as you fairly step out of the door, if you wish to know the *true* character of the people you might have lived with, turn around quickly and look at the faces which have settled down, behind your back! This is what we did for two days and a half. We exhausted the list which friends had given us; then we drove slowly up and down the streets where it would do to live (by the way, there are not more than a dozen of them in all this great city), and looked at the signs, and whenever we saw one which we thought promised the least chance of success, out we got, and up we climbed. In one place we would find a parlor so sunny, so comfortable, that we could not leave it; then the bedrooms were wrong; in another the bedrooms could be made to answer, but the parlor was a den, and cold as a barn; then we were taken with great love of a view, or of the blankets, or of the china and glass, which we would have liked to take away with us, to use in the other house, which we still firmly believed was awaiting us somewhere. Then we came upon one quite fine and comfortable and sunny, and then the rent would be at least one hundred and fifty dollars a month, and we would meekly say, "Troppo," and go away, followed by pitying looks between the landlord and lady. By the way, I never thought be-

fore of the composition of the word "land*lord* and
lady": no wonder they are so lordly in their ways.
At last we found our house. It was my inspiration, and
I take great credit to myself; high up on the Via
Quattro Fontane (four fountains), just opposite the
Barberini Palace, on the corner opposite Miss Hosmer's
house. Think of that! Are n't we in luck? Well,
it happened oddly that the good people, being modest,
had stuck out " Piccolo appartamento " on their sign.

Longingly I had looked at the corner twice, as we
neared it, and said to S———, " I suppose there is no
use in looking at anything which an Italian *calls* in
the outset ' small.' "

" O no," she said, " not the least."

So it came to be near night on the third day, and
we were still homeless. We were driving back to our
hotel and passed this house. Still the same little sign
which had seemed all day to have a magic fascination
for me! I said, " Let us look at it; it will do no harm."
A strange sort of delight took possession of me as
I first trod on the stairs; they were stone, but clean;
the flights were short, and the halls were comparatively
light. Such a beauty as opened the door for us! Ah,
if you could see her! Just now she came to bring me
an egg beaten up in milk, and as she set it on the table,
and said, " Signora," the grace and gentleness of her
motion, the sweetness of her voice, — ah me, I believe
I had tears in my eyes to look at her. I never saw
just such a human creature before! Well, the beauty
opened the door (she is only a maid of all work, this
beauty, our Marianina), and then she called the Padrona, who came, having the same sweet, gentle ways,
but looking so ill, so ill. She, poor soul, has had the
fever. The rooms were charming, — a parlor on the
southeast corner, two windows; a dining-room, two
bedrooms, and such a kitchen, resplendent with
copper. But that I'll tell you about later All
except the third bedroom, this was our place. How

we looked at each other, and went back and forth through the dear six rooms (there was one great dark room), trying to make them count more than they would. I began to feel like the "fifth kitten," and think I might as well be drowned. O dear, only three out of you dear twelve will have the least idea what "fifth kitten" means; never mind, I can't help it, perhaps you can find out. Suddenly I said, "Why need we have a dining-room? We are not grand; we shall not entertain any but our own sort; we can have dinner in the parlor, and the dining-room will make a good bedroom." So it did. So it does; and L—— sleeps in it, and here we are! And now I wonder if I can tell you how the rooms look, and if you will care if I do; at any rate, it is Roman housekeeping, so you might like to know how we do it. Ah, if you would all come and do likewise! I don't believe it is in the least "as the Romans do," though; poor souls, I have a lurking doubt whether even the Dorias and the Borgheses are half as comfortable as we are. The two Romans who have come to see us go away out into the northeast corner of our little parlor to sit down, and look with dismay at our great wood-fire, and say, "O, thank you, I will sit here; we do not have fires." "I think them *exqueesetely* beautiful," said Signor L——, the other day, meaning to be very polite, "but I find them very hot!" I really think he supposed we kept our fire for ornament, and endured the discomfort of the heat as the price of the pretty display. But this is not telling you about the house; only, from this you will see that we have wood-fires. Ay, that we do, in the parlor and in two of the bedrooms; mine crackles at this moment as lustily as if it were of Vermont maple, instead of little round sticks of I don't know what, but something quite worthless and small, which I amuse myself with by building it up into cob-houses on the hearth, and then the fire trips up from side to side and in and out, like an acrobat. Well, well, now I will be exact, and describe a thing or two. You see this old Rome goes to one's head, and it is not easy to keep a steady hand.

Firstly, comes our parlor; it is cosey, and that is a rare thing here; it is long rather than square, and it has one window to the northeast and one to the east; we make much of the east window, for out of it we see such lovely red-tiled roofs, and a bit of an orange-garden high up above the roofs, and a whole cypress-tree; into it comes straight sun, and that is worth solid gold, inches deep, for every inch that it covers on our carpet. We don't spread down any Cranford papers! not we! Our northeast window looks out unterrified on the Barberini Palace. There is the lovely, sad Beatrice, who will be my friend in rainy days; I have not sat with her yet, because there has been no rainy day when I dared to go out; and on the pleasant days there is always some artist or other copying her, which I should so dislike that I could not see her well. Clouds, I think, could not cut off so much light as one man.

At first our parlor had so much glass case and stack of flowers and marble-top table, that we did not know what to do; now it has only two marble-topped affairs, and they are covered with books; then there is a marvellous square dining-table which can be stretched into any size, and I firmly believe also into any shape; I have n't yet seen it in an octagon, but I expect to. As soon as I have learned the Italian verbs, I shall attack this table and find out how it goes. Then we have great arm-chairs, called *poltronas;* (why? for lazy cowards who shirk sitting up straight, I suppose;) and a sofa and common chairs innumerable; and all these are green, and the paper is green, and the carpet is green and red. The mantel is covered with red velvet, with a deep fringe; on it is a pretty clock under a glass case, and a shepherd and shepherdess, who hold candles. There were two china vases, big as hay-stacks, but we banished them to our art-gallery in the dark room! Our parlor would delight us unqualifiedly, if it were not for the pictures. We have banished so much of the sweet Padrona's china and glass finery, that we have not the heart to ask to have all the pictures carried off; I think we shall do it ultimately, though, and are wasting our strength in this interval of martyrdom; — it is incredible till you have seen it, this profusion of awful pictures. Out of the parlor opens a bedroom, Miss C——'s; high iron bedstead, lace-curtained, handsome dressing-table, wardrobe with full-length glass, bureau, etc., all marble-topped; then comes the dark room; ah, chaos itself! trunks, chairs, — there! I mean to go this minute and count the chairs in our house. There are *thirty-two*, in this tiny little house; it is very droll to see so many; only four small rooms and thirty-two chairs. I am not certain that there are not more, for I could not count those very well which were piled up in stacks in the dark room. Everything is of the nicest quality, solid woods, black-walnut or mahogany, with seats of morocco or green or crimson damask. But now I shall tell you no more about furniture, excepting of my writing-desk; this alone proves that the house was predestined for us. Miss F—— says she never saw such a thing in a Roman house before; I never sat to write at anything half so fine; solid mahogany, quite finely carved, four drawers, then a desk covered with green morocco which lets down, and reveals a shelf with a looking-glass back, and five drawers; (one with a false bottom; how I pine for a secret!) then above this another drawer, and on the top, room for many of my dear books, if they ever, ever get here. This stands across one corner of my sunny little bedroom, and one window on my right hand opens on a little ledge called a balcony, and looks out on the wall of the Quirinal. Ought I not to write to you better than I shall from such a corner as this?

Now I must tell you about our kitchen. This is, after

all, the crowning glory of this wonderful little "apartment," our house. Such sun as lies in our kitchen, two windows full! and such copper as it shines on! They must have made ready for a minute prince and princess, who would give dinners to retinues of small people in the little dining-room; twelve shining copper *casseroles*, all sizes, up to big ones so big an orchard could be made into apple-sauce in them; copper jars with handles, copper basins, copper kettles, all hanging on the wall in the sun; all new, shining like mirrors; white wooden table, solid log, on legs, to pound beefsteak on; I think the log must have come from America; it is huge and looks like hickory. Ah, but the place for the fire! — I don't believe I can tell you how odd it is. Every time I go into the kitchen, I stand and look and look at it, and Marianina comes in and finds me, and looks so anxious, because she is afraid something is wrong. Imagine the biggest range you ever saw, only not a range at all, just a great stone table with an arch under it and a chimney above it; you can look right up the chimney; all the steam from things you boil goes up this big chimney. You keep the charcoal in this arch under your stone table, and you build a fire *on* your stone table, anywhere you like, and then there is a little square hole on one side, and you fill that with hot coals from your fire, and set your teakettle on them; and then you put a great gridiron above the whole of your fire, or half of your fire, and set your copper *casseroles* on the gridiron, and that is the way you cook. People who know say great and delicious dinners can be gotten up by these fires on these tables; we don't cook our dinners; they come in a tin box on a man's head, and are smoking-hot when we get them; so we only try the wonderful table-cooking to make our tea, and boil our rice, and bake our potatoes for breakfast; but we are going to stew pears, and make oatmeal pudding, and L—— and I have our eye on a surprise of a hash some morning, if we have a chopping-tray, which we have n't yet remembered to find out. I must not forget our well; that is in the kitchen too, and it has a door to it, a little square door, black like the door to an oven ; and it is close to the stone table and chimney, so I said, "Of course this is the oven"; and I popped my head in, — such a stream of cold air! and a slender iron chain, and a dark wonderful place, which did n't seem to begin or end. Then I looked up and I saw the sky; and I looked down, and way, way down, near China I should think, — or is it *you* who are at bottom now ? — there was a gleam of sunshine on water; then I drew my head out, and there stood the Padrona laughing hard. How this water is carried about I do not yet understand; but there it is, ready and flowing, day and night; sun on it by day, and stars by night, and it comes from the fountain of Trevi. So we, of all people in Rome, are sure to get so spell-bound that we shall return and return, since we not only drink once, but daily, of the charmed water; and not only drink it daily, but bathe in it daily! From each story in this house opens a little black door into this secret well-turret. Many times a day I hear the chain clinking up and down, as the people above draw water.

Now one thing more is really part of our house. It is on the floor above; a little open *loggia*, out-doors room, where, when it is warmer, we shall sit and study and work; this is over our parlor, so looks down on the palace, and off over the roofs; to the east and north it has a railing, and rows of geraniums and orange-trees in pots around it, and chairs more than we need. This is the best thing of all, perhaps.

Upon this upper floor live our sweet Padrona and her husband and little girl. The husband is a master-mason, and his name is Biagio Frontoni; the Padrona is Vittoria and the little girl who has, like two thirds of the lucky little girls in Rome, the lovely low broad brow and straight nose and curved lips on which mothers here look all their days, is called Erminia. Erminia owns four hens and a cock; and they live very happily on corn up five flights of stairs, and never go out. All the money for the eggs is Erminia's, and we are so sorry that we don't eat a great many. I take one every noon, beaten up in milk, partly for love of Erminia. Yesterday Marianina came running at eleven o'clock into the parlor, and, talking very fast, just as if I could understand her, laid one of two snow-white eggs against my cheek so that I might feel how warm it was! not more than half a minute old I should say! Then, seeing that I was so pleased with that, she darted off, and in a minute more came back with the very hen cuddled under her arm, as quiet as a kitten! The hen looked as if she must be purring. I dare say she was — in Italian, which I don't understand.

Now what remains for the house-warming, except to tell you what we have to eat? Soup, roast-beef, or lamb, or mutton, with potatoes; a chicken or a pair of pigeons, with cauliflower, or spinach, or celery; one dish of *dolci* for dessert; sometimes boiled rice, with wonderful sauce made of raspberry-jelly; sometimes puffy pie, which people who eat pie would like; sometimes charlotte-russe; sometimes stewed pears with raisins, *very* delicious; always four courses. This all comes in a tin box on a man's head from a restaurant, and we pay for it daily only seven francs; always there is meat enough left for our breakfast and lunch the next day. Then when we add Graham bread from the English bakery, almost as good as home-made, and butter fresh each day, a bottle of cream each morning, and oranges and apples by dozens, it is plain that we are feasting.

How much does it cost us? Ah, we don't yet know; we are a little afraid that when we add all up at the end of the month, we shall be constrained to decide not to eat two oranges apiece at every meal any longer. But just now we don't count costs. The rent of our house, with the service of the beauty Marianina, who does all we want done in doors and out, is seventy-six scudi a month, about eighty-one dollars and fifty cents. The dinners cost us about forty-five dollars a month, — about forty-three dollars a month each, this makes, all told, — and we hope to get in the wood and the oil and the bread and the butter and the cream and the oranges, etc., within twenty dollars a month more (for each). This is not very cheap living, but then it is Rome. If we had come earlier, we could have found cheaper rooms; and if it had been last winter instead of this, everything would have been cheaper still; but if gold will only "stay put" or not get above 135, we shall not grumble at paying sixty-five dollars a month for such life as this. Now what will there be to tell you next month, since I have told you all this now, and I am under bonds never to write about ruins? We shall see; perhaps it will be Ostia, after all; for if we go down into those depths with Signor L——, the archæologist, who promises to take us, I think there will be something worth telling, in spite of its being *ruins!* If I do not hear regularly *each month* from you all, I shall write no more. How shall I know you care to hear? How shall I know you are alive? God bless you all. Good by.

ROME, Tuesday Eve, January 19, 1869

DEAR PEOPLE: What do you suppose we do with letters? I'll tell you. We read them over and over and over and over, until we know them just as well as we know our alphabets; and then we put them on our table, where we can see them all the time till we go to bed; and then, the next day, we read them a great deal more, and carry them in our pockets, and feel every now and then to see if they are there; and then, the next day — Well, there is no use in going on forever with the story; but there are Americans who have been seen reading over old letters in the Coliseum! There now, if you don't all write to me after this, you are the nethermost of millstones; and, once for all, let me say (because this is my last appeal for letters), do write all the most insignificant details, — what you have for dinner, and the color of your winter bonnet; what was your last ailment, and whether you took aconite or calomel; if your front gate is off its hinges, or your minister has had a donation-party; who came in last to see you, and what they had to say. Don't suppose that anything can be too unimportant to tell. You don't know anything about it. Wait till you have been hungry yourself. Here ends the "Complete European Letter-Writer."

And next? To-night it shall be about ruins. Don't think I forget your savage injunctions, dear young woman of N——, who said to me, "Don't write about ruins, whatever else you do." For all that, I shall tell you where L—— and I went this afternoon. At divers times, thick envelopes had been left at our door, containing the most learned prospectuses of the British Archæological Society, and setting forth in terms which sounded fine the rules and the advantages of being members of the same. We thought we did not know enough, and we did not know anybody who belonged, and so it slipped along and we did n't join, and yet we had all the while a hankering after it. They have a lecture every Friday night in which some especial ruin is described, and then the members of the society take an excursion on the next fine day to see the ruin. It is the fashion to laugh at this, you know; therefore very few Americans have anything to do with it, for which they are silly; though I dare say I should have laughed too, if I had got my first impression of it, as one of my friends did, from seeing the whole crowd, one day, rushing pell-mell down a steep place, not into the sea, but nearly into the Tiber, and knocking each other over in their wild eagerness to get down to the lecturer, and hear his explanations; and perhaps I should have found it a bore if I had begun with a lecture. But we took the excursion first; and it is that from which we came home, cold and tired and hungry, three hours ago, but from which I am rested now, and about which I shall tell you, if I can get to it. I shall have all the names wrong, but you won't care. I shall not have the first name wrong, though, for that is Trastevere. I love the very sound of the word; they never mean to live or die out of it, these proud poor souls, who think themselves more Roman than other Romans. I fancy they are all nobler in their looks over there. If I were a man I should certainly go and live in Trastevere and find out some secrets. Painters like to paint the Trastevere women; but About says people have died who looked too curiously at them: I can easily believe this.

Well, we drove over an old, old bridge (I know the name of that, too, but I won't tell it) into Trastevere, and wormed our way in and round the lanes and under all the washerwomen's wet clothes hanging on lines

from window to window, and came to the church of
San Crisogono, from whose steps the Archæological
Society were to get out at precisely 2 P. M. (Sounds
a little bungling for the name of a pleasure excursion,
does n't it?) There was the church, solemn and still
as death. Not a soul to be seen; we ran round the
other side; worse and worse. There were the empty
carriages in which the A. S. had come (lucky there is
only one S., for I must really abbreviate it) to Trastevere, but no A. S.! The coachmen, many of them
private, looked at us with the becoming nonchalance of
British coachmen who drove the A. S. about, and we
thought we would n't ask them any questions; so we
prowled a little, and presently a sunny Italian face
said, "Ecco! Ecco!" and pointed to a door. He knew
what we were after, and so, for that matter, did the
British coachmen.

Into the door we went, and down a winding stair,
and plumped right on the A. S. before we knew it.
There it was, large as life; it had about a hundred
legs, all pretty badly dressed. I don't know which
were ugliest, the trousers or the petticoats. A gray-
haired man in the middle of the group was talking
earnestly and showing photographs, and everybody
was crowding up to see; the place they were in was
like a great open cellar with high walls, and several
other cellars opening out of it. L—— and I felt a little dashed at first, but in a moment our friend Signor
L—— stepped up, and took us under his wing, and
there we were launched as archæologists.

I must tell you about Signor L——. Miss C——
had a letter to him, and we were told that he had
charge of government excavations, and could do more
than any one else to show us curious old ruins, was a
distinguished archæologist, etc., etc. So the letter was
sent, and we waited patiently for the first visit from
the archæologist. We thought he would be middle-
aged, rather stout, wear gold spectacles, and be a little

bald. Ha! the bell rang one night, and in skipped a slender figure in full evening dress, lavender kids, and a violet in his button-hole; he sank down with a mixture of timidity and vivacity perfectly overwhelming, on the tip of a chair, and with a burst of infantile laughter said, "I do not speak any Eenglis but a leettle." This was Signor L——, and we had hard work that first night to keep grave faces. Now we know him very well, and find him entertaining and clever; but he has still the same infantile way, and I begin to doubt if Italian young men ever grow up. He told us the other day, with perfect gravity and evident sincerity, that his mother "would not permit him to leap in riding!"

But I forget that I left you "in a cellar." In this cellar, too, were hidden secrets; it was the old barracks of a Roman cohort in the time of the Emperors. In the court-yard the soldiers had lounged and scribbled on the walls. There they were still, the uncouth faces and figures they had drawn; names and dates; the name of the consul at that time; and, best of all, the date of the Emperor's birthday; and that, Signor L—— said, was the only record of that Emperor's age.

In a little niche on one side were figures of Mercury in rough fresco; this was a little chapel dedicated to his worship. In the middle of the court-yard was a stone rim of a fountain, star-shaped. On this lay bits of all sorts of old marbles which had been dug up in the different rooms; and the gray-headed man laid his photographs on them: so the years met!

I am quite sure that we were the only Americans there, except Professor G——. Everybody else was as British as British could be. We did not stay long in the cellar, of which I was glad, for it was colder than any place ought to be into which the sun shone. I felt as if ghostly breaths blew on us from every corner. Then we climbed up the stairs again, and the A. S. which drove got into its coaches, and the A. S. which walked took to its very strong legs, and the procession moved off. It was a little like a funeral, but we did not drive far; the first carriage stopped, and then all the others stopped, and the gray-headed man, who had on a cloak with a pointed hood and kept the hood over his head, led us down on the banks of the Tiber, to what looked to me like the mouth of a drain, if I might be so bold. I gave most irreverent inattention to all he said here; I gathered only that he believed that the priests used to wash their knives at that particular spot. I did n't believe it for all that, and I looked at the Tiber while he talked. "Yellow Tiber" sounds well; Macaulay never could have got on without that adjective; but it is such a license, no poet any nearer than England would have ventured on it. The water looks just like the water in the puddles in brickyards, dirty, thick, dead, drab; as for "shaking its tawny mane," it does not look as if it ever stirred so much as a drop, and all the craft that are on it look as if they had roots like pond-lilies and would n't come up. They are all tipped a little to one side, and seem to lean on the banks, and I don't believe one has been in or out for five thousand years. I have looked and looked in vain to see even a little boat in motion there; and the longer you look, the thicker and the stickier the water seems, and the more lifeless and useless the ships and the two or three hulking steamboats look, and the more real and intent the old bits of stone ruins become, till it would not astonish you to see Julius Cæsar himself step out from under one of the gray lion's heads and knock all the sham of modern shipping into a cocked hat, before you could say Jack Robinson. Surely it takes quite a long time to say Jack Robinson; so if any of you know how this bit of slang came about, please tell me when you write. But, I forget! you never write; so it's no use asking you questions.

Presently I found that the A. S. was moving off again; dear me, they did look as if they knew all about that drain (it was n't the Cloaca Maxima though, I took care to find out that much); but I made up for not having attended to the drain when we reached the Emporium. This really did thrill my insensible soul; here were the old wharves, in the old days, and here lay the blocks of marble which were brought and unloaded and never carried away; who knows why? Like pebbles under your feet were strewn bits of old red pottery, where the unlucky or the thriftless broke the jars in which had come oil or dates to be sold. Ah, this was really worth looking at!

From a hole in the side of the bank stuck out a huge column of dark marble, only half unburied; this is the largest column known of its kind, and when the great council meets next year, they are to set it up on some hill in Rome; then the A. S. said the other end of the column could be seen by going into another hole, farther back. Why we all wanted to see the other end of it, Heaven only knows; but we all ran like sheep; hopped up and down over the great blocks of marble, and then, when we got to the hole, only one could go in at a time, and nobody could see anything after getting in. This seemed to make everybody more anxious to go in; and when you saw that you had to bend yourself nearly double, and poke in head foremost down a slope, with every chance of falling on your nose, it became irresistible. Everybody said breathlessly to those coming out, "Did you see it?" and the come-outers said deprecatingly, "Why no, I can't say I did exactly; it's pretty dark." And so we all asked, and so we all replied, and that was the end of that.

Then the Baron V—— arrived, who was to give some explanations of these ruins; he came running, with the light of joy on his old face, and a little bit of stone in a white paper, which he showed to the gray-headed man in the hooded cloak; and they both gloated; and everybody crowded up and looked over, and after all it was rather worth while. A bit of stone they had just found, yellow jasper from Sicily; very, very old, and very, very rare. Then the Baron put it into his mouth and wet it, as if it were a small jewel, and held it up again, rubbing it in the sun to bring out the colors. And then the British A. S. stretched up its fifty necks to see. Then the Baron began to talk, and dear me, what should it be but French! So being of an ingenuous and just turn, I slipped off, and gave up my good place at his elbow to somebody who could understand modern French on the subject of Roman ruins, spoken by an aged Baron without many teeth; and that was about the last of the archæological excursion.

Then L—— and I drove home by way of the Piazza Navona, where are more oranges and apples to sell than all Rome could ever eat, one would say. The orange-stalls dazzle you like the setting sun's light on a great front of glass windows, on a hot day. We wanted some sour apples; Romans don't know what the word means; there are no sour apples here; but there are some which are just *not* sweet, and they are better than nothing. When I begin to stammer out my few substantives at the stalls, the men and women gather round and laugh so good-naturedly, that I don't mind their cheating me, which of course they will do in spite of all I can say. Once, though, I did make a stand with a little black-eyed rascal who sold oranges, and asked me two *soldi* apiece for them, when I had that very morning been told by Marianina that I should give but one. I shook my head and said " *Un soldo, un soldo.*" How he did asseverate and reiterate, and at last said a *soldo* and a half; on which I told the driver to " drive on "; and in two seconds my orange-boy had signalled to the driver to stop, and was pouring the oranges into the bottom of the carriage, and laughing just as roguishly at me as if it were the best joke going that I had detected him. " *Sì, sì, signora;*

un soldo!" Of course strict morality would have refused to compound felony (or whatever they may call it, to encourage dishonesty) by buying oranges of such a little liar; but I only laughed as hard as he did, and bought two dozen.

Thursday, P. M. — Now something better than ruins; we have seen the lambs blessed at the church of St. Agnes. Did n't somebody who did n't know tell us it would be at 9 A. M.? and as the church is outside the walls, did n't we get up at seven, and breakfast shivering at eight, and see *icicles* in the fountain in the Barberini Piazza as we drove out? However, the sun was clear and bright, and the mountains looked like clouded sapphire against the sky, and it was only an hour too early.

We had time to see the church thoroughly (it is a cellar, by the way, rather cold on a frosty morning) and get good seats, before the mass began; I have given myself papal absolution from my vow never to sit through another high mass; because, you see, they are so wily they put the things you *do* want to see after these tedious masses instead of before them, so you have to sit it out. The crowd grew tremendous, and began to push and scramble long before the lambs came. Luckily a priest had moved a huge *Prie-Dieu* just in front of us; so we were sure not only of a barricade, but of something to mount upon in crises.

At last came the servants of the cardinal with their droll long-bodied coats trimmed all over with upholstering gimp, elbowing a passage through the crowd; behind them two men in uniform, each bearing a good-sized lamb on a red damask cushion, its eyes tied, its head half covered with red and white and green flowers, and bows of red ribbon stuck here and there in the wool. You would n't have thought they would look pretty, but they did; it is so hard, I suppose, to spoil a lamb! But what they did to the lambs after they carried them behind the high altar I don't know, we could not see; but they were presently brought out again, and laid, cushions and all, under the great marble dome over the altar, and at the feet of the statue of St. Agnes herself. While they lay there the cardinal and the priests and the choir, and the sackbuts and the dulcimers and the fiddles, were all chanting and singing and going on, and the lambs once in a while said "Baa, baa," which was the only thing I understood of it all, and produced the most marked sensation in the crowd.

I had a dear little Italian boy to hold up on the top of the desk; and when the lambs baaed he laughed out, and his nurse from behind, who had consigned him to heretic hands with about equal misgiving and gratitude, reached over and jerked him and told him to be still. But I encouraged him to laugh. One poor little lamb kept lifting up its head and shaking the flowers, and the man who held it pressed its head down again, till you could hardly see that it had a head at all. Then the men cleared a way again through the crowd, and the poor little creatures were carried off; and good Catholics pressed up to touch them, as they were carried by; and then we came away, only stopping on the staircase to try to read some of the odd inscriptions from the tombs of the early Christians, which are built into the walls, — the inscriptions I mean, not the early Christians. This sentence is about as good as one in Murray where he speaks of this ceremony, and says that the lambs "are afterwards handed over to the nuns of a convent in Rome, by whom they are raised for their wool, which is employed in making the palliums distributed by the Pope to great Church dignitaries, and their mutton eaten!" It is true about the wool, but the lambs are never killed. They are usually given to Roman families, and kept as pets; an English priest told me so to-day.

We are luxuriating now in clear cold weather; at least I am. There are misguided souls (or bodies) that like the warm days; but I find them insupportably enervating. As for the sirocco, when that blows all hope forsakes a person of nerves; you feel as if you were a thousand needles, assorted sizes! Good by and good by, and God bless you all!

x

ROME, Monday, February 15, 1869.

DEAR PEOPLE: Will you be relieved, I wonder, or appalled, when I tell you that I have decided not to try to send you more than seven days in this letter! Such a seven days as it was, though; if I could only have photographed the seven sunshines, each bluer and whiter and yellower than the one before it! Spring is spring nowhere but here, I begin to suspect. No matter if a possible fever does lurk in every golden hour, and a certain weariness and lassitude in every whiff of the hot south-wind, you don't care; you glance up and down and run swiftly into the sunny spots with no more care than the lizards, who outstrip you, do your best.

Well, it is to be a week that you are to spend with me, and you came a week ago last Thursday morning, February 4, and I said, "Good, you are just in time for a delightful excursion to the Palace of the Cæsars, with the Archæologicals, this afternoon," — so we set off, P—— and I in a little low carriage, and the rest of you on your broomsticks in the air, as you always go nowadays with me everywhere. When we got to the door of the enclosure, there was the Archæological Society at bay! door shut! the old gray hat of John Henry Parker bobbing up and down above its worthy wearer's excitement and indignation, as he was parleying with the custode, and explaining to the crowd of Britishers that, owing to an unfortunate misunderstanding, we could not go in. There had been some mistake, some informality; of course there had, and Mr. Parker, being by nature a blunderer, had made it. Then danced up the gay Signor L—— with his violets in

his button-hole, and his little cane,— ineffable mixture of
infant, archæologist, and Marble Faun; and he chuckles
in his broken English over Mr. Parker's blunder, and
says, " O, I am so *emused* to see such many people so
deesappointed!" we laugh till we are ashamed, and
have to slink behind other people not to be seen. The
crowd is quite large, fifty or sixty people; — some
drive off; some follow Mr. Parker, who dashes across
the road, past the Basilica of Constantine, with its
three grand old arches, and in among the blocks
of everybody's house, and everybody's temple, and
everybody's road, all lying about in centuries of con-
fusion, between the Basilica and the Coliseum. We
saunter along after them, but not of them, and finally
sit down on what was a doorstep, I dare say, in the
days when Romulus went to late suppers; and there
we talk, and knock the sacred bits of marble with our
parasols and canes, just as if we had hobnobbed with
ancients all our lives. At last Signor L—— says, "This
is too stoopeed; we will not do it more; let us go into
the Coliseum." So he shook hands with Mr. John
Henry Parker as respectfully as if he believed he had
not been in the least to blame for the *contretemps*, and
off we went into the Coliseum, which had all that
while seemed to be beckoning us with its gray arms.
You all know just how it looks, I knew that before I
came; but how it feels, that is something which don't
photograph! — the unspeakable quiet; the dance of
lights and shade in and out of the arches; the distance and the nearness of the Gothic spaces of sky, set
in settings of stone, and looking like sapphire gates on
which, if you had but wings, you might knock and find
them opening to you! The noise of the city comes
in muffled and dulled, you hardly hear it, and, if you
do, you can hardly remember what it means; you are
more tranquil than you supposed this world would ever
let you become. I have wondered if one could not
even sit still under one of those arches and be happily

and unconsciously changed into wallflower or moss, without a pang of death! The wallflowers look perverse enough to have been the result of some such uncanny spell cast over human beings; they hang and wave and flaunt everywhere but where you can reach them,— great blazes of yellow darting and swaying like fires on the very tops of the most inaccessible places. By and by there will be more, I see, lower down; but at first, while they are a marvel, in these early days of February, they are only in spots where no human hand can touch them. We went up to the third tier, and out through one of the openings, and sat down; my feet were in a fragrant bush, looking and smelling like the old-fashioned "southernwood" in country gardens. Below us, the mass of mingled earth and ruin was a sharp precipice; we dared not look over. Just on the edge, a smilax vine tauntingly held up a cluster of claret beads,— I thought them seeds; the Archæologist said they were buds, and, before I could stop him, had picked them, to prove his theory true. I felt like throwing them on the ground, as King David did the water for which a life had been risked; instead of that, we quarrelled still longer over them, neither of us knowing enough to prove ourself right, and when I got home I found they had fallen out of my bouquet.

Suddenly we heard a sound of chanting below. There was a procession, going from shrine to shrine, kneeling down before each one, and chanting their prayers; there were a dozen men shrouded from head to foot in coarse brown cloth, like linen,— only two small holes left for the eyes. "These are they" who beg from door to door, shaking a little tin cup on every threshold, speaking no word, and turning away almost instantly if nothing is given them. I have been told that they are many of them noblemen who do this,— some of them as a penance, which is imposed by their confessor, and they have to walk the streets till they have got a certain sum; some of them belong to a fraternity or society, and are pledged to do this so many days in the year. They are uncanny objects to meet in the street. For two days after this scene in the Coliseum I saw them repeatedly, in different parts of the city; in fact, one of them walked by my side one morning as I was going to my Italian lesson, and I saw that his eyes were black and fiery, and his feet were white and finely veined. (Their feet are bare, with only a leather sandal.) A monk went before them, with a cross, and some twenty or thirty poor people had joined the procession. They all fell on their knees, and crossed themselves, and chanted aloud before each shrine. One poor man, who had a white beard fit for a patriarch, carried a sort of square board, perhaps some relic; at the end of each prayer, he threw himself forward full length on this board, face down, for a second, and seemed to be kissing the earth. Meekly, at a little distance, followed another smaller procession, all women. A nun carrying a smaller cross, a few sisters walking on each side of her, and a dozen poor women following; they kept in the rear, and knelt at a respectful distance from the monks and the men, but joined in all the prayers. O, you can have no conception of the wild sense of yearning tender pity which sweeps over you sometimes in looking on such a scene. You think you cannot bear it one minute longer! You must spring down among them and say, "Poor souls, poor souls, this is nothing; do look up, and see the sun." I watched Signor L——'s face while all this was going on, but I could not fathom his expression. I could see nothing beyond a sense of the picturesque additions which the veiled figures and the chanting and the high black crosses made to our view, as we looked down on it all from the upper chambers of the air; and yet he is a Roman Catholic, — so good a one that he has for five years gone, every spring, into a convent for *eight days of entire silence.* Think of that! Not one word to a human being for eight days!

There are some of us who would go mad on the seventh, if not sooner. It seemed malicious in the sun to hurry down on this particular afternoon, as he had not hurried on the day before, but I am sure he set an hour earlier! We were suddenly frightened by seeing that arch after arch began to lie in shadow, and that Mount Gennaro was turning pink; we almost ran down the stairs, for you must know that nobody may see sunsets from the Coliseum. As for that matter, it is at risk of your life you see them anywhere in this land of malaria, but in the neighborhood of the Coliseum it is worst of all; so this was the end of the first of our seven days, dear people.

Then came the Saturday on which we started out early for the *Baths of Caracalla.* You *would* have the Guide-Book carried along, you remember? and I called up to you, in the air, as we drove, that you might read it for yourselves; that I would not be tormented with its husks of information; that all I cared to know about this most wonderful ruin was that it was begun only two hundred years after Christ, and that emperor after emperor kept adding and improving till it grew to be one hundred and forty thousand square yards big, and sixteen hundred people could bathe there at once. I don't know whether the historians mention about *towels!* perhaps they did n't mind drying off in the sun! If they had much such sun as this Saturday's, it would have been easy (and perfect bliss besides). There were great halls for exercises; great round rooms big enough for churches, where a thousand or so took a vapor-bath if they liked. Then there were the cold rooms and the hot rooms, and the porticos, and the tribunes and the galleries; and the walls were painted and the floors were mosaic, and everywhere there were grand statues, so that the naked men could never have found themselves or each other beautiful. And I don't suppose there was a Roman of renown for five centuries who did n't have his turn in the tubs! That was the way it began, but now you see it is quite another sort of affair. You cannot follow out the plan of it, even if you keep Murray's map under your nose every step of the way, and break your shins, in consequence, over the great clutter of old stones lying about you everywhere; so presently you reflect that it does n't make the least difference to you which room was the "Cella Frigidaria," and which the "Cella Calidaria"; and as soon as you settle that, you can be happy. Then you can wander through great-walled square after square, and see on which floor there are most daisies; they are like fields now, — what were the old floors, — thick grass, ivies, vines, thistles. (Ah, the beauty of a Roman thistle! Some day I'll try to tell you just how they look; they are almost the most beautiful of the roadside things here.) All about you are these jagged broken walls, which look as if they might topple over any minute; where windows used to be are irregular great gaps, with vines growing in them; and presently, as you get used to looking up higher and higher, till you see the tops of the walls, you see what seems to be another earth, midway between you and the sky, and there are small trees growing, and vines and bushes hanging over the edges and reaching down to meet their kindred who are climbing up from below. Then it first dawns upon you what gigantic ruins these are, and by that time the custode knows you are quite ready to scramble up to the top; so he comes along with his key and unlocks a door in the wall, and there in the wall is built a narrow ladder of a staircase, up and up and up which you go, and when you come out at top you find that the "other earth," whose fringes you had seen hanging over, is a magic wild garden, on the tops of the old walls, with here and there a bit of what was *roof* in Cæsar's day, but is now more solid ground than the rest. Then you sit down on the safest-looking spot you can find, and lean up against a great stone, and think you will never go away. You dare not look over; too dizzy by half. I did wish I knew how high these walls were, but of course *that* was n't "put down" in Murray. The few rare bits of knowledge that I do hanker after never *are* in that unpleasant red book. But I can tell you a little by this; looking over into the great chamber where I had been picking daisies, I could see no daisies, only dark, still, solemn green. In another room men were at work digging down, down, for what they might find; they had struck the floor, but from our height it looked like a shapeless dark hole, and the men looked like children.

Here too were the yellow wallflowers, setting their torches where only the wind could reach them. O the cruel lure of a flower you cannot possibly touch! I shall remember some of *these* wallflowers as long as I live; and those I pick I shall forget, I suppose, though I nurture them tenderly for many days in my room.

We were so blessed in the day we took to see these ruins, that we were absolutely alone there: only one stuffy old Englishman came, and he did not stay; he wheezed up the staircase, and almost as soon as he caught sight of us he went down, looking frightened to death at the thought of two independent American women sitting with no hats on their heads, alone, on the top of the walls of the Baths of Caracalla!

But I nearly forgot to say that besides the wonderfulness of being on the top of these walls, and scrambling about dizzily on the brink of jagged unroofed chambers, where such thickets of laurestinus and myrtle and all other green-leaved things that grow so hide the real edge that you feel as if the tiny brown path before you might be an illusion and a snare, and the next step would be your last; besides all this, you look off over all Rome, and all the wonderful hills which encircle the plain, — hills so unlike any others I have ever seen that I do not know how to describe them. It is not their height, — they are not very high; it is not their shape, — their outlines are not unique; and perhaps I have seen other hills as pink and purple and gray and blue; but their beauty is like a subtle beauty in some faces, which cannot vindicate its claim by a feature or a tint, but which ravishes you, and holds you forever! The artists say it is atmosphere. There is an atmosphere to faces too; so I think perhaps there can be no better word for it than that.

Now have I given you a shadow of an idea of what it is like to roam about for four hours in and on the Baths of Caracalla? I am afraid I have not; and what is still more stupid of me, I skipped over from Thursday to Saturday, and never let you stir out of the house on Friday, which was the day for the Villa Pamfili Doria; and there we went and saw the whole of it, and picked anemones, — yes, purple and white anemones and painted crocuses on the 5th of February.

The word "villa" I have always had an unreasoning dislike for, and I went one cold, raw day last month to the Villa Borghese, and increased my dislike. It seemed to me more dismal than a cellar, and more set and lifeless than a checker-board; and as for the damp chill there was under the trees on that day, I have no words to express it. So even in the sun of this Friday I set out for the Villa Pamfili Doria with no great glow of expectation. Now I must tell you that, by Murray, the grounds are four miles in extent, and that it was given by a pope to his sister-in-law more than two hundred years ago, so that they have had time as well as room to make a comfortable home of it; and having told you this, we will begin at the gate, — a huge and high gate with three entrances, statues on the top and in niches; then a broad, smooth road, — broad enough for three carriages abreast, and on each side smooth greensward half white with daisies, — you can't think how daisies cuddle in the grass, where they have it all their own way all the year round; then another gate, less high, with one entrance; at the side stands a ser-

vant of the Pamfili Doria, in a long blue coat, down to
his heels, and trimmed with what looks like chintz
trimming on the collar and sleeves and pocket-flaps.
He takes off his hat to everybody that comes in, and
looks as proud as if he represented the hospitality of
long lines of Dorias. It is really a princely thing to
do, to throw open such a place as this, to the whole
swarming public, two days of every week, and let
them eat oranges, if they choose, under the trees, and
pick all the wild flowers they can. On each side
of the road are century-plants, seven and eight feet
high, — grandest things for a wall; behind them
great towers of something whose name I don't know,
— a sort of tall grass with soft tassels or plumes
that stand up eight feet high instead of falling over,
but look as light and airy as if they drooped. Presently
the house appears on the right, — big, and quite ugly.
I think nobody can look at it much; yellow and white
in panels and patches; statues, in niches, of all the
things in the Book of Ezekiel, I think, — but Murray does not mention. Past this, and you are in shade
of a great avenue of evergreen oaks. It would be
just as easy to believe that Adam set them out as that
Innocent X. did, only two hundred years ago. Then
the road winds in and out, and up and down; there
are groves, wild tangles of bushes on sides of hills,
paths that lead nowhere, ravines, meadows, swamps
which have not been touched, and swamps which are
made into ponds, and on which swans sail towards
the road at sound of wheels. From all the higher
parts of the road are exquisite glimpses of Rome, of
the Alban Hills, — which are always blue when the sun
shines, and which have white villages set like white
stones along their sides; these glimpses are most beautiful, when they struggle through among the stone-pines. There are no such stone-pines here as those at
this Villa, and there cannot be anywhere a tree more
beautiful than the stone-pine; no wonder Theodore

Parker, when he saw them, said, "Let one be set over my grave." A stem straight as a mast, up, up, into the air; then a sudden outstretching of fairy-like fingers and arms which hold up a canopy of the darkest and vividest green; — a great platform it becomes in some of them, from which another magic company of slender fingers holds up a second and then a third or fourth canopy. So slender are these arms, that from a great distance you do not see them, only the soft, dark, mysterious canopies against the sky, and below, the one shaft which rests in the ground; that is a stone-pine! Closer, you see that the needles are set thick and firm on the stems, and point up; and that they are like our soft-pines at home, only suddenly seized with a heavenward purpose. So, like all other things with heavenward purposes, they make themselves seen everywhere, and everybody soon learns their places.

There is one stone-pine, all alone, on Mount Mario. Years ago, some Englishman paid a large sum of money to have it left there undisturbed forever. In every view of Rome stands out that one stone-pine. You remember I told you we had one grand one in full sight from our parlor windows; the Barberini Palace stands in line with it, and seems so much less a thing! I shall see the pine always, but I can't even remember *now* exactly how the palace looks. All this in parenthesis! Dear me! shall I ever send you seven days at once?

When I first saw the open meadow on the right hand of this broad road, where I left you a page back, it was dotted here and there with bright spots of purple, so bright they looked almost like red. " O, what are they? what are they?" said I. " Only anemones," said S——, quietly. How soon I knelt at the feet of one! I have it yet, — my first Italian anemone. It was not unlike an ox-eye daisy in shape, but vivid purple, and the petals were larger. Then I found two other kinds, — one white, and one pale yellow, — next, a painted crocus, and then there was no time to look for more, for the sun was on the wrong side of the middle sky, and there were yet more than two miles to go in these wonderful pleasure-grounds. Everybody was there: several sets of Catholic boys with their priests at their heads; some in long scarlet gowns, some in black with stove-pipe hats. These last were really running and playing, and it looked about as droll as it would to see the Judges of the Supreme Court kicking up their heels! The red ones wound about among the trees, and shot out their gleams of color at unexpected places, so brilliantly that I was very glad they had all joined that particular shade of Catholicism if they could n't be Protestants! There was a farm-house with a tiled roof, and sheds in a good deal of disorder, and a barn full of hay, all of which we saw, because the barn was only a roof on eight stone pillars, and the hay all bulging out for its own wall! This was so picturesque that you could not help suspecting it of having been done on purpose, instead of because the climate is so mild. Then there was a garden, — a perfect specimen, they say, of the ideal Italian garden, — a flat square, laid out in the most absurd little shapes and strips, edged with green. They looked like the first pages in Euclid, or still more like a cook's table after the doughnuts have been all cut out, and the corners and bits of the dough left. How I laughed! It was the most ridiculous thing for a thing that meant to be fine! I can't imagine anything but small caricature puppets of flowers growing in it. This is the only thing in the grounds of the Pamfili Doria Villa which is not enchantingly beautiful! But I must not say another word about this Villa, except that, besides all I have told you, it has old tombs and columbaria, and fountains and greenhouses, and a little church, and a little monumental temple to the French soldiers killed in 1849, and a casino, and more violets than there are in all the rest of Rome put together! And here endeth Friday.

On Sunday we went to church at San Pietro in Montorio. We did n't hear much of a sermon, to be sure, nor stay through the services, because the church was very cold. But we made up for it by going into the cloister of the convent adjoining, and going into the little temple which somebody built over the very spot on which Peter was crucified. You don't doubt about that spot, do you? What is the use? and then wait till you hear the circumstantial evidence, i. e., we saw the very hole in which the cross rested! What more could one have! It is in a crypt (that is Roman Catholic short for a dark, damp cellar) under the temple, and there is an iron grating over the hole, and a sacred lamp perpetually burning in it. The old monk who showed us in had a long stick, hollow at one end, which he poked down and twisted round and round a few times at the bottom of the hole, and brought it up full of sacred earth, and then held it out to me, just as butter-men hold out to you the samples of their butter from the bottom of the tub. I realized afterwards that I ought to have taken the earth and carried it away as a relic; but I only stared at it and him and said nothing, and he put it back again with a sigh. However, he liked our franc just as well as if we had been Christians.

The cloister was the most shut-up spot I ever saw: high walls, brick and stone pavement; only the sky for relief, and that looked so far off it would very soon have discouraged you more than it would have comforted you, if you had been shut up there; in the middle, the cold, white, still, round temple with a dome, and a row of gray pillars around it. I thought it very beautiful, and was quite surprised to find it one of the things set down in Murray as proper to be admired. A few little weeds were struggling up between the stones in this cloister, and I thought if we did not escape pretty soon I should find my Picciola. The poor monk looked wistfully after us as he let us out.

I suppose he goes out too when he likes, but that can't
make much difference if you know you must go back
at night. O, I long to get out of hearing of the clank
of these chains!

This church and convent stand on the top of one of
the highest hills; behind the church, a few rods farther on
the road, is the fountain Paolina, — such an ugly thing;
all but the water, which is beautiful and makes you
leap about to look at it, — three great streams rushing
out of a wall into a semicircular basin; while the wall
and the basin and every head and corner and post are
so ugly, it only shows what water is, that it can be
so beautiful in spite of them. Some pope — a Paul, I
suppose — made the fountain more than two hundred
years ago; that is quite modern here, in fact, a mere
thing of yesterday. The water comes all the way from
the lake of Bracciano, and after this one brief minute
of jollity and beauty plunges down into the city, and
does — what do you think? — turns all the flour-mills!
How it must chafe when it remembers its frolic in
the pope's fountain, to which it can never, never get
back!

From the plateau in front of this fountain, and in
front of the church, is a grand view of Rome, — the entire campagna and the mountains. It was so warm
that we sat down on the grass and looked and looked.
The gay Roman people were flocking up and down,
keeping their out-of-doors Sunday. Poor souls, it is
no wonder this becomes part of their religion! Three
women sat in a group by the roadside, with huge piles
of some sort of salad, which they were getting ready
for market. They ate almost more than they put into
the basket; munch, munch, munch, — away they ate
and talked, and talked and ate, and laughed, as if clear,
cold, raw spinach were the most delicious thing in the
world. Before we went home, we took a turn in the
Coliseum, which was sunny, and had more flowers in it
than on Friday; from the topmost pinnacle they brought

down asphodel to me, and when I saw that, I was sorry
I had been so unsocial as to choose sitting alone in my
old arch, with my feet in the southernwood bush, rather
than climbing up with them. And here is the end of
the fourth lesson.

Now Monday can be told in few words, because it
is only the Villa Pamfili Doria over again. We went
early and we stayed so late that we were half sure we
should wake up with fever the next morning; and all
that time we were picking anemones, and lovely green
things to make into bouquets to throw at the Carnival
on Tuesday. Yes, absolutely to throw anemones at
the Carnival! Now that it is over, I see that it par-
took of the nature of sacrilege, but at the time it
seemed to me wise and good. O, such a basketful as
I brought home! and the next morning I spent two
hours and a half tying them up into lovely wild-looking
bunches; snowdrops mixed with them, and great ivy-
leaves set round like a bouquet-holder. I felt afraid I
had left no anemones for anybody else, and thought I
had enough to make at least a dozen bouquets, and,
after all, I had only seven! Then I had a basket full
of other flowers, and I had a white cape trimmed with
purple, and a fine wire mask, — and L—— had a white
cape trimmed with blue, and a wire mask, and a big
basket of flowers; and Tuesday afternoon we set out
with Marianina, our beautiful little serving-maid, bright
and early, after lunch, for the Carnival. You must
know that all this week Miss S—— and I had been the
owners of half a balcony on the Corso, and L—— had
been the owner of a seat in a fine balcony with other
friends, and yet we had been only twice to look on,
and found the whole thing so stupid, and the horse-race
so cruel, that we did not care to go again. But at the
last minute I was seized with a sudden desire to enter
into it wildly for an hour or two on the last day, and
see if I could by clear, sheer force of will compel myself to be amused! Would you believe it? in less

than ten minutes after I took my stand on that balcony,
and spread my flowers out before me, and began to
pelt people, I was just as excited as if I had been the
granddaughter of Julius Cæsar himself! I hit everybody I aimed at, and I caught every bouquet that was
thrown at me, and I worked for three hours harder
than I ever worked anywhere except in Dio Lewis's
gymnasium! It sounds silly. I am half ashamed to tell
of it, except that it would be a pity not to let you have
the laugh at me, and you can't laugh harder than I
do to think of it; for a woman of — well, of my age!
to be heartily amused for two solid hours throwing
bouquets to a crowd, and being pelted back by bouquets and sugar-plums! it sounds like a sharp, short
attack of being crazy. But I did it. Some of the
bonbons were very pretty, but I threw them all down
again to other people. My anemones, though, I did not
shower down promiscuously, you may be very sure;
our balcony was low enough for us to see the faces of
the people perfectly, and I threw anemones to none
excepting those who looked as if they knew the difference between anemones and miserable bought flowers
on wires. Then, when it grew dark, everybody lit
candles, and we had a few minutes' fun with those.
The people from below threw bouquets and hit them
and put them out, and the people from above knocked
them out of your hands, and the people from the next
balcony switched them out with their handkerchiefs;
and everybody screamed out, "Senza moccoli, senza
moccoli," and as you looked up and down the Corso,
the dancing lights were like a shower of stars blown
about in the wind. But this lasted only a little while,
and few people in the street had candles; so that it
was quite unlike what it used to be in old times. In
fact, the whole thing from beginning to end has been
no carnival at all, they say. The Romans do not
choose to be amused any longer. There are too many
sons in prison, too many waiting for one more chance

to fight; a hairdresser said to L—— one night in a half-frightened whisper, when she asked him why the Romans did not give themselves up to the Carnival as they used, " The whole city is in anger, miss ! " Even in the little contact which we have with the Romans we see smoulderings of the fire. I can't help wishing they would wait till this mild, gentle, good old Pius is peacefully put away under (or in) his sarcophagus. He cannot live long; I do not want him to be disturbed. After that, I could stay and fight myself to set this poor people free.

Well, that was the end of the Carnival; we left a dozen great bouquets in our balcony, and Marianina lugged home a few of the best ones which I thought might possibly do to take to pieces in the morning, and rearrange. Alas! in the morning the poor things showed what they had been through. The history of one bouquet through an afternoon of the Carnival would be a strange record. I do not doubt that sometimes the same bouquet goes through thousands of hands. Some of them had live canaries tied on them. That seemed to me even more cruel than the goading the poor horses for the race, which is a bit of cruelty of lineal descent from the days of the Gladiators.

Now I have made these days so long, that of the next one I can tell you nothing, except that it was just as sunshiny and warm as the rest, and we went to another villa, — the Villa Wolkonsky. Here are old Roman aqueducts, covered with ivies whose stems are larger than my wrist, and which branch and spread like trees! And here is an old tomb, which in the time of Nero one Mr. Cladius built for himself in a fine, conspicuous situation, as he supposed, and put his family names on the front; but now his tomb door is many feet underground, and the curious few go down into his tomb, and tumble about the bones of his kindred as much as they like. A Russian princess owns this villa, but has not lived in it for five years; so in what is she better, said we, than American princesses who own no villa?

What do you think of this for a week? We don't live quite so fast every week, but then we might, if it never rained, and if we were never tired; so the Roman calendar becomes, you see, quite another thing when you count the days in Rome. In spite of it all, however, I am hankering after a hill country with only its own legitimate dead about! Not that I mean to reflect on the family records of the Cæsars and Antonines; but I think it chokes the air a little too much to dig down into so many layers of sepulchre. Sufficient unto a century is the dead thereof. I shall like Switzerland better than Rome, and I shall say a new kind of prayer at night when I get into a country where I can go to bed once more with my window wide open.

Good by now, dear souls, one and all. Tell me all the smallest things you do, and keep a little green spot in your every-day hearts for me.

Rome, March 15, 1869.

DEAR PEOPLE: I have been to an exhibition of delegates from Babel. Don't think this is a figure of speech, it is naked truth; the other name for it, though, is the Exhibition of the College of the Propaganda.

O the wily wisdom of this Romish Church! the fineness of the web they spin! Nothing ever showed it to me like these thirty tongues, — Hindostanee and several other dialects of India, Arabic, Greek, Persian, Hebrew, Chaldaic, Syriac, Armenian, Curdo, Telegunese, Canarese, Coptic, Latin, French, Celtic, Danish, Illyrian, Bulgarian, Albanian, and I don't know how many more. But first I will tell you how we got there, and I might as well say here, that about this price has to be paid for everything you see and hear in this city. The exercises were to begin at half past two; we arrived at the door at quarter past one. Already a few determined spirits had taken their stand close to the great padded curtain to make sure of being first in. Soon there was a solid phalanx that could have battered the door down if they had gone at it head foremost. I never saw the water let on at a dam; but I have seen women let in at these Romish doors, and it must be pretty much the same thing. Perhaps you think you are a free agent in such a crowd; anything but that; you feel as if you were nothing but one great elbow that somebody else shoved with! Each time I think I will never go again, but you can't stay away.

It was a very narrow passage-way into which we were let by the opening of the first door this day.

Were we free now? O no, by no means; at the other end of this passage another door. In it one of the Swiss Guards, red and yellow and big with his towering plume: past him but two could go at once; first come, first served. Then such pushing! such elbowing! disagreeable, insufferable, only that you *have* to suffer it; and as if this were not enough, up comes one of the authorities, and drags through, by main force, two women who were at the rear end of the crowd, came late, and had no sort of right to a seat at all: women at the front remonstrate; man coolly says, "If you don't let these ladies pass, you sha'n't come in yourselves, that's all," and jerks them along. A—— V—— and L—— C—— get in several shots before Miss H—— and I. When we are handed into the small gallery, there they sit, stowed each in her appointed chair, A—— in the first row, L—— on the third, and I am mounted to the fourth. This gallery is like a little section of the family circle in our theatres; it will hold perhaps forty, — that is all, and there is no other place; so, instead of grumbling, you begin to thank your stars you got in at all. Still the men pass the women along twos by twos, and don't the last couples look black who have to climb up to the top seats? They might as well be in St. Peter's for all they can see or hear of what is going on in the hall below, down into which we look. It is half filled with the Propaganda boys facing the gallery; a great sea of black cloth with gleams of red lining, and a featureless white face once in so often, — that is how they looked.

Then there were three fiery blotches on the front seat, cardinals' caps and cloaks of hottest red; behind them, the next shade of dignity and righteousness, the monsignori, all purple (half mourning, I suppose, because they are not cardinals); then came spectators, chiefly priests and monks; in two balconies, opposite each other, the music, — the leader had gray hair, and held a violin under one arm all the while he beat time with his baton; it was droll to see him leaning out of his balcony, and gesticulating with both arms to the other half of his orchestra way off on the other side of the hall. I forgot to listen to what they played, but it was very fine. Then there were windows opening from an outside gallery into the hall, and at all these windows stood the women who could n't get seats. Every year there are fights at these windows; nowhere, they say, are there such fights seen as at these ceremonies at the Propaganda, — there is so little room and so much interest.

P—— and N—— saw a shocking scrimmage there to-day; in fact, that was one reason they came away, N—— remarking in an audible tone that she came to hear the young men speak, but she had heard nothing but quarrelling and fighting, and she should not stay to hear any more. Fancy hearing well-dressed women, who can speak French and Italian and English, and perhaps German, abusing each other face to face in a public crowd.

"Madam, it is evident you are no lady."

"Madam, I will call the police and have you taken out."

Well, we all got our breaths, and the boys had theirs beforehand, and it began. Nobody spoke more than five minutes; those who could, sang at the end of their little "piece" a few lines of what I presumed to be a national air. Some of them were very wild and pathetic; most of the Asiatic ones reminded me of the songs of the sailors at sea. It was a great joke that when the "Inglese" came we could not understand it much more than we had the Persian. It was spoken by "Signor Giacomo Burns," of Glasgow, and, so far as I did comprehend it, I must say it was anything but shrewd or Scotch-like in its ideas. I forgot to tell you that we all had had given to us a pamphlet programme of the exercises, in which was printed each speech, in

Italian, with the man's name and country below it. Some of these brought up strange pictures just by their very look. "Signor Michell Chenaja di Yelchife Nella Mesopotamia," "Signor Gulielmo Samba dell Isola di S. Maria Nella Senegambia." Ah, he was the man that it would have warmed your heart to hear! Black as the ace of spades, a great, full voice like a river, and the presence and the motion of an orator; how they clapped and clapped and clapped him! He wore gold glasses, and a side light kept flashing on them, making his eyes look like yellow topazes at the distance from which I looked at him. He sang an African song which was so exactly like a plantation "break-down," that I began to think the whole scene was a weird dream; the candles, the scarlet, the fresco, the Swiss Guards, the erect black man in his solemn black gown, and out of his mouth coming these ludicrous "Hi-yi's." But I think he was the strongest man intellectually of all who spoke. I have observed him many times before, walking arm in arm with the white students. You hardly ever go out without meeting a procession of them taking their walk, and I have always been impressed by this man's face. How long before we shall be great enough in America to see such a thing in Yale or Harvard?

Everybody grew tired, but I did n't. Many went out, so that I finally clambered over and down till I was in the front seat. After the exercises were done we leaned over the railing and looked down. Up steps the guard, and says, "It is against orders for women to look over!" I could n't see what more harm we could do to the poor men by looking over. We had been set up there in full sight for three hours, for them to look at and find out how nice we were! But we turned meekly away, and A—— and I ran home alone through the Duc Macelli and past the Capo la Casa, through the Via Felice; then she to the Via Sistina and I to the Via Quattro Fontane, and it was quite too dark, but nobody troubled us. Do you like the sound of the names of the places where we walk? I do. If one could only walk more! But these torturing pavements! Somebody said in the "Pall Mall," the other day, that ·a pilgrimage over the pavements of Rome without peas in your shoes was quite enough to atone for most sins. Sometimes I think one hour of it has cleared my scot! O, how they twist you and turn you! ˙ Everybody hobbles, nobody walks.

The next day we drove out to Santa Maria Navicella, one of the oldest churches in Rome, way out and up on the Cælian Hill. We went through lovely old lanes, walled up high on each side, with ivies and vines of all sorts; then under the arch of Dolabella — did you know him? — and then we came to the church. We knew it by the great marble boat in front of it, — solid marble, gray and black, and split in the middle; a boar's head on the prow, much chipped on the edges, and with fools' names scribbled over it, — chiefly in English, I am sorry to say. Leo X. made this one; there used to be a much older one, which came to grief, and this is the model of it. I am sure all the little boys on the Cælian Hill for centuries have wished they had it.

In the church were thirty men mumbling off a sort of lay service, and a slipshod monk at the altar, and the two Misses ——, nice old maids from Massachusetts, patting about among the pillars. Over the tribune — that means the round place at the end, on which the altar stands — were such odd mosaics, you laughed before you knew it; Christ and the Apostles and the Angels all put in little bits of marble, and looking much more as if they came from the court of Japan than the kingdom of heaven; in the ninth century they were stuck up there, and I suppose they will stay forever. Next we went to San Stefano Rotondo. This is still queerer and older; used to be part of a meat-market in Nero's time. In the court-yard we saw an old well, which somehow reminded me of getting ice from the butcher's shop next door, at home.

The church is just one huge round room, high and gloomy and bare, with a row of columns, and what do you think for frescoes? — *all* the possible and impossible martyrdoms! panel after panel, the whole dreary circuit; and you get into such a horrible sort of spell that you can't help going on from one to another, till at last you feel as if you had been head-executioner to the Inquisition for a hundred years, and would have to chop off heads, and broil people on gridirons, like a kind of Wandering Jew, till the end of time!

Under each picture is a slab with a Latin inscription telling you who did it, to whom, where and when, and all about it, and you spell these out with a dim sense of finding out that it is all a fancy sketch. This is all there is to this church, except some grotesque mosaics in the tribune done in the seventh century, two big saints and a little Saviour, and in the vestibule a great marble chair in which St. Gregory sat and read his "Fourth Homily." I hope you don't think I know who he was, or what his Fourth Homily was about. All I know is, that, if the Homily were long, the Saint must have grown uncommon stiff and cold.

Monday we went all over the Quirinal Palace, — twenty-six rooms of it at least, all they show; I dare say they keep twenty-six more locked up. Such a dreary place as it is! O the poor lonely Pope! I hope the Vatican is better. Marble floors, or else inlaid wood; walls marble half-way up, and never stopping; such distant ceilings; many of the walls hung with crimson damask, which looked as if it had been frozen, spite of its red; chairs in nearly all the rooms of solid wood, some of them black walnut, but some painted in imitations of marble and malachite, all with Pius IX. on the front, the poor *garde nobile*, and anybody else who lives there, must have a hard time sitting on them; crucifixes in every room, and in several of the state rooms a throne with a canopy over it. I kept thinking the Pope had run off with my beggar, and lucky enough he would be if he had!

We saw his bedroom, all crimson and gilt, but quite plain; that and the study were the only rooms which looked small enough to live in; he has a study table, like any other man, with a place in the middle to put his legs under. I sat down in the chair, and put my heretic feet on his damask footstool, where nobody saw me. I should like to write one of my encyclicals there.

But the spittoons! Ha! that pleased me! I hope somebody will tell Mr. Dickens; I never saw so many in a hotel in America. They are in almost every room, but their purpose is cunningly hid in this fashion: the box has a lid, — it is all of wood, — and a broad band like a bell-pull fastened to this lid, and then going up to a sort of high post, which is attached to the box, and the whole thing looks rather ornamental, and it was n't till after some time I smelt out the trick; then I slipped back into the Pope's study, and I lifted up the very one by his sacred chair, and sure enough there it was, sand and all, a spittoon! The *custode* never missed me, but I wonder what he would have said if he had caught me at it.

A dear honest old priest from the country was taken round at the same time with us, and his tender adoration of everything was pathetic to see; he went on tiptoe round the most sacred spots, and talked under his breath. The *custode* would speak English with us, and we could hardly understand a word he said; but we were ashamed to ask him to speak in Italian, for fear we should understand still less.

The Pope's private chapel was the only homelike-looking place there; that was really cosey, if it is proper to say such a thing of a room with arches on each side and a high dome, all one mass of gilt and carving and fresco; but it really did look comfortable, it was so small in comparison with the great giant caverns we had been through. In this chapel is a Guido, — The Annunciation. The Virgin is a good-looking. woman in a great blue gown, and the Angel is another good-looking woman in as much more yellow gown, and with the things which artists have agreed among themselves to call wings growing out of her shoulders.

Tuesday was the day for the Villa Albani. I have told you about the Villa Pamfili Doria. That is my love, no other villa will wean me; but the Villa Albani has a great collection of statues and pictures. I sat on the balcony all the afternoon, and looked at the view: Alban hills all in shadow, deep blue; Monte Gennaro also in deep shadow, but the whole long range of the Sabine Hills between, one kaleidoscope of light and shade; the clouds lay low and the sun was bright, — cloud effects here are rare, for the sky is usually clear, too clear for the beauty, of the landscape. I shall never forget the Sabine Hills that afternoon. Among the statues was one old Bacchus that I think I should like to have come to supper.

Wednesday I drove about all day with P——, who was doing last errands before starting for Sicily. It always seems more unreal to do shopping in Rome than anything else; to stop in one of these old streets at a glove-cleaning place seems such a flagrant violation of unities; after the errands were done, we went to the Coliseum for our good-by, and sat there till the sun looked in in level beams, it was so low. The wallflower is blazing out now from all the high places which you cannot reach,— such great swinging masses of vivid yellow, it is more than human nature can bear to see it, and the larks sing among it like divine flutes. While we sat there, some poor working women walked through, and all knelt and kissed the great cross in the centre, — to kiss that cross makes you free for a certain number of years from Purgatory, — after them came two priests, and took off their great flapping hats and kissed it too.

Thursday we went to the Ludovisi Villa; that is really a villa which one could go into a rhapsody over if one had not sworn allegiance to the Pamfili Doria. O, that reminds me I have not told you that in the Pamfili Doria the real anemones are out now, and on Friday, the 19th, we went there, and I picked a great basket full. The meadows were literally covered; we trod them down, we could not help it; I could have cried; I did not dare to look where I had walked; they are white, they are buff, they are scarlet, they are crimson, they are lavender, they are pink, they are purple, they are white with purple veins, white with pink tips, buff with dark crimson base, buff with purple, and besides all these many more! Of course you don't believe me; I should n't if anybody told me. They are like a small single poppy, made a little more neatly, and the leaves pointed a little and setting up in a cup shape; they are all sizes, from a tiny buttercup to a good genuine poppy size; they are close to the ground, or they get up as high as six or eight inches on their stalks; and all the world can go two days a week to this villa and pick all they want, and, whatever else the house of Doria does or does not, that is a princely bit of good-fellowship with the world, is n't it? Now to go back to Ludovisi, it was there that I had your last letter. We had found it at the bankers on our way, and I carried it in my pocket through great avenues of ilexes, walks with hedges of box and laurel twenty feet high, past a bird-cage as big as a small house, with a wire dome, and a big tree growing under it, and a fountain at the foot of the tree, and a hundred canaries doing as they liked there, which was chiefly to sing and to spatter; past statues of Hercules and all the other old heroes, and a grand head of Juno; past great frescoed rooms where are an Aurora by Guercino and a Night by somebody else, both of which are lovely in photograph, and not a bit lovely in plaster, — way up and up to the third floor of the casino and out on

the terrace, where we sat down with our backs to the
sun and our faces to Soracte, and I read your letter.
L—— read one from her brother, and we said no word
to each other for an hour. Then we walked about and
picked violets which should be called Tyrian, they are
so purple. All of a sudden there came a dark cloud
in the midst of the blue of the sunshine, and without
one second's warning a sharp shower. It really seemed
as though some mischievous little heavenly boy must
be doing it with squirt-guns, for the sun shone as brightly as ever, and at first we could not even see the cloud,
it was so little a tree hid it; but we had to run all the
same as if it had been big, and we got wet, too, before
we could reach our carriage, and that was the end of
that day's sight-seeing. And that must be the end of
this letter.

We long for the country. Albano gleams out cool
and white high on the hillside only twelve miles
away, and beckons and lures like a magic strain of
music in the distance. Perhaps my next letter will be
from that fairy spot. Farewell.

VENICE, Sunday P. M., May 16, 1869.

DEAR PEOPLE : We came away. It was harder than you could imagine. Rome is a siren of sirens. It was so hot that we could scarcely breathe from ten o'clock till four, and there was nothing to eat except ices and strawberries with no flavor to them, but we clung to the very stones of that city. I went in from the beloved Albano on Friday, the 7th, supposing that we should set out for Venice on the following Tuesday; but P—— and N—— were not ready, and we did not get off until Thursday. At first when they told me this I said, "I will go directly back to Albano. I will never stay in this ill-odored oven five days!" But I stayed, and when Wednesday came I privately hoped that some dresses, or marbles, or pictures would not come home at the last minute, so that we should be kept a day or two longer. There are still so many things in Rome that I have not seen. I feel as if I had made only a beginning, though I have been there more than four months; in those five last days, however, I made good use of the time; if I had been as industrious all winter, I should have accomplished more. Among other things I did, which had been inexplicably postponed in the winter, was the "Palace of the Cæsars." I could not tell how many times the day had been set to go there. Once, as I wrote you, I stood at the gate, with the whole Archæological Society at my back, and could not get in. I had grown superstitious about it; but at last I really did get in, and then, O my countrymen and women, what a fall was there! I had all along anticipated seeing ruins grander than any other except the Coliseum. As I saw them from the distance they looked imposing, and looked wild and overgrown, like the Baths of Caracalla, and as all ruins ought to look. But what do you think you see when the gate is first opened? (It is owned, you must know, by Napoleon, sold to him for $40,000 by the King of Naples, "that very stoopid young man," as Signor L—— said, in telling me about it, "for $40,000 this whole grand ruin; and the water privilege alone is worth more than that." So the Emperor has walled it in, and is carrying on excavations in a masterly manner, and the public only go in on Thursdays; but I went in with Signor L——, who has always the right to go anywhere on any day, so far as we can discover; and we went on a Saturday.) When the gate is opened, you see a broad walk and a sort of *café*-like building, and very much landscape garden, nice little beds, such as you might see in Brooklyn or Springfield, bushels of roses, and white thorn and box borders; if you are like me, you stand stock-still and burst out laughing, and say, "Where is the Palace of the Cæsars?" and then your archæologist leads you along, up and up, into great spaces, some of them floored with mosaic, some of them bare earth, but all cleaner and more swept and garnished and scrubbed than any old maid's parlor you ever saw; great columns set here and there, and grand bits of marble, fragments of acanthus, and legs and arms, etc., such as you see always in the ruins of Rome; but *here* they are all set by so neatly that, upon my word, you don't feel as if they were ever in any other place in their lives. Then, as I say (if you are like *me*), you laugh still more, in fact, you get positively irreverent; and you look round, expecting to see old women with pails and mops in every corner, and there is nobody in sight, except workmen wheeling away things in wheelbarrows, and you think they must be carrying off the old women with pails and mops, for there does not seem to be anything else to carry off! All this time the archæologist is delivering a little lecture by your side;

how this is the old audience chamber, and this was the dining-room, and this circular mosaic at the end is the place where the emperors used to sit, — and very likely *lie*, if they ever got "under the table," — and this is the bath-room, and this is the academy where every day a poet read a poem, or a philosopher or historian an essay, before the emperor; and at last the archæologist sees that you are shaking with laughter, and, having previously found you more than sentimental enough on other occasions over other ruins, he thinks you are laughing at his English, and stops short and says, "What are you doing? what have you the matter?" And then you, that is I, sink down into a thicket of purple foxglove, and begin to sneeze violently (for rose-cold happens in these days, because Italy is one great garden in blossom). Then I try to explain that I think it the funniest thing in life to see a ruin so scrubbed up and put in such horribly good order; that there is such an eminently French look about it all, that it seems to belong to the Rue St. Honorè, and to have nothing whatever to do with Rome either ancient or modern; and that I very much doubt if ever an emperor set his foot in it! Then the archæologist, being the gentlest little soul in the world, loses his temper, and says, "You are very provokking"; and that completes my nervous amusement, and all is "up" for that day. However, when I was fairly underground, walking along an old street, many feet beneath the landscape garden, and looking into stuccoed room after room, and up steep stone staircases, on one of which it seems to me quite probable that Caligula was killed, I found my usual faith and reverence reviving, and patched up a sort of truce with my archæologist. But I shall never forget the comical effect of that first look at the palace of the Cæsars.

Among other good things of those last days in Rome was an illumination of the Venus of the Capitol: daytime too! It happened on this wise. We went to the room at just that one minute of noon, when the sun flooded in through the upper panes of the window on the right, and lit up the whole statue with a positively supernatural color. Even the *custode* exclaimed he had never, in all the years before, happened to hit that precise moment and such a sun. The face smiled, and the right arm trembled a little as the sunlight flickered over it. We stood breathless and silent, and it would not have surprised us in that instant to have heard a voice from the lips. On the left of the Venus stands a dear little girl in marble, looking like anybody's little girl in the next street, only that her gown is all one great square piece of something gathered up in what were folds in those days, but would look uncommonly bunchy, I think, if we were to try them now. She is holding a little bird up in her arms, to keep it safe from a snake which stretches up behind to reach it. We wanted to wait till the sun had come to the little girl's head, but we had not time; so we ran to take one more look at the black marble Centaurs, and the Infant Hercules, and then went home.

At the last, the leaving Rome was quite picturesque. We went at night; for of the two evils, to ride all night seemed less than to get up at 4 A. M. and ride all day in the heat. Poor little Marianina had haunted the hotel all day; running in and out to see if I did not want something done, and finally standing in the dining-room door while we took our tea, and looking at me with the piteous eyes of a dumb animal. Every now and then she would say, "Iddio mio! Iddio mio! O signora mia!" till I could not stand it, and had fairly to pretend to be stern, and send her off. I said to her though, "If I were rich, Marianina, I would take you with me." "O, but you *are* rich, signora mia!" she said, with the tears in her eyes. Poor soul, I think nobody has ever been very kind to her before, and this one month with me (with good wages and nothing to do!) has been the one *festa* of her life. Giovanni, the girls' old courier, went with us to the station, and Marianina, who had insisted on carrying my bundle and bag, appeared with a cousin to carry the bundle; so we filed up past the little garden and the soldiers and out among the fire-flies, quite a procession. Marianina knelt on the step of the car till the bell struck and the guard pulled her off; then she kissed our hands and walked slowly away, looking over her shoulder at the guard out of one eye, and at me out of the other! The guard said something to his fellow-guard about her beauty, and snapped the door, and we were off, — we three women, good friends, good travellers, — off for Venice, with Rome written on our hearts!

If there be any greater misery short of rheumatic fever than to ride all night in the cars, I do not know what it is. So long as there is daylight, and one can see that there are peace and dry land and homes and human beings to the right and left, railroad riding is bearable; but the minute I am in the dark, every whistle sounds like the shriek of fiends, every jolt and jar seem to me the wrenches of a rack on which I am being torn; and when people sleep on either side of my misery, I am aggravated to that degreee that I am dangerous. Each time I spend such a night, I think I will never spend another, come what will; but by the time the next occasion arrives, I buy my ticket, and go on board as docilely as the best sleeper among you. And I dare say, before I see you again, I shall have spent a month, all told, in night railroading. It seems to be considered the thing to do here.

At Foligno the cocks crew, and the passengers got out and ate, and we could see what color the fields were. Then began a royal progress through a garden; all the way to Ancona, four hours, nothing but wheat-fields and vineyards; in the wheat-fields, scarlet poppies and purple foxglove, and bright blue something, I don't know what, but as we dashed by it looked like

bachelor's-buttons flying off in the air. Under the
vines, which were trained on trees, were such fields
of crimson clover as you would not believe in if I
were to tell you about them. Fields of crimson pe-
onies set close as they could stand would not be more
crimson. In Ancona I found some peasant-women
who had walked into town with huge loads of this
clover on their heads, and were resting by the roadside.
I jumped out of the carriage, and asked them for one
of the flowers. O, how brown and handsome the
women were, and how they laughed when I broke off
one blossom and laid it carefully in my book! I shall
slip a bit of it in this letter, and you can see for yourself what fields would look like where such clover as
this flowered in spikes three inches long! We liked
Ancona, but did not see so much of it as we should if
we had not gone straight into our beds at 9 A. M.
and slept till 1 P. M.! It is enough to make an engineer officer's mouth water for a war, to see such hills
and such fortifications. From Trajan's day till now it
seems somebody or other has always been building
forts there, and somebody else firing at them. No
wonder. The very sight of the place is a temptation,
and the build of it as much a proof of the divine
intent of war, as flesh-teeth in animals. We saw Trajan's arch, and a statue to Cavour, and a cathedral up
in the air at tiptop of hills and forts and town and all,
and a gay-looking theatre where *Faust* was to be played
that night, and ever so many nice shops with muslin
waists and straw things, which we wanted to buy, and
a man peddling boiled dinner round in a big iron pot in
a handcart. Yes, really boiled beef and peas and potatoes, and it smelled savorily; and a poor ragged creature came out of a forlorn house and bought a plateful,
while we were looking on. Then we bundled into a
little cockle-shell of a boat, we and our five trunks,
and were rowed off to the steamer, where we found
an American family at dinner in the cabin, as if they

had lived there all their lives, — a thin, yellow mamma, with tight hair, which savored of sewing-societies and rigid principles; a papa who was all gray, grizzled good-nature; and a miss who did French for them both: and they had been on the Nile all winter, and were just from Corfu; and were in Madeira the winter before; and, dear me, for all that, how very inexperienced and uninformed they looked!

Almost as far as we could see the shores of Ancona, we could see the bright patches of the clover-fields. They gradually faded from crimson to claret, and then at last looked like dark woods in the dim distance. I remembered Mrs. Howe's "I stake my life on the red!" Wonderful color, which makes such road for itself through space.

Think of our not getting up in time to catch the first glimpse of Venice rising from the sea! It was stupid, but we might as well own up; we did n't do it. However, it looked odd and unreal enough when we did get on deck. We were squeezing along in water that felt thick, — piles all about us, as much land as water, and not enough of either to make it seem like anything set down in geographies; and the bell-towers and domes in sight, like a gray mirage against the sky. Somehow I could not feel as I expected to. Generally you don't, I find. I felt more like Mrs. Partington than like Rogers, or any other man of them all who has touched bottom in Venetian romance. If I had opened my mouth, I am afraid I should have exclaimed, like the worthy female above named: "Laws sakes alive! What an awful freshet they must have had! And what on airth are these poor people going to do, supposin' they can get there, which seems no ways likely?" Then, when we began to be surrounded by the dismallest black craft I ever saw, uncanny enough to have come straight from the Styx, and I was told exultingly by my companions, "There are the gondolas!" I was still more "taken down." I could n't say either that they looked unlike the photographs of them, and that was the most provoking part of it. I can't tell you how comical and melancholy they looked to me that morning, — and look still, for that matter. The body of a hearse set down low in the middle of a gigantic peaked snow-shoe, the whole black and sticky, and stamped with sepulchral designs. It is an understood thing now, that I am not to be expected to "ride in that kind of kerridge" again. Once I tried it, but I wriggled and stumbled out instantly, and told the girls if they were going with *me*, that hearse-top must be taken off. Rain or shine, I will take my chance with an umbrella. When this top is off, a gondola becomes the most fascinating of boats. I could glide about forever in them, and you have the feeling all the time here that the next minute the whole city may go under, and perhaps you can pick up a survivor or two. So it seems well to be on hand with your boat. I suppose I shall become accustomed to this miracle of a stone city at anchor. We are to stay a month, and I must begin to do something else besides try *to look under* the houses, which is all I have done yet. Even the floors seem to me to go up and down like the old "China" I came over in. If I were not an uncommonly good sailor, I should be seasick all the time; and when I am walking in what they call streets (Heaven save the mark; they are just cracks in the walls, that is all: a big soldier and I nearly got wedged trying to pass each other in one yesterday, and I had on no hoop at all), I half expect to "slump through" at every step. As for the Doge's palace, that's another blow! It may be imposing; I suppose Ruskin knows; but somehow it won't impose on me, and I can't get it to! It looks low and undignified, and the "edging" at top is not half so good in effect as I have seen round summer-houses at home. And the windows are not in line, nor sufficiently out of line (like our dear old up-and-down windows in Rome) to be picturesque;

and the colonnades look to me very shoppy; and there, you see, I am, and, like Martin Luther, "I can no more"; and I suppose you will think there is no fun at all in having such an unappreciative friend in Venice, especially if she does not know enough to keep quiet about the sacred things she is too ignorant to admire. I have been up and down the Grand Canal twice, and seen more old palace fronts than I can count. They are fantastic and gorgeous, and it all looks Arabian Nights-ish; but I cannot make it look to me otherwise than overloaded and mixed. All the time I find myself recalling the stern simplicity and beauty and grandeur of arches and walls and churches in Rome, and Venice seems to me tawdry. This is at end of the second day, however; so it is premature. We have begun to read aloud the "Stones of Venice," and we are going to be praiseworthily conscientious in attention to all that Ruskin tells us is admirable; so at the end of our month I may be as enthusiastic an admirer of the city as he. But the one thing I expect to be made really happy by, and to bear away with me to keep the rest of my life, is the color of Titian. Michael Angelo is the god of shape; I think Titian must be of color; and no wonder, when he fed on such sunsets. Last night, beside all else, we had a rainbow over the sunset. It broke up and floated about in pieces; and the Doge's palace looked like amber in the yellow light; and on the three great scarlet flagstaffs in St. Mark's were three huge flags, which floated from the tops of the staffs to the ground, — green and red and white, so that all things seemed turning to rainbow.

We are most comfortably established at the Hotel Vittoria, *not* on the Grand Canal, thank Heaven! When at first N—— said that she did not dare to stay on the Grand Canal, because she feared too much sea air, I was quite dismayed. But now I am thankful enough to have dry land; that is, a stone floor laid on piles, on *one* side of our house. I look down from my window into one of the cracks called streets; the people look as if they were being threaded into the Scriptural needle's eye, and a hand-organ looks like a barricade. Yesterday I threw down four *soldi* to a man who was grinding at one under my window, and made signs to him to go away, for I was almost frantic with the noise of seven different bells ringing at the same time. I am in mortal terror now to think of my indiscretion, for that man, having discovered the "vally of peace and quiet" to me, I presume will become a regular pensioner on my bounty for the rest of my stay.

VENICE, Wednesday, June 2, 1869.

THERE is so much to tell you about here, that I see plainly my only way will be to keep a sort of journal, and if, so doing, I make my letter into a book, I hope enough of the color of the days will get into its pages to repay you for struggling through them. We finished up our May with a christening! — Venetian twins, in the church of San Giovanni e Palo, called in the guide-book vernacular (if there be such a thing as vernacular for men who write guide-books, bless them!) "the Westminster Abbey of Venice."

We had wandered about among the tombs of the Doges, and the statues of generals, and the altars and the candles, and the pictures and the scaffoldings, and the workmen and mortar, and the begging men and boys and old women, till we were perfectly exhausted, and did not care whether Venice ever had a Doge or not, or if the beggars died of starvation at our feet; and we were just going off, when we saw a woman hurrying into the church with a glass box in her arms. P——, who had seen them before, exclaimed, "Oh! oh! there is a baby to be baptized!" and we almost ran towards the woman. A baby indeed! there were two babies, rolled up tight, like mummies, to their very throats; little knit caps on their heads, which were about as big and red as Baldwin apples, and rolled about from side to side as if the stems would n't last long. The box was perhaps a foot and a half or two feet long, and a foot high, — a wooden framework, with knobs at the corners like bedpost tops; the sides of glass, and holes around the edges in the wood-work to let in the air. The babies were twins, and were just one day old!

The woman set the box down on a bench by the wall as indifferently as if it had been a bundle of old clothes, and walked away. There they lay, the two poor little gasping things, all alone in this huge church, with effigies of dead Doges and great equestrian statues all about them. I never supposed anything so uncanny could happen to one in the first forty-eight hours after getting into the world, even if one had the luck to land in Venice! P—— and I stood and watched the poor little creatures; they hardly seemed human, though their eyes were really bright and they were unusually wide-awake-looking babies for their time of life. One of them was quite uncomfortable, and gasped often as if it would cry if the bandages were not too tight; the other, which had a red string in its cap, and by that token I thought was the older of the two, seemed to look upon the grimaces of his brother with positive philosophical scorn. He would look him steadily in the eye for a minute, and his mouth seemed quite pursed up with contempt for such babyishness. Presently the woman came back, and with her a priest, slouchy and unneat, with a purple vestment slipped on over his old coat; a little ragged boy carrying a candle; and a stout handsome fellow, evidently a workman, whom I took to be the father. It turned out afterward that he was only the godfather, which relieved my mind of some anxiety, because I did not at all like the stolid, uninterested way in which he looked down on the baby's face while he held it. The father was in the sacristy through the whole ceremony, and did not so much as peep out. The woman who brought the babies was evidently a servant, and there was no attempt at holiday attire about her; in fact, the whole atmosphere of the thing would have led you to suppose that baptism of twins was an every-day thing to them all, and it was much as ever they could do to spare time for it. Fancy the group, — the priest, the little boy with the candle, the heavy godfather holding the baby, the listless servant, and two eager and horrified American women looking on! An old beggar-woman hobbled up too, and stood near. The other poor baby meantime was left alone in its glass-walled bed half-way down the church; the door ajar, and nobody to watch! Such a chance to steal a baby! The priest mumbled and galloped over a Latin service; once in a few minutes the little boy said something which sounded like "Nan! Nan!" The priest put a great pinch of salt into the poor little thing's mouth, breathed on it, put oil in its ears, on its breast, and on the back of its neck, the godfather holding it bolt upright with the poor little one-day-old spine bending and lopping in all directions! The sacristan spilt some of the oil, and the priest almost laughed out; then they all laughed; and the servant took twin No. 1 back to the case, and brought up No. 2. But we did not stay to see the ceremony over again; it was too horrible.

The only things I shall remember about this church are these twin babies; the ornamental effigy of a general, who died of grief after a defeat in battle; and a fine Gothic arch in the wall over a sarcophagus, — "*the tomb of an unknown person*," says Murray. It is wonderful, the spell of that "unknown person." One day in the Protestant cemetery in Rome, I found a grave without a stone to mark it, and white violets growing above. I am not sure that the white violet I brought away from that grave has not a voice sweeter than that from the grave of Shelley! Who can tell why?

To-day we have had a picturesque day: first, the school of San Rocco, three rooms full of Tintoretto's pictures, about which, since I do not like many of them, and am not competent to speak, I hold my tongue.

Next we went to the church of San Crisostomo; and here is a picture, by Giovanni Bellini, with which one can form an intimate friendship! I should like to spend mornings with these saints: St. Jerome, high up on a rock, with his book; poor harassed St. Augustine, in his mitre and vestments, on the right; and on the left, St. Christopher with the loveliest baby boy astride on his shoulders, holding on tight by one little hand to Christopher's black hair. O, it is delicious! but then it won't sound so, and it is stupid to take up your time with empty names of things.

When we left San Crisostomo we supposed we were going directly home. Surely we had seen enough for one day; but as we turned into a narrow canal we found all the houses decorated with flags, and the flags trimmed with black. "O Signora," said Luigi, "there is a great funeral in the church on that street." Now a funeral was the very thing we had wanted to see! We had seen how Venetians began, and we had curiosity as to their end! We had asked Luigi, the day before, if he could not find a funeral for us, and he had replied quite sadly that funerals were just now out of season. Nobody died in Venice in the spring! We did not wonder that nobody wanted to; but still it seemed a little queer, looked at from a statistical point of view, that nobody did.

However, here was a funeral, ready to his hand, and a grand one too. We hurried down the little street; every house had the national flag hanging from a window, and the staff wreathed with crape; people were all hurrying in the same direction; in a few moments we saw a bridge crowded with men and women, all looking eagerly down the canal! "O," said we, "we are just in time; the funeral cortege is coming up in gondolas"; so we pushed and elbowed in among them, and looked down the canal too! Nothing to be seen, and while we were looking, the crowd dissolved and left us. That is the most mysterious thing about an Italian crowd; it gathers dense and black and resolute in five seconds from nowhere, and in five seconds more it has gone like a cloud, and no trace of it left, and why it went or why it came you will never know, neither does it know itself!

Again and again I have asked a man or a woman why they were waiting, and they have answered with a laugh, "Because there are many people here!" Lamb-like children!

The church was near and we ran there, hoping to catch the funeral yet. The walls were hung with black; great pyramids of white flowers on the altar; a mass going on, and many people kneeling; so we sat down. In a few minutes two men came behind us with a ladder, and began to take down the black hangings! This looked unpromising, and at last we did what it would have been sensible to do at first, asked if there were a funeral to take place there. It had happened at nine o'clock in the morning, and now, I suppose, they were saying masses for the soul! The men flew about, tearing down the black cambric with most unseemly haste, and scattering dust on everybody's head, and we walked away quite crestfallen.

It was a most picturesque little street, about six feet wide, and set thick with stores on each side; bread-stores with piles, of all imaginable shapes and colors, of bread on the open window-sills, (everybody keeps store on the window-sill or the door-step here!) great baskets of boiled beets, round and flat like pancakes; and young potatoes, size of nutmegs, also boiled ready to eat, were on every corner. Stockings and lace collars and China toys and yellow handkerchiefs hung and swung and stood and waved to right and left of the beets and potatoes. A big butcher was asleep in his little cupboard of a store, and on his window-sill stood six round earthen cups of what I think must have been the dreadful blood-puddings I have heard of; it looked simply like blood cooled, with stiffened bubbles on top! It made you faint to think that it could be put there to sell to human beings. Then came a fish trattoria, — a scene for Rembrandt to paint, — a dark cavern of a shop, lit only from one door and window in front; a stone furnace in the rear, from which came a fiery red glow;

two men, with arms bared to the shoulder, standing in this firelight, frying fish! crockery plates set up in rows on stone ledges above the fire; and flat wickerwork platters of fish, round, long, flat, whole, sliced, curled, straight, floured, and peppered, ready to fry, standing in tottering piles in the window! This was a picture, and I stayed so long to look at it I nearly got lost going back to the gondola alone. Then I bought out of another window a big round cracker, which I hoped was made out of unbolted wheat; but it proved sour and uneatable, like everything else we find here, except the dazzling white fine bread of the hotels, which is sweet simply because it is lifeless, and has no more nutrition in it than so much cobweb.

As we rowed home, Luigi told us all about the funeral. He had been gossiping with the street in our absence, and had found out that it was the funeral of a Countess Somebody, who had been very patriotic, had run great risks in the times of the wars, had been three times in the Austrian prisons, and had lost most of her property in consequence! She was much beloved by the people, hence the flags and the kneeling crowds at the mass. Some day he is to take us to see the house in which she died; though why we want to see it I cannot imagine.

Sunday the Sixth. — O, if I could but catch these swift days and clip their wings! Dear people, will you not all come to Venice in spring, some year of your years, and have our Luigi for gondolier, and be as content as we? All I can write you is dusty, dry. You do not know in the least what I have seen. For instance, on the Thursday which followed the Wednesday of the good Countess's funeral, did I not spend a whole forenoon in the rooms of Rieti, a Jew with spectacles, who hires a palace to keep store in, and who fattens on the decay of Venetian families, buying up every shred of thing which they have to sell, and setting them, one above another, in these palace rooms, to be sold again to American men and women? And would not the catalogue of the beautiful and weird and uncanny old things I saw there fill a volume? Chairs and tables and chests and sideboards and mirrors, from time of Doges down! Glass and china and tapestry; workboxes and crickets and candlesticks and pans and busts and gravestones! Yes, old gravestones there were, and hall lamps, and an old medicine-chest, out of which came dusty scent of poisons which helped to thin out the eleventh century, I am sure! The old leather case was dropping and crumbling to pieces, and the green baize lining seemed half turned to fungus. It was most curiously studded with silver nails, and surely belonged to a physician of degree.

There are six of these stores of antiquity and works of art here, and we have been to four of them, for my lucky friends have a house, and a room to be refurnished. I feel now as if I had had "the run" of all the Venetian palaces from the tenth to the sixteenth century. I have lifted off the lids of their soup-tureens, tried the hinges and handles of their sideboards, and pulled out all their secret drawers. I only wish I had a thousand dollars to spend to-morrow morning in small articles which would never be missed out of these bewildering confusions. I would buy for one of you a stool, whose seat should be crimson, and should be held up by a black Moor, a cunning little fellow six years old, called Abdalla, I "calculate," and clothed as to the loins in a tunic of green and silver. Should you mind sitting on him? He looks very happy, and shows all his teeth. For another, you who give little dinners, I would buy a fish, a China fish, to hold your salmon; the platter is gay with flowers; the fish is purple,— mullet, perhaps; at any rate it is purple and silver, and a lemon at top of him for a handle, and by the lemon you lift off his upper half, and there will be your salmon; and what Doge ever had so good a fish out of it before you! For you who have made a million since I

came away — ah! for you, my dear, there is a set of
furniture in ebony inlaid with white ivory tablets, and
the tablets covered with fantastic designs and patterns,
like fine etchings! Such a little wardrobe of drawers
as stands on a table of this set, three feet high, doors
always to be kept open, and twenty little drawers
ready to hold all your letters! If you like it better,
there is a set of brown nut-wood inlaid more elaborately with ivory, not an inch left plain, and all sorts
of carved ivory figures set in the impossible places.
These are four things out of thousands; but I can tell
you no more, because in the afternoon we went to
Torcello, and that is better worth talking over.

I am tempted to put in a little guide-book about
Torcello, because I knew so little about it myself
before coming here that I think some of you may be
equally ignorant. But I remember that I promised
never to do guide-book at all, and so I will not yield to
the temptation! You will know that it is an island,
and that before Venice was Torcello, and had churches
and bishops and palaces; it will be easier for you to
believe all this than it is for me, — though, to be sure, I
have seen the Cathedral and one church and a bit of
one palace, but, for all the rest, I find no real faith in
my heart. Nothing in all Rome, not even the loveliest
old aqueduct stones in the farthest silence of the campagna, ever gave me such sense of desolation, of forgotten life, as the atmosphere of this little island. We
sailed to it through sunshine, — swiftly too, for we had
taken an extra rower. The lagoon was astir with fish-
ing people, and the smoke of work went up from
Murano, as we passed it, and bells rang from old towers
on two other islands as we drew near Torcello. We
had been told that many of the great barges which we
had seen at sunset coming down the Grand Canal,
loaded with cherries and salads and artichokes, and
all sorts of good garden things, were bringing vegetables from Torcello; so we thought we were going to

a thrifty suburb of Venice to find some old churches we knew, but we supposed to breathe the air of to-day. We had not glided ten steps into the silent Torcello canal before we felt the hush of a burial-place. So low lay the fields, lapping up the slow green water, that it seemed as if we might slip over at any minute, and be floating above the grass. The silence was indescribable; old stone bridges spanned the canal, and as we rowed under them the grass nodded down to us from the sides and the top! Had human feet ever brushed it? We grew afraid; the white honeysuckle was in blossom; and raspberry-bushes, with pink flowers, made long thickets of hedge, over which here and there a scarlet pomegranate looked, as if holding court; bits of old stone-work gleamed out among these wild growths; hardly more than a door-step at a time, a corner-stone, or a few inches of wall, all so sunk, so bedded in the green, that but for knowing that a city and palaces had stood there we should have thought them no more than natural stones. After a time we found a house or ·two; then an old bell-tower rising up suddenly and ghost-like in the waste, walled in as if it were the keep of the powers and principalities of the air! Then we came on a little brood of ducklings, — they looked more human than you could conceive, — and then, after another turn, on a Custom House! This took our breath away. I do not know yet what it meant. If I were the right sort of traveller I should have found out. But its stone steps answered for us to land on, and nobody stopped either us or the ducks who stepped on shore with us; and we all crept along together. I felt somehow as if they were so much safer than we.

An old woman, whom I *almost* believe to have been alive, showed us the old church of Santa Fosca, and the Cathedral. I can't tell you about them. Nobody could. The church is a dome on top of a Greek cross, and a portico with tumbling pillars all around it. The cathedral stands close, almost joins the church, and has a floor of mosaic, which makes St. Mark's look new; high marble reading-desks; and around the semi-circular apse, behind the high altar, marble seats rising up in tiers one above the other, like the Coliseum; in the middle, the Bishop's chair, and all so old that it looked crumbling, — though it never can crumble, and it is not so very old, after all, not more than a thousand years; but it feels, for some inexplicable reason, older than anything I ever saw. Fresh annunciation lilies were on every altar; their odor filled the air, and drowned out the smell of fungus; the old woman's shoes clapped, clapped at the heel with every step she took, and echoed in the dark corners.

Down in the crypt there was a poor old wooden Christ, all cobwebs and dust, — a most pitiful thing. As we walked by she kissed it, and drew her withered hands down the legs to the feet with a lingering touch of tenderness and passionate devotion which I never saw equalled, and which made my eyes wet for some minutes. It must be that which has kept her alive in Torcello, — this poor, haggard, hungry old soul. The air is poison there! It was that which drove the people away, and put this melancholy end to the city; only a few poor souls live there now, who are too poor to live anywhere else, and cannot, perhaps, resist the temptation of ground to cultivate; for green things thrive and produce in Torcello, though all the children look as if they had just left their beds for the first time after some terrible illness. They crowded round us, and begged, more by their hollow eyes than by their words. I sat down in a great rough stone chair which stands in an open space before the cathedral, and in front of the old bit of a stone house in which the Bishop lived, and gave all the children bonbons which I had cribbed from our hotel dinner, — a questionable charity, I know, but I had no pennies! and beggars have such digestions in Italy, one feels less scruple about giving them unwholesome sweets.

One little girl, six or seven years old, with great gaunt brown eyes, and a weight of tangled auburn-black hair, grasped hers firm in her little hand, and never opened it. The other children were tearing open the bright papers, and munching down the candy, like monkeys. She looked at them wistfully, but did not offer to touch hers. I explained to her that it was good to eat, and tried to make her taste it; at last, after I had asked her a dozen times why she did not eat it, she whispered so I could but just catch the words, — she was so frightened, — that she kept it for her little brother! Did n't I turn my pocket wrong side out, and find one more for that little angel? and did n't she bite into it in about the shortest second? and do you think I believe in original depravity? As I turned back for my last look at the desolate grass-grown piazza, and the cathedral, and the church, and the bell-tower, the children were all scrambling to get up into the stone chair (they call it Attila's chair, — because he never sat in it, I suppose); three were already in, two more climbing up, and a poor little two-year-old tugging away at one of the six legs hanging down in front, and trying in vain to lift himself up by it.

Yesterday I was heroic, stayed in the house, and wrote all the forenoon. In the afternoon we rowed over to the Enchanted Island, that is the Lido; the girls and Mrs. and Miss T—— went into the water in Venetian bathing-dresses, hired for two francs, and swam about as if they had been brides of the Adriatic all their lives! I sat on an upper stair and watched them and the sea; mostly the sea, which was pale, soft gray in the distance, and green close at my feet. There were many people rowing back and forth on it, and some of their sails were orange, and some looked rose-pink against the sky. Why do not all sailors have orange and pink sails, I wonder? it is all a sail needs to make it as beautiful as a cloud, and it signifies so much more.

Sunday the Thirteenth. — This Sunday was the anniversary of the adoption of the Constitution by Italy, and all the houses were bright with flags; the square of St. Mark's was gay with red and green and white, and in the evening there was to be music on the canal. We commissioned Luigi to buy an Italian flag for our gondola, to show our sympathy with freedom, and anticipated a fine night on the water. Alas! at six o'clock the sky was black, and it thundered mutteringly in the east; however, we would not be kept in, even by its beginning to sprinkle as we took our seats in the gondola; actually under umbrellas we rowed up to the Rialto, and displayed our flag. Some of the gondoliers saluted us as we passed, and they all looked pleased and smiled.

The band was playing on a great barge in front of the prefect's house, and a few determined people were creeping about under umbrellas, as we were; but it was a failure. The sky grew blacker and the drops bigger, and, against our wills, we went home. To be out in the rain in Venice is too much to be borne by the stoutest soul. To be between two fires is always accounted a bad thing in battle; but to be between two waters is as bad. Going home we passed a grave-looking American family, singing psalm-tunes in their gondola. It sounded very pleasantly, but I could not resist the suspicion that it was a kind of a sop to their consciences for being out on the Grand Canal so near sunset of a Sunday.

Wednesday went for looking over photographs in the morning, and for three or four not especially interesting churches in the afternoon; but you know, without my taking time to say it, that simply to go from one place to another, in this wonderful sea-city, is a delight in itself. If it waited for me to say where we should go, we should never go anywhere. It never seems to me to make the least difference. I feel as if the gondola knew, and would go of itself. I should sink down, if I were alone, and give no orders to the invisible Luigi. Luckily for me, N—— and P—— are more wise. N—— is our guide, and has always something to propose for each day, which is just the best thing to do. Thanks to her, we have in this four weeks seen Venice most thoroughly. On Thursday we spent the whole morning in the Academy, with the beloved pictures. I feel that I am so entirely ignorant of art, that I have hardly right to say what I think about any picture. But I am sure of one thing: pictures and poems are one. All the pictures I have seen which have impressed me are poems; and I see that even to my ignorance it becomes clearer and clearer in what measure they are written. Also, I see that it is as silly to like, or even to be ready to like, *all* the pictures painted by one man, simply because they are his, as it is to believe that one's favorite poet could not write a poor thing. Did not Browning write "Mr. Sludge the Medium," and Wordsworth "Peter Bell"?

I am wondering about many things in these days, of which I have nobody here to ask, and no books to help me. I am sure that if one knew literature and art well enough, close parallels could be drawn out between poems and pictures; and I wonder if there would not be historical agreements too. Some of you who know, write and tell me what you think about this. Now, I find Carpaccio to be a man who painted ballads! All his pictures have the ring and the movement, with the light touch. There is a series of them in the Academy, which tell the story of St. Ursula. I sit and read it over and over and over, as you can, "How they brought the Good News to Ghent." He does not forget what the little page said, nor that on that day the maiden was ill at ease; nor that while the ambassadors asked the king for the hand of his daughter, outside of the gate sat an old stern woman who liked not these foreign wooings, and muttered that ill would come. Every picture is a complete ballad in itself; as you look at them, you involuntarily walk with steps set to the sound of a singer.

Then there is Bellini, whose pictures are gentle and tender, and are like quaint sacred songs. Always he puts at base of the pictures little angels or babies sitting with crossed legs, and playing on lutes the accompaniment to the song. Most of his pictures are called "Madonna with two Saints," "Madonna with four Saints," Madonna and Child," etc., etc. I always think of them as "The true Song of the Day when Catharine and Agatha met Mary and the Child Jesus," or "The Greeting of St. Agnes to the Infant Lord," or "The Words of Sts. Jerome and Christopher to Augustine the Monk." But for all this Bellini has painted many Madonnas whose faces are like faces of wood; and one frightful picture of his has in the clouds over the Madonna's head seven cherub heads of fiery scarlet, like lobster! There are two pictures in the Academy by a Martino da Udine, a rare man of Bellini's day and school, who has left only few things. One of these is the Angel of the Annunciation; the other is a Madonna — both single figures, severe, alone, no accessories, but an air of heaven about the one, and of sanctified earth in the other, which it is good to see. I know lines in George Herbert — written, is it one hundred or more years later? — which are like these pictures. Titian's single heads and single figures are the sonnets, either solemn and slow, with the whole of the man's life concentrated into that day's voice, or vivid fiery, like the passionate outpouring of one moment! His "Presentation of the Little Virgin at the Temple" is the picture I like best of all the pictures I have yet seen, except the "Last Communion of St. Jerome," by Domenichino, in Rome. It is a grand epic poem. There is the whole of Jerusalem and the worship of the Temple in the figures of the high-priests, all Jewry in the crowd below, and all Christianity and redemption in the figure of the little Virgin. All my life, blue will be more sacred to me by reason of this little Virgin's gown! And as for red, it has always been to me like the key-note of a universe of hidden things, like a very spell in the air; and now I know that Titian had been taken inside of its mystery, and signed with its sign. Every day I see men in the Academy sitting down calmly to copy Titian's red! and I wonder at their being suffered to go about without keepers.

From the Academy we went to the house of two old Venetian ladies, sisters of an artist whom P—— and N—— knew when they were here before, and who made a copy of one of Bellini's pictures for them. She was sick and deformed and poor, but had great talent as a copyist, and had worked with great industry, for all the rooms of the little house were hung with her drawings and paintings. She died some two years ago, and these two poor old sisters were so gratified and touched at her being remembered and sought out by strangers for whom she had painted, that it was hard to know what to say to them, especially if you did not know many words of their language! But the sight of the house and their way of living was most interesting. After all, one such interior picture is worth scores of common outside views; they must once have "seen better days," — everything in their manner and surroundings showed this. They have now no servant, and one sister could not see us this morning. We knew by the stir and the odors that she was cooking their dinner; and who but she could it have been who snatched and hid the string of onions which, when we arrived, was hanging on the hat-rack in the front hall, — by side of an old cotton umbrella! — and when we went away was no longer there? The sister we saw was perhaps seventy years old. Her eyes were faded, and her lips very shaky, but she must once have been handsome; and the woman had not by any means died out of her old heart, for when

I recognized as her portrait the face of a handsome woman of not more than thirty-five, among her sister's paintings on the walls of the little parlor, her wrinkled cheeks flushed with pleasure, and she smiled a little as she might have smiled the day the picture was painted.

She wore, just as such pitiful "genteel" old ladies do at home, — and, I suppose, all the world over, — skimpy black clothes, gray with age, and a forlorn, dusty black lace thing on the back of her head, — they always look more like palls than like caps on that kind of old lady. They asked high prices for their sister's pictures, and I am afraid they will not sell all of them. The girls bought a lovely little picture of a picturesque palace on the Grand Canal, at which we look almost every afternoon. They could hardly have found a more vivid bit of Venice to carry away with them than this little sketch by the poor dead Raffaella.

In the afternoon we went into the house of another Venetian family. Such a contrast! This family's name is Giovanelli; and the Prince Giovanelli married a Contarini, and, of the Contarinis, five have been doges! and the house in which this Giovanelli and Contarini live is the most splendid palace in Venice. Did we not do well to go to the poor old sisters first? It was like the one bit of red which Titian throws in at last, in the distance of his pictures, which brings all the other colors out. But you see plainly that of this palace I cannot tell you much, because there is a limit to a letter, though you may think I don't know it; neither did I half tell you about the other little home. I shall remember it quite as long as the grand one. Mrs. Contarini Giovanelli is the only palace-owning lady that I have envied. I would not have taken one of the superb palaces in Genoa as a gift, if I were to be compelled to stay in their great ghostly rooms. But this Giovanelli palace, superb as it is, is cosey. Think of that! — a cosey palace! — a boudoir of blue, blue damask from ceiling to floor, and a ceiling like a hollow shell, and a rounding blue satin sofa, on which she sits and mends her husband's shirts. How do I know? By this token, that in a costly glass toy on a little table before the sofa, and among a thousand dollars' or so worth of other trifles in the way of baskets and statuettes and boxes, were three old shirt-bosom buttons!! close to her work-basket, — which might have been yours or mine, it was so neat and simple. Their bedroom is regal, — ebony and yellow damask; but — O the but, even in a palace! — on this gorgeous ebony stood, in easy reach from one of the yellow satin beds, *cold-cream* and — a bottle of *magnesia!* Heartburn, you see, even for a descendant of doges, in this dream of a palace. I, who never had heartburn, and would die before I took magnesia, chuckled and passed on.

A crimson room, satin tapestry, on walls with raised velvet figures; a yellow-and-white room, the tapestry woven to fit, with the coat of arms wrought in here and there; a picture-gallery hung with claret velvet, and holding rare pictures, — Titian and Veronese and Bellini and Durer and Van Dyck and Rembrandt; a dining-room with carvings and purple velvet and China, which was a study in itself; a sitting-room with a grand piano and a marvellous bird-cage of gay latticework alternating with transparencies, on which were painted morning-glories and honeysuckles! In the cage, seven little Japanese birds, drab and scarlet and gray; on the piano, cigars of several sorts, ready for the prince after dinner. This is a skeleton glimpse for you of the Giovanelli's ways of living.

I shall never forget the glow on the faces of some of Titian's portraits of doges, which hang in the crimson room; not all the heat of the red tapestry of Lyons can dull the glow of the orange and red mantles, or approach the kindling fire in the faces.

"Is there a library?" said we.

"No," said the courteous and elegant creature, called servant, who had showed us his master's house. And somehow I instantly felt as if it had been quite impertinent to ask, and as if perhaps, after all, books were a superfluous indulgence. The prince must read, for he is "Syndic of Venice" and "Senator of Italy"; but not a book did we see, except some ornamental ones to match the crimson furniture.

Yesterday, two more churches,— San Zaccaria, which is the first church in Venice I have liked; and San Giorgio degli Schiavoni, a little one-room, upper-chamber sort of a church, in an out-of-the-way quarter where are nine quaint old pictures by my favorite ballad-man, Carpaccio, sung when he was young; with too many adjectives, but ringing, ringing like all the rest. I shall grow to remember his things better than any others if I study them much more. That also is like the hold a ballad gets on you; it haunts your downsitting and uprising, as no other verse can.

I must not forget to tell you about Murano. We rowed over there on Saturday afternoon to see the famous glass-works. The minute you get away from Venice, and row off towards the other islands, it all looks more and more unreal; the islands look like nothing but mirages, and Venice itself looks like a gigantic colored phantasm, just that minute set up against the sky by some magician. You have not the least faith in getting anywhere, unless possibly you might be cast up, gondola and all, like a bit of sea-weed, at foot of the Apennines or Alps or Himalayas, whichever they are, that stand up sharp and real along the coast, whether south or west I do not know,— I can't find out, I never shall; but there they are, the only actual-looking things to be seen. You feel as if the world began at their base, and you were drifting around outside, part of a great miracle-play. This is not wild talk; it is the way everybody must feel after half an hour of gondola in these waters. Perhaps they do not analyze their bewilderment so closely as I have; but if they did they would find it all there. I see it all in their faces as they glide by, even in the most stolid and Jewish of them all.

Well, after three quarters of an hour of this, we bumped up against a wharf, which did not really elude us and fade out of sight, and a very tangible old beggar hooked us fast, and we stepped out on the thin crust of stone, over Murano piers, and began to look for glass-houses. Of course we were pounced on instantly by Murano loafers, who scented our errand and our inexperience. We are a tempting-looking trio, — three not bad-looking women, tolerably well dressed, and usually on the broad laugh, with any amount of desire for information in our faces. Of course we are as plainly meant for *custodi* and *cicironi* as fish are for gulls; but we are growing sharp in Venice, there is too much of it here, and what with Ruskin and Howells and Murray and Baedeker we know so much more than the guides do that we are quite justified in scorning them. However, in Murano we were helpless, and we were led off meekly as lambs by a horrible old simpleton, who pretended to understand us, but I think did not comprehend one word we said. Into one dark furnace-depth after another we plunged, at his heels, and into aisles of astonished-looking workmen, and saw them blow glass bottles (just as they do in Sandwich, Massachusetts), and draw out long hollow threads of fiery glass, and snap it off like pipe-stems; and we paid odd francs here and there to people who had not done anything to earn them; and we stood about till we ached all over and got quite cross; and then all of a sudden we "struck" for lower wages and no guide; frightened the simpleton off our track, jumped into our gondola and rowed off to the Museum! Murano was such an uncanny place, I was horribly afraid we should be turned into something or other, and have to stay there all the rest of our lives. It is a kind of a ghost of a poor relation of Venice; canals and houses and bridges, and old carved corners and balconies, and black gondolas, but all beggarly and ghostlike. The Museum was a great stalwart building which looked out of place there, and fresh signs of offices of one sort and another on the first floor made us afraid we had lost our way; but we soon found the *custode*, and he trotted us about through five rooms of the most wonderful glassware we ever dreamed of.

Do not suppose there is anything which cannot be made of glass if you set about it in Murano: chandeliers, gigantic and of really graceful shapes, all glass; tables which looked like mosaic, mirrors framed in glass, and roses and convolvuluses, and green leaves wreathed about them, all glass; a bonnet, with daisies on the top, and openwork lace strings, all glass; a high stove-pipe hat, light brown, quite pliable, nothing but glass; a portrait of an old doge, frame and all glass; portraits of Victor Emmanuel and other people by the yard, run in a long stick like a stick of candy, and wherever you sliced it off there would be the perfect portrait, so wonderfully were the colors put in. Then there were all possible shapes and sorts and sizes of vases and tumblers and pitchers and cups and candlesticks, white and yellow and green and red and opal, and lapis-lazuli and malachite; some painted in old styles, the secret of which is now lost; some threaded in and out with threads of color, or of white, as fine as cobweb silk; — five rooms filled with these, and many others that I do not remember.

When we came home the light was so beautiful on the Grand Canal (O, if one could be permitted to call it anything but a canal!) that I could not go in; so we dropped N—— on our watery door-step, and P—— and I rowed off again for the moonlight. We found a great steam-yacht anchored in front of the Doge's palace, and the canal gay with gondolas and music. No less than the Viceroy of Egypt had come in the yacht, and the Duke of Brunswick was in the hotel, and the serenade was just as good for us as for them; and we rowed up and down till ten o'clock, and heard the whole of it, and then we went home silently, so as not to break up the dream.

To-day has been such a day that I have hardly courage to try to tell it. I can only give you the barest skeleton. If I were to really describe the hours, my letter would be forty pages long.

In the morning we went to the Doge's palace, stood on the Doge's balcony, and looked seaward; walked over, I mean through, the Bridge of Sighs; saw the door which shut the prisoners who went to the Council of Three from those who went to the Council of Ten; looked into the cell where Marino Falieri was confined, and sat down on Carmagnuola's bed. O the horror of those cells! no light except through a small round hole, by which the food was put in; the door so low I had to double to step through it. The Mamertine prisons in Rome were not much worse. One of these cells is still lined with wood, as they all were in the days of these terrors; the guide gave me a piece which he broke off in a dark corner over the door, — it is quite worm-eaten. I suppose the prisoners now and then, perhaps, could hear a little nibble.

Then we went up into the grand Hall of Council, and saw Tintoretto's great picture of Paradise, the largest picture on canvas in the world. I should hope so. It would cover two sides of Dr. T——'s church, I think; and what do you say to it for a conception of heaven, when I tell you that even at that size it is crowded with figures; packed, jammed, wedged, they are, — the saints of Tintoretto. I would rather be any kind of a sinner in any other place where there was elbow-room. The only thing that gave me pleasure was to see that St. Mark had got his lion in. The sagacious beast is looking up in St. Mark's face with such an earnest, inquiring expression, puzzled and uneasy, as if he said, "Well, really, master, is it possible you like this kind of thing, and do you mean to stay long?"

Now I will take you to a concert on the Grand
Canal. We are in our gondola, quite close to the Viceroy's steamer; it is not quite twilight, and the lamps
are lit in the cabin, and the great people are at dinner.
Brown Egyptians, who look much like Marshpee Indians in red fezes, are clambering about in a kind of
busy idleness all over the boat; and the Viceroy's little
boy, ten years old, also in a red fez, is on deck with
his tutor, a gray-headed old fellow, who does n't look
half so wise as the boy. Poor little soul, to have been
put through all this before twelve! What a sucked
orange his world will be before he is twenty! I never
see these experienced children without thinking how
much better off they are who begin with mud-pies
and a "cubby-house" of broken crockery, as we did.
Did n't you? I did, at any rate, and the consequence
is that here am I to-night, ——! years old, but deliciously delighted and amused with the outside of the
Viceroy's ship, and the show, and the music, while this
baby of ten sat and twirled his little cane, and looked
on as indifferently as an old loafer. The bands of music
were on two gondolas which had been fastened together
and draped with blue and white, making a great fairy-like barge, which was towed up and down by three
other gondolas draped in white, and rowed by gondoliers in white and black velvet. We all raced about
after this barge, sixty or a hundred gondolas of us, and
tried to get as close to it as we could, which was foolish; but all people are sheep when they are in crowds.
This is n't quite true, however, for we did not like to
be in such jams, and kept moving off as well as we
could; but, in spite of us, we were wedged much of the
time. On the Viceroy's steamer was a band, — African,
should say, and made up two thirds of cymbals and
tambourines; but it suited the fezes and the color of the
men, and the red and yellow and green lights with which
the whole ship was illuminated. Did n't we believe in
Aladdin just then? I think the Viceroy lives in his
palace.

Then came a gondola waving with green laurel-bushes, with colored lanterns swinging among them. This was the most beautiful of all; on this were singers who sang songs, and if they were singing still, we should still be there listening to them, because to come away from the Grand Canal in Venice when Venetian men are singing on the water is not in the power of human beings. The Ten Commandments can be kept perhaps; people are said to have done it; but this is harder.

The ships in the harbor were gay with colors, and there were rockets and Bengal lights and Roman candles in all directions; and after the Viceroy and his guests had done their dinner, they stepped into *such* gondolas, — the royal gondola blue velvet and silver, with six gondoliers in blue and white; the others green and purple and yellow, — and away they all rowed up the Giudeca.

Later in the evening we were near the Rialto, and all of a sudden the whole *cortége* shot past us. O the sweep of a gondola with six rowers! Several of the gondolas had Bengal lights at the prow, and the effect of this light on the old stone fronts of the palaces and on the bridge was something that sobered and saddened you in a second. The very stones seemed to cry out, "We are dead, we are dead." After all, Venice is a ghost. The banquet is over, and these shows of to-day make the old palaces scornful in their tombs, I dare say. Now who could sleep after such a night? But one has a duty to one's eyes; so good by.

On Monday I went alone to the Academy, and had a feast off a few pictures which I like. Do not be afraid I shall tell you much about them. I have told you about Titian's little Virgin in "The Presentation," — have I not? That is a picture for which one might almost sell one's soul, if taken in the right moment! My love of this picture has almost cost me the loss of all the others in the building, I find it so hard to leave it.

Then there is a St. John by Veronese, which one could look at and grow happier for a lifetime; and such grand old ballad pictures by Carpaccio, and lyrics by Bellini, with cunning little angels playing accompaniments at the base of altars.

There is a head of Homer by Caravaggio here which is grander than Milton's Hymn. The darkened air and those sightless eyes! You have a fear of blindness hanging over you wherever you go, on the day in which you look at this picture.

In the afternoon P—— and I roamed (and wriggled) through the cracks in the walls where the shops are, and looked in at the windows, and said what we would like to buy, and went in and "priced" things, after the manner of women, for two hours or more, but did not spend any money, which I hope is set down to us for righteousness.

On Tuesday was the Arsenal, not very good to tell about, but worth while to see. Stacks of old armor, complete suit of Henri Quatre, and a helmet of Attila's, and the visor of Attila's horse among them. Some old monster's instruments of torture, a thumb-screw and a collar, and a pistol of poisoned arrows, and an iron helmet. I had my thumb in the screws for a minute, and the guide squeezed it down for me within one of the point at which I should have abjured Calvinism (if that is what I believe.) There were all sorts of wooden models of all sorts of ships and boats and forts; two sides of old Venetian galleys, carved in great figures, and all gilt and red, — they must have been gay things afloat; a mast of the old Bucentaur, and a picture of it; and the model of it, eighty feet long, which the Austrians carried off with them, the thieves! A great torn and patched and faded shred of a flag which came out of the battle of Lepanto; a suit of armor made for a little boy eight years old, the son of some Doge, who wished to inure the poor baby to war, and kept him on the walls in war time in this frightful suit of mail. It was on a lay-figure of wood, and even the white round wooden face looked scared, just as, no doubt, the poor son of the Doge did!

A patronizing officer went about with us, and said he had been in Boston and Montreal, and that people had to be very rich to live in America. Ah, we knew what that meant,— that he expected a big fee! But afterward he asked N—— if we had all been married; so for his impertinence we gave him only a franc, and he looked quite taken down when we came away.

Wednesday we went over the Viceroy's yacht. At first the Marshpee Indians — I mean Egyptians — did not seem inclined to let us go on board; but we coaxed and wheedled them as well as we could at six arms' length, rocking in a gondola under their stern, and at last we prevailed.

Going to sea would not be a bad thing to do in the Viceroy's yacht. Mrs. T—— said it was far handsomer than the Queen's. Such a luxurious cabin you never dreamed of,— satin damask of the most exquisite gray color, with bright rosebuds and vines over it, on every chair or sofa or cushion; mosaics from Rome for tables; inlaid work in woods and in silver on the walls; above every lamp a convoluted shell with mosaic and mother-of-pearl in it to reflect the light; — does n't it sound comfortable?

They did not show us the bedroom, and we were afraid to ask, for they crowded about us, and their black eyes gleamed with something which did not impress us as being the pure respectfulness to which we were accustomed; and I, for one, felt a little happier when we were fairly out of the ship. But we had seen Ismail Pacha's cabin and all his men; most of their clothes, too, which looked like the shirts and trousers of any other nation, and were all hung out to dry on long lines forward. They were very busy getting ready to leave Venice the next day, as soon as the Viceroy should return from Florence, and I dare say it did not please them to be interrupted by five women's questions.

In San Giorgio are some fine carvings in wood. They were made by a Flemish somebody. There are sixty seats or stalls for the priests in a semicircle; the backs and the arms and the railings in front, and every available inch, all are cut into the most exquisite and effective picturing. It is the life of St. Benedict which is the theme of the largest panels, those making the backs of the seats. It begins with the St. Benedict baby and Mrs. Benedict in bed, and the nurse and the doctor, and the rest of them giving the Benedict baby its first bath; and so on down through the saint's whole career, about which I was ashamed to know nothing. One dies daily of shame at one's own ignorance here. But these lovely carvings are as fine and telling as bronze; some of the faces I shall remember always, and the riotous foliage and ornament everywhere. The Fleming must have lived long and put his best years into this wood.

Thursday we saw the Viceroy and his whole suite come down the G—— C—— in the royal gondolas, and go on board the small tug to take them to their steamer. Ismail Pacha looked like any Mr. Smith of America, full brown beard and fat cheeks; the officers blazed with uniform and orders; the bands played, the singers sang, and Venice looked on from the air with her old palace front as strong and regal and unmoved as ever. O the queenhood of the face of this sinking city! three inches in a century it goes down, — did you know it? — so the end is sure!

On Friday we went to Murano again, and saw the colored and twisted and flowered glass and beads made, and I had two tumblers made for little H—— and A——, and, like the smaller child I am myself, cracked one on the voyage home, in my hurry to get it out of the cooling seaweed it had been packed in, and smashed the other on the stone stairs as I went up to bed!

On Saturday we went to the Lido, looked at clover and buttercups, and ragged-robin, and green fields, and old Jewish graves overgrown with rank grass, and piled up shells on the shore of the Adriatic.

Yesterday we went to a Scotch Presbyterian meeting in a little room on the Grand Canal. Think of the antithesis of the thing!

BERCHTESGADEN, BAVARIA, Tuesday, July 6, 1869.

DEAR PEOPLE: This is what we do of an afternoon, if the afternoon happen to be this one just going. After dinner we saw from our front window a priest bearing the crucifix, and little boys with candles going into the church which is opposite; in the morning P—— had seen a man and woman digging a grave in the graveyard, which is also opposite our house. (Don't think we dislike it; on the contrary, it is the cheerfullest place I ever saw. The crosses almost elbow each other, they are so close; they are gay with wreaths and bunches of flowers, and on every grave are growing forget-me-nots or roses or sweet-williams.) So we thought there would be a funeral soon, and were on the watch for it; but, just as it was in Venice, we were a little too late. It must have happened while we were at dinner, and when we got there, — now you will never believe me, but it is true, — there was nobody left in the graveyard but three old women and two little children; and two of the old women were sitting on a grave knitting, while the third was filling up the grave with a kind of hoe; the two babies were leaning over the edge and looking at each fall of the earth on the boards! We were so horrified that we walked immediately away, and in our excitement sat down on one of the praying benches with our backs to a huge crucifix, and never observed what an irreverence we were guilty of, until an old peasant woman came by, and, with a stern look at us, knelt directly before us and made the sign of the cross. We fled again, this time out of the churchyard, and down a staircase path which leads to the river, by way of much zigzag through two or three people's grounds. This wonderful little village is so up and down hill, that you are always coming on bits of staircase, built in for a short cut, where, without it, you would have to go miles round. Pretty soon P—— found it too warm and went home, but I kept on till I found a shady place under an old stone wall, where I camped. It was on the edge of a thoroughfare path from one part of the river road to the top of the hill, so I had sight of everybody who went on foot that way for an hour. An old woman with a fishing-pole and trout in a pretty wooden firkin; — I peeped at the trout and said "guten," and pointed to the hotel where we stay, and she nodded and said "Ja"; so I dare say we shall have these very fish for supper. Then an old man on crutches,— how he was ever to get up that steep climb I could not see, nor for that matter how he could walk anywhere, he was so old, and the crutches so poor; but the very poorest, most tottering old people here bid you good day with such a cheery, contented, good-fellowship, voice, and smile, that you would not be afraid to change places with the forlornest of them. Probably you would be the gainer. I never saw such beautiful souls shining through such hideous faces. Really the transition from the average wayside face of Italy to that of Germany is a severe cold bath to one's artistic sense, — such persistent and unconscious ugliness! At first I was vexed with them for not looking humiliated; but presently I perceived that it was grand in them not to discover that they were hideous, — a positive pre-apple innocence of all vanity. Already they have grown beautiful to me, and their hearty recognition of every human soul they meet is the most divine thing I have ever known a whole community to do. I intend, all the rest of my life, to smile and say "Good morning" to everybody I pass on the road; and be set down for a mad woman? Yes, I suppose so. I did not mean in New York or London, though; I meant in the blessed country. I said "road," if you observe. After a time "Barefoot" came by with a great pail of strawberries on her arm tied up in a yellow silk handkerchief. I peeped into this too, and they looked so ripe and red and dewy that I thought perhaps for once they *would* taste like strawberries if I bought them out of her hand and ate them on the highway. For you must know that from the 1st of last May till now I have been steadily eating strawberries, and not a strawberry of them all has had the real strawberry flavor. They have a name to live and are dead, — these "Alpine strawberries," which have such a fine sound to the ear. I would give a bushel of them for a saucer full from Bethlehem, New Hampshire, any day. I held out a kreutzer to her with one hand, and made signs that she should put the berries into the other; she gave me a large handful, and wanted to give me more, but there was no room. I ate them slowly from the tip of a sharp grass blade, and discovered that they were a little less lifeless without sugar, which will be an economy for the landlord of the Watzman; several of them rolled away in the grass, and were at once pounced upon by mysterious crawling people of many kinds, who fell to with a less fastidious appetite than mine. I burst out laughing all alone by myself, to think how droll it was that there should be such a difference between an ant and me, — I eating the berries down by the handful, and he stretching his neck up to get a nibble off the great red mountain! Then I picked some purple thyme, and some vines of yellow "money," which straggles all about the roadsides here, and then I washed my hands in a little brook which ran under the thyme and "money," and then I went home and went into the dining-room and turned the German waiter's head by making signs that I wanted two toothpick dishes. He kept tipping out bunch after bunch of toothpicks and giving them to me, and I kept putting down the toothpicks and clutching at the dish, till I got into such a fit of laughter I was afraid he would never treat me respectfully again. However, at last I triumphed and bore off two of the dishes, leaving him looking at the toothpicks scattered all over the tablecloth. On the stairs I met our little "Special Providence," as I call him, — a fat curly boy who speaks English, and I told him I wanted the dishes to put flowers in, so I hope he explained to the other. They are dear little oblong dishes of glass, four or five inches long, and one and a half wide, and I have had my eye on them, ever since I have been here, for thyme and "money." Now one stands on my right hand on my writing-table, and one on the centre-table in P——'s room; and anything lovelier you could not see than the pale purple and the bright yellow, and the tangled sprays falling over as if they were still by the roadside.

To-morrow I suppose I might as well tell you how we got here, and what sort of a place it is, which it would have been more business-like to do in the beginning of my letter, only that one never does begin where one ought, nor leave off where one should. But you are going to be let off easy this time! no such thirty-six pages as the last! Upon my word, such a sight as I just saw from my window, — a man and a woman coming up the road, the woman carrying a load of wood in her arms, and the man carrying only an umbrella! And just as I was getting hot at the look of it, do you think he did n't march up and give her the umbrella too!

Wednesday, July 8. — Really these people make me cry. I have been rambling about the village this morning, sitting down in shady nooks and reading over a great delicious parcel of newspaper extracts from America; and three different blessed old souls stopped and spoke to me in such a way that I could not keep the tears out of my eyes. First, the poor old man on crutches; I meet him everywhere. I don't see anybody with legs who walks so much. He thinks he knows me now, and so he adds more and more courtesy and benediction to his greeting every day. I do believe he is inspired. I never saw such a radiant look of content on any human face, yet he is very, very thin. I do not believe he ever has enough to eat, and his clothes are very poor. I would give a hundred dollars (if I had it!) to be able to speak to him. I am sure I cannot put into my simple bow and smile one half the reverence I feel for him. Then, as I was sitting on some stairs in the heart of a meadow hill, midway between the church and the river, came by an old woman with a rough wallet holding two loaves of black bread and her shoes! She stopped and nodded, and nodded and smiled, and said "Good morning!" and then added, "It is good here," or, as they say still more effectively, "Here is good." I said, "Yes, yes," and smiled back again as hard as I could, but, dear me! what would I have given for a few words! Then I struck out of the path, and half ran and half rolled down the other side of the hill, and came into a Brattleboro' path, on the edge of a stony brook and set thick with purple vetch and tiny sunflowers, and white "snowflake" and "pride of the meadow," and half a dozen more of our common field-flowers. I made a big bunch of purple and yellow and white, and fringed it with green grass and odd leaves, and then sat down bare-headed under a tree, and plunged again into my newspapers. John Weiss and Frothingham and Emerson! how good their voices sounded under this sky! I was quite lost in listening to them, when a great, gruff voice said, "Ja, ja, hier ist gut" ("here it is good"), and there stood a Berchtesgaden carpenter, his foot-rule sticking out of his pocket, and a bundle of boards under his arm, looking with such genuine sympathy at my flowers, at my hat hung on my umbrella, and at me. I nodded and said as nearly as I could the same words after him. Then he laughed a little at my German, and lifted his hat, and kept it in his hand till he had passed many steps beyond me. Think of the air of such a place! I positively begin to wonder if they sin here! I suppose somebody must. But none of these people who smile and look so serene and say " Good morning " to me do; I'll go bail for them, all of them. They seem to me just as true and beautiful and harmonious as the trees and the butterflies; and as for going back from this atmosphere to that of the rest of the world, I do not believe I can. I shall stay here till somebody comes to carry me away. I already feel as if never of my own free-will could I turn my back on these hills. And how can I tell you what they are like to the eye? Like Brattleboro' and Bethlehem married and come to spend honeymoon in the Alps! Now I have exhausted my fancy on that figure, and how you will all laugh at it! But it *is* like Brattleboro'. There are soft-wooded hills that lap and circle; and there are paths everywhere by little brooks, and roads everywhere by stony foaming rivers; and such pine woods as Brattleboro's will be when they grow up. These are, well, forty or fifty feet higher! Never did I think a fir could be so tall and not snap. I am afraid, driving between them. Then there are mountains, like Mt. Washington in its best October days, purple or gray, with patches of snow *dazzling* white; and then there is the giant Watzman, the king of them all, and he has a glacier. Also there are lakes, only one of which I have seen, and that is so wonderfully beautiful that I cannot try to tell you anything about it, but I shall put in some little photograph pictures into this letter; from them you can build the air castles for yourselves, and put in the mountains and the woods and the lakes and the people.

The " Guest House and Brewery " at which we are staying looks much better in reality than in this very bald little picture. It should have been taken so as to throw in the whole of the hill on the left, which has pine-trees at top, and is one of my morning haunts. It is quite as high as the hill behind, on the top of which you will see a house gleaming out among the trees. Now you can understand from these why we go up and down stairs all over the village. It is not six minutes' walk from the Watzman to that house on the top of the hill, but more than half of the way is up stairs. On a small clear plateau of this hill, overlooking the whole village, and in full sight from every part of it, is a large shrine in which is a fearful representation of the Crucifixion. The Saviour and the two thieves, figures of wood, and large as life! We have found these at every step of the way since we entered Germany, of all sizes, colors, and degrees of the horrible. At first I could not look at them, and felt only a sense of repulsion and antagonism against the religion which had put them there, but I have now entirely changed my feeling about them. I believe that much of the sweet beautiful recognition which the people give to strangers and to each other has grown out of the habitual reverence of their daily lives for these images of Christ and the saints. The smallest child, the coarsest man, uncovers his head in passing one of these shrines. We are very bigoted and stupid, it seems to me, in assuming that it is the *thing* which the Roman Catholic reverences, when he kneels before his poor tawdry saint, or kisses the feet of the silver Christ. We who have pictures which we kiss daily ought to be more just than that.

Opposite this hotel is a most picturesque old church and graveyard; O, I remember, I told you so! Well, joining the church is a little shrine, with a group of figures in it which I defy anybody to see without laughing, they are so grotesque, so hideously absurd; and yet I cannot now look out at them at night, and see the little solitary beam of the lamp burning before it, without a thrill. I think there will be some hard moments in my life to come, when, if I think of Gethsemane, I shall think of this dreadful little shrine in the Tyrol, and of the earnest, pleading, praying souls I have seen kneeling before it. It is the night in Gethsemane; the Christ and all the Apostles have wreaths of artificial roses on their heads. The positions of two or three of the sleeping Apostles are so ludicrous that I should not dare to describe them. Several little fat angels, also with wreaths, are hung by wires from the roof, and a big angel, worst of all, is directly in front of the kneeling Christ, supporting him. Never in the poorest country church have I seen anything so frightfully grotesque, and yet I have seen men kneel before that iron railing with that in their faces which it smote me to the heart to see; I should never have done justice to what the Roman Catholic religion was intended to be, if I had not come face to face with it in these honest, earnest, solemn country people of South Germany. In Italy it was no more the same thing than if it did not bear the same name. I wonder daily if this be not its very strongest hold, — I mean, on the *masses*.

July 14. — Well, dear people, I could not put in, if I tried, all that we have seen since I wrote these last pages of rhapsody over country Catholicism. Such a tumble as we have had, and such a scatter! At first I thought I would not try to tell you the story, it would be so long; but it is too good to keep. To begin back, we were told, before coming to Berchtesgaden, that the hotels here would not "keep" people, that everybody had to go into lodgings; but, being of the self-asserting sort, we did not quite believe this, it sounded so incredible. We thought *we* should get kept, if nobody else did; and as for going into apartments to live, that was something we never would do, not we! I was strongest of all on this point. Never again, so long as I live, do I wish to see my dinner coming into the door in a box on a man's head. Well, so we settled down in our comfortable rooms at the Watzman, as I told you; and are not the H. H. written in the photograph over the very window of mine? And did not the good-natured chambermaid and porter lug out the second bed to make a nice place for my writing-table? and did I not hang up my "Council of Friends" on the walls, and Paul Veronese's little St. John, and the dear convent of San Lazzaro, and set all my sixteen books in their appointed places, and say unto my soul, "Soul, thou hast six weeks before thee in this room; it is a good place to do good work in"? and that very night did not Franz tell us at tea that we could only have the rooms a fortnight, he thought; that nobody ever stayed, everybody went into lodgings? Still we thought we would let things *slide*, and trust to sticking on somehow; at least, I did. The best part of all the fun is, that at this crisis, in these early days, P—— and N—— were a little bored with Berchtesgaden and intimated that they might not be contented here a month. "Very well," said I, "you can go off to as many watering-places as you please; out of this heavenly spot I do not stir for six weeks. I do not care if there be not a human being here to whom I can speak." People kept coming and going every day, — Germans, chiefly; now and then an English party. Nobody stayed over two days or three; the house filled and emptied, and filled and emptied, like a railroad station. One day we saw the landlord send away three carriage-loads of people in one hour; no rooms for them! Then my heart sank within me! Still I said, "I will pay for that second bed which has been taken out of my room; then I shall be as good as two." So I clung to hope.

Last Friday the blow fell. The poor Franz, with great suffering in his face, told us that a party of court ladies were to arrive from Ischl Saturday night, (the Queen had already arrived at her villa with a large suite,) and that every room in the house was required. "I told you so, mees," he said. Yes, he had told us so, —

we had nobody to blame but ourselves. In midst of my discomfiture, what triumph that my friends did not, after all, wish to leave this quiet Berchtesgaden! Did n't we take an *einspanner* and drive to seven different lodging-houses, one after the other, in vain? No rooms in Berchtesgaden which would do for us. This little town is absolutely brimful of people. At last I found in the house next to the hotel, only a minute's walk, two lovely rooms, which by some strange chance had been left unrented, — a little bedroom, and a corner sitting-room with four windows! Into these I moved in two short hours, having all my "Council of Friends," and my pictures, and my books, and my tooth-powder, and my india-rubbers carried over in a clothes-basket. And then I was magnanimous enough *not* to laugh at P—— and N——, who had absolutely no resource left them but to drive back to Salzburg, to stay there a week, before they could have rooms at Ischl, where they had intended to go a little later! It is only fourteen miles off, to be sure, and it is a beautiful place; but it is a large city, and we had seen it thoroughly, and last, not least, it cost us fifteen francs a day at the hotel there, and to go back there and stay seven days would have been the very thing of all others which we should have said nothing would induce us to do. At first I felt a little nervous about being left all alone in this little German town, one word of whose language I cannot speak. But I wanted to stay so much that I decided to try it, knowing that I could join the girls at any minute if I found it too lonely; thus far I enjoy it immensely, and think now I shall stay two weeks, while they take a look at the gayeties of Ischl, for which I do not hanker. I have my breakfast and tea in the house, and go over to the hotel for my dinner; and Franz, the little curly-headed "Special Providence" who speaks English, begs to be allowed to come over and translate for me, — "if there might be anything what you will like to say, mees," he tells me every day; so

I am writing away at things I had wanted to do, and taking long walks, and reading Morris and Emerson, and having the novel experience of being, for the first time in my life, absolutely and entirely alone. It will only be so for a few days, however, for next week I expect friends from Venice, and probably some from Rome. In fact, it is partly because I do not want to miss seeing them that I stay on. Meantime I see more and more the reason of the landlord's not keeping permanent people in his house. Carriage-load after carriage-load they come from both ways, for a day, a night, a dinner. In August, Franz says the gentlemen sleep in the barn often, or camp on the hill, and he has *four* beds in my room! And I, poor simpleton, thought perhaps I might bribe him by paying for two! In the parlor and bedroom opposite mine, in this house, is a German lady who looks so like Mrs. Dall I am sure she belongs to the same class of workers; she has a writing-table, too, all covered with papers and work just like mine. I have caught her "peeking" through at mine, just as I do at hers; I presume we wonder equally at each other. She has two sons, — fine, tall fellows, students, I think, — who come to see her every day, and they go off for tramps together. Now you see the mistake of my life in not having had the gift of tongues. If I could only speak German, all sorts of things would happen. Among others, I should be able to get out of the director of the Salt Works, who lives in such a lovely stone house joining the old church opposite, all necessary information to make a wonderful story about the Bavarian salt. It is the most marvellous thing you ever heard of, — the way they carry this salt-water about in pipes from town to town, over mountains two thousand feet high; sixty miles it goes on one route, — from Berchtesgaden through Reichenhall to Transtein. The other day in Reichenhall, I saw, in a great dripping chamber, two wheels, forty feet high, rolling slowly round and round, dipping down into water under the floor, and working all sorts of mysterious pistons and things, and that is all I know about it; but I shall go into the salt-mine after the G——s come. That will be one thing I can see without speaking German. But now I must tell you a little about the pictures of the wonderful lake Kœnigsee, so that you can understand them. Look first at picture No. 1; that is the end of the lake to which we drive from Berchtesgaden (three miles); those little houses are boat-houses, from which you push out in a ticklish little boat, rowed perhaps by two women, — there are as many women as men who row. You row down between those two points in the centre of the picture, and turn round the one on the right, and there you see the view which is given in No. 2. But you can hardly form any idea of the immense distance, except when I tell you that the little chapel of St. Bartholema, which is shown in No. 3, is the tiny white spot which you see apparently near the end of the lake in No. 2. The mountains are all five and six thousand feet high, and there is hardly a spot on the lake where even a foothold could be got on the shore, these mountains rise so sharply from the water. When the king comes to hunt, the peasants drive the chamois down these steep sides into the water, and the royal people shoot them from boats. If I am here when it happens I must see it, and yet I shall want to shoot one shot for the chamois into midst of the court. O the cruel thing that it is to do!

The picture of Berchtesgaden does not give you a good idea of anything except the big Watzman, with its glacier; you see only part of the town, and get no idea of the lovely sloping hills which lie all about it, with houses and farms set like white and green stones in the framing of dark fir forests. The little villa is a capital picture of the average style of country-seat in this neighborhood. Almost all have as many vines as this one, and they all have the projecting roofs and stones laid along the narrow cross-boards to hold them down. I meant to have sent a picture of the royal villa, but forgot it. That has a solid wall of woodbine over the lower story, and is very picturesque. But my letter is heavy enough now.

I don't tell you anything about Salzburg, nor about Innspruck, nor about the Grand Ampezzo Pass through which we came up from Venice here. It was a fine two weeks' journey, — better even than the Cornice road, about which you never heard, for the luckless letter went nobody knows where. O, I must tell you that your next letter will be from Innspruck, from the Schloss Wyerburg, an old hunting castle of the old Maximilians! Does not that sound well? Some pleasant English people, friends of the S——s, are boarding there, and are anxious to have us join them; so that is likely to be our next move; and from Innspruck there are many pleasant excursions, — it is nearly the centre of the Tyrol. I feel as if I had told you nothing in this letter. There is a wedding dance I have seen, and a ride all by myself in an *eilwayen* (omnibus), and a trial of a fire apparatus here in the streets of Berchtesgaden, and a trip to Reichenhall, and a dinner in a garden. Why cannot one write as fast as one could speak?

Good by; love, and love, and love to you all.

WILD-BAD-GASTEIN, AUSTRIA, August 11, 1869.

DEAR PEOPLE: I had half a mind to send you this month a treatise on European cookery, or politics, or anything else rather than where I am, and how I came so. It looks like such a tangle of a story to tell. But I suppose if I said I was not here, but somewhere else, somebody would be sure to turn up and contradict me. I always got found out in all the lies I ever told, and a good many I did n't. I dare say half of this story will be taken to be fiction.

The last you heard of me was at Berchtesgaden, Bavaria, leading the life of a hermit, and feasting on mountains. I think I wrote you all about the general stampede of strangers there, and the utter impossibility of getting rooms in the hotels. How little I thought that in less than two weeks I should see a place by comparison with which Berchtesgaden is a roomy solitude! But dear me! I am giving you hints; that spoils all. The last week of my stay in Berchtesgaden, however, I must not forget to mention. I led anything but a hermit's life, having no less than twelve friends and acquaintances in the town, so that I was sorrier than ever at the prospect of coming away. But the girls wrote from Ischl, entreating me to join them at Salzburg, and take a run down to this Bad-Gastein before we went to Innspruck. Gastein I had longed to see, so I packed up in an hour and posted over to Salzburg; and for Gastein we started on Monday morning, August 2, — a capital pair of horses, an easy carriage, and a respectable old body for driver, who had been in the service of the Goldener Schiff (the hotel from which we set off) for twenty years. How gay we were! The

girls had so much to tell of their doings at Ischl,
where they had been driven from pillar to post, in
matter of rooms, just as they were at Berchtesgaden,
but where they had managed, in a sort of Israelite
fashion, to have a grand time; had seen the Empress of
Austria and her papa and mamma, and the wonderful
little town of Hallstadt, which clings like swallows'
nests to the mountain-side, and never sees sun above
the mountain-tops from November 17 to February 2.
Think of that! I had nothing to give them in return
for these traveller's tales except faint, shadowy sketches
of the conversation of the Baroness von M——, who
had spent several mornings in Berchtesgaden in telling
me about the life at court, the experiences of her sister-in-law who is Maid of Honor to Queen Somebody,—
I forget now who,— and the ways and manners of German people generally. The little Baroness is an American, but has married an officer in the Prussian army,
and lived seven years in Germany. Her head is a little the less steady for having so many relatives at court;
but she is very amusing, and has quite a fund of American good sense left in her yet. Fancy the poor Maid
of Honor having to sleep all alone in a small pavilion,
some little distance from an insignificant and inconvenient villa which the Queen had seen fit to buy of a
tailor, and live in for the summer, though it was far too
small to accommodate her suite. At night the Queen
says, "I will go at seven in the morning to take a walk."
So by seven in the morning poor Maid of Honor must
be at the door of the Queen's bedchamber, dressed,
ready for the walk. No queen! Hour after hour passes.
Maid of Honor can't stir, because at any moment
Queen may come. Perhaps at eleven Queen comes
out and says, "O, it is too late now, but we will take
a drive!" Off goes poor breakfastless Maid of Honor
to drive for two hours! And so it is all day; and then
perhaps at midnight the Queen takes a walk. It sounds
so real when it is the Maid of Honor's sister-in-law who

tells you. I never had any idea of it all before. Madame d' Arblay's Memoirs sounded as mythical to me as the labors of Hercules. — Well, with our queens and our empresses, and our maids of honor, we rolled along over such a lovely road that I could tell you nothing, if I tried, which would make you see how it looks. The great Salzburg plain is the most beautiful I ever saw. Hadley meadow, perhaps, enclosed in an amphitheatre of mountains eight and ten thousand feet high, with a city in the middle of the plain, and a great gray turreted castle perched upon a crag in the middle of the city. It is all highly cultivated,— the plain,— wheat and flax and grass; avenues of linden-trees cross it here and there. The flax was blue as the sky, the wheat was yellow, and much of it stacked in the queer fashion they have here, which is to build the stack up of tied bunches, "criss cross" round a pole; three bunches at bottom stick down in the ground like legs, and every stack looks like a grotesque Esquimau. A field full of them in rows and squads is as funny as Beard's bears.

At ten we reached Hallein,— a dingy, close-built little town, which looked like an Italian town baked over. Here we stayed four hours, and went through a salt-mine. Can't write that up now; only I will mention that we went in at top or near the top of a mountain twelve hundred feet high, and we came out at bottom of the mountain. Yes, honor bright, we did, and I shall send you the pictures of it in this letter, to show you how we looked. They are very good pictures. Some of the slides down which we went, squatted on poles and astride the track, exactly as you will see in the pictures, were hundreds of feet long, and just as steep as they look, the first one almost took our breath away with terror, but after that we did not mind it. The most wonderful thing was the pull across that black lake, lit by shimmering lamps all round the outer edge, and the rock roof close over our heads, and we towed slowly over by invisible hands on the farther shore. It reminded me of the Car of Padalon in the Curse of Kehama.

The Bloomer dresses we had to put on are made of stout white twilled cotton. They also give you round woollen caps; but those we declined for many reasons, and wore our own hats. Coming down from the mine into the town, I was so tired that I stopped a man whom I took to be a post driver by his top-boots and yellow trousers, and asked him to take me to the inn. I mean that N—— asked him, I seconding the appeal by the mute language to which I am confined in this country. I thought he looked uncommonly astounded at the request; and awful misgivings crept over me, inch by inch of the way, as I looked at his heavy costly gloves and whip, and the superior make and get up of his horses. "Of course," I said to myself, "here I have been and gone and jumped into the wagon of a baron or an archduke or something, and I can't even say, 'I am quite sorry, sir, but really your face is so red I took you for a postilion.' But he was only the Herr—something or other which I can't spell,—and he only had to carry me a few rods; we were not so far off as I thought; and I dare say he is very glad of the story to tell, to illustrate the manners of American women, and how they don't know better than to offer a gentleman money.

We ate a good dinner of trout in the queer little stuffy dining-room of the inn, with dishes set up behind slats on the wall; and I came away and forgot my lovely bouquet of edelweiss and cyclamen, my farewell gift from the head-waiter at the Watzman in Berchtesgaden. Always at these German inns they give you, when you go away, a bouquet of flowers; sometimes you will see a carriage full of people driving off with four or five beautiful bunches of flowers. When we left the house of the Golden Star, kept by the five sisters Barbaria, in the Ampezzo Pass, at Cortina, they gave us each a bunch of the most superb great geranium blossoms and roses, all cut from the plants in their dining-room. How they could have had the heart to cut off so many, I don't know; though, to be sure, the windows looked just as full of flowers when we drove off as when we arrived.

At four o'clock, Golling. Pouring rain! O, how we chafed and fretted, for at Golling is the waterfall! "Scharzback, one of the finest in the German Alps," said Murray, and supposed to be outlet of our dear Kœnigsee at Berchtesgaden, and this we meant to see before dark. Could we drive to it? "O yes." So I said resolutely, "I shall take an einspanner and go." The girls went to bed, and I and my little dwarf man of a driver started off. The rain delusively held up for me to start; once down in the meadow, then it had me, and began to flood the very road. Poor Dwarf shifted his seat from puddle to puddle on the seat; now and then he looked back imploringly at me; but I was snugged up under the boot as dry as a chip, and they had told him that the dame could not speak a word of German; so what could he do? Then it began to thunder and lighten; and the horse plunged, which is n't a nice thing in an einspanner. (O, I have never yet told you about an einspanner, I will.) At last the man drew up in front of a little house, or room rather, for beer drinking, and made signs to me that I should jump out; so I did, and there I waited till the worst went by. A good-natured German woman came in, hoping to sell me beer, and we talked about the weather; with my eyes and hands I talked, and a few ejaculatory substantives, and then I made a pun in German, which tickled her and the driver so that they roared. I said (never mind the German), "I wish see waterfall, much waterfall!" pointing to the sky. Waterfall in German is "wasser fall"; that's how I happened to know it, it is so like the English. Then they both began to talk German to me in torrents; and I was glad to escape into the carriage. The man led the horse up a gully road for quarter of a mile, and then stopped and said I was to walk the rest of the way. . . . .

Monday, August 16. — This letter is sure to be the worst I ever sent you, dear souls. It is a kind of washing-day-dinner letter. You 'll eat it because you can't get any other, and you won't be as hungry as if you had eaten nothing; but don't we all hate Monday dinners? Now you see there is nothing left of that waterfall, for since August 11, when I began this letter, I've cooked it for a newspaper! It fitted and slipped in so naturally into a letter I was writing I could not resist the temptation to serve it hot *à la carte* to those customers, and this is all you'll get of it, unless you look up the waiter who carried it off. But nobody else but you will be told how funny it all was when we did really reach Gastein. It was at noon of Wednesday. We began to grow nervous as we drew near the town, because we had had no answer to our telegram for rooms; and the minute we drove into the little Platz before the Straubinger Hotel we had an instinct that there was a clear case for Mr. Malthus in this town. A pompous fellow in a white waistcoat met us. Yes, he had received our telegram. Sorry he could not give us rooms in the house. He had taken them for us in the Schloss, the great stone house opposite. So we drove up the side of a house, — I mean hill, but it was as steep, — and faced the proprietor there. Big man, big hall, big blackboard with numbers of the rooms in the house, and the occupants' names written in chalk on it! Yes, the landlord of Straubinger had taken a room for us; this was it. "No. 16, Lord Cavendish"! Now if anything in this world could be plain, one would think it might be the fact that three American women were not "Lord Cavendish"; but for half an hour poor N—— and the landlord bowed and jabbered to each other in vain to clear up this point. Back we drove to the hotel again. Yes, that was our room. Lord Cavendish would not arrive till Saturday. We timidly said that we had telegraphed for three rooms, and that however double or triple Lord Cavendish might be, and yet be satisfied with one room, we wanted three. At last we got one more, a flight higher up; P—— and I took the noble lord's apartment, and N—— went up stairs. A very fine room ours was; four windows, two beds, and wardrobes and tables and secretaries in quantity. But such a noise! It was over the waterfall. A waterfall three hundred feet high, in the very centre of the town, is the most picturesque thing I ever saw; but the effect of it on the human ear is something not to be endured. You feel as if you had just got into New York in twenty steamboats, and they were all letting off steam at once under your stateroom window. "Well, Lord Cavendish," said we, "you are welcome to your room on Saturday morning. English nerves may stand this racket better than American." In the night P—— and I called out to each other, "Are you awake? don't you think it gets louder every minute?" We felt as if we were part of it, at last, and going down head-foremost over rocks. Breakfast and tea in our room, not bad; dinner over at the Hotel Straubingers at one o'clock for a florin, at three o'clock for two florins; being bent on economy, we went at one. Babel let loose! Why people talk about American *tables d'hôte* I can't imagine; we don't make half so much noise, nor make knives fly in and out of throats, nor do some other things which Germans do, but which I could not even bring myself to write. We are much more civilized than I supposed we were in comparison with the peoples I have seen thus far. Not a window open; a German would think he was sure to die, with an open window at his back. One hundred people in a room which ought to hold only fifty. A narrow plank-wide table in the middle, and one a little broader all round the room. Hungarian to right of you, Russian in front, French and German to left, and English silence just beyond. Waiters bringing, first, soup, with watery bread in it; roast beef, done black, and swimming in gravy, and cucumbers served with it; junks of fat bacon, and an indescribable bean-mush served with that; roast veal, and stewed plums to eat with that; and then fried griddle-cakes, chopped up and spooned out for dessert. That is the wholesome and nourishing dinner you get at Straubinger's for one florin. There are other hotels here, worse. At three o'clock, for two florins you get several more courses, and a good deal of fol-de-rol for dessert; but it is all of a piece, and you may as well save your extra florin, and spend it for fruit at the peasant woman's stand opposite the hotel. We cruised about town; smelt and tasted of all the hot springs and cold, poked into the cavern where some of them are dripping, got drenched with the waterfall, looked at all the booths and things to sell and went to bed, having engaged our driver to take us back to Salzburg on Saturday morning. On Friday afternoon I was attacked with a sore-throat. Saturday morning, no better. Lord Cavendish impending. Gustav, the kind and pompous head-man at Straubinger's, in despair. I bundle up, and go over to small room in his hotel; girls in another. Sunday morning, no better. Driver behaved like a villain, refused to release us from our bargain, and insisted on being paid ten dollars a day while he waited. Of course I could not get better in such a state of things; five English people coming to take these rooms on Monday morning. Never, I think, in all my life did it appear to me so inconvenient and perplexing a thing that I should exist as for a few hours that Sunday morning. At last I made a *coup d'état*. I conspired with the good angel of a doctor, engaged a room in the priest's house, a few doors from the hotel, and then told the girls I should stay two weeks and they must go. I knew, as far as one can know anything, that I should be entirely well in two or three days. I wanted to see more of Gastein, and I promised to telegraph to them instantly if I were not so well. The doctor speaks English perfectly. I knew that friends from New Haven were coming in a day or two, and I was sure I should never get well so long as I felt that I was keeping my friends here, and we were paying ten dollars a day for the rascally driver. It was hard to make them go, but I succeeded; and in less than twenty-four hours after they left I was quite well; the third day I walked all over town. I hurry to this consummation of the story, because I know just with what dismay you will have been reading the last page. Now I will go back and give the picture of the days a little touching up. Sunday afternoon I moved down to the priest's house, — one of the nicest in town, and crowded full of lodgers; only just this one delightful front room vacated for me the day before, and to be vacant just three days, and no more, — just the length of time which must pass before the dear doctor could give me a room in his own house. All things seemed to work so singularly that I began to feel as resigned as a log, waiting to see into what corner I should drift next. The girls came down and took tea with me in my new quarters, and I was all unpacked and in order in an hour. At nine o'clock a tap at my door, and there stood the sweetest-faced, saddest-faced girl, perhaps seventeen or eighteen years old, but hopelessly dwarfed and deformed. "I heard that you were English and did not speak German, and I came to see if there were anything I could say for you to the maid before bedtime," said she, in the gentlest, but most pathetic voice I ever heard. Do you suppose you can any of you have an idea how I felt at that moment? I did not know till then that I had had a shade of misgiving about being alone; but by the warm rush into my cheeks and eyes at sight of her I found out that I had. I think I shall never see any face which will look to me so beautiful as does the face of that poor dwarf girl; but it is not beautiful at all. The next morning she came and sat with me for a long time, and I have seen her every day since. She is a Hungarian. Her father is the president of the highest tribunal at Pesth, and he is here for his health. Her mother is one of the most glorious specimens of what a woman can be at forty-five I have ever seen. Think of her walking last week up the Gamskogel and back, — nine hours of hard and even perilous climbing; and she laughed when I asked her if she were not tired. They urged me to join the party and go on horseback, — several members of it (all Hungarian) speaking English well, she said, — but I dared not try it even on a horse. How can one keep that tenth commandment in presence of such strength as this! Legs and languages! Let nobody expect to be happy in Europe without two very strong specimens of the one, and at least four of the other. I could not tell you if I tried how kind and lovable and bright these people are. I have always heard that the Hungarian nature was a rarely fine and sensitive one, and since I have known this mother and daughter I can easily believe it. There is a subtle something in their atmosphere I never before found, and cannot put into words; a fine aroma of soul all the while making beautiful the smallest word or gesture. The radiant tenderness with which the mother looks every moment at the daughter whose life is so blighted, and the brave gayety and love with which Jozsa looks back. I forget to speak sometimes, watching the marvel of it. Jozsa has studied English but six months, and she speaks well and understands all I say. This puts me to such shame when I think of my six months in Italy, and that to-day I could not do more in Italian than perhaps to order a dinner or dispute with a *cochiere*. Well, there were three days at the priest's house; dainty breakfasts and teas served by the most ruffled and linen-clad of housekeepers; horrible dinners sent down in layers of stone-china from Straubinger's; long talks with Jozsa, and sametimes four or five calls a day from the kindly doctor, who, having only sixty patients to see each day, is so running over with benevolence and good-will that he is constantly doing odd jobs of helping for everybody he can find in need of him. "Is there anything I can order for you?" he would cry out almost before opening the door, and down stairs again before I had half said, "No, thank you." Then it would be a book, then a newspaper, and then my letters and papers, for they took to coming, too, just at this crisis in my affairs. Ah! you need n't suppose those three days in the house of the Gastein curé were dreary. I spent half the time lying on the sofa, and looking out over the waterfall at the mountain wall to the west; green to the very top, and so high, the sky seems resting on it like a ceiling. I ought to have written, but I did not, and that is the reason your letter is late.

On Thursday I moved again, — the fourth lodging in a week, — up to the house of the good doctor. He was much concerned, because in the priest's house I had been somewhat sumptuously bestowed (for Gastein and his simplicity), and in his house I was to come to an attic chamber and plainer furnishings, and he did not know me well enough to be sure I would not miss the gilt curtain-fixtures and the big looking-glass. I could see some distress in his face as he ran up stairs before me, carrying a lovely little rosebush in his hand, which he set on my window-sill. Ah, if I had not been satisfied! An attic room, to be sure, and only a bed and bureau and washstand and lounge, and two tables in it; but from each window such mountains to be seen as I have never yet looked on. This Gastein is almost at end of roads! You can drive four miles farther to Böckstein, and there the mountains close in like an army of giants, and there is no more going that way, except on horseback or on foot, through dangerous and difficult passes. Four of these mountains I see from my windows; from my writing-table I look down on the whole town; for I forgot to tell you that the house is high up above everything, a quarter of the way up the west wall of the Gastein valley. It only takes me ten minutes to walk down to Straubinger's; but it is all the way like going down stairs.

Then came Marie the housekeeper, and kissed my hand; and she, too, brought a rose with her, and a few forget-me-nots. Then I hung six of you, dear people, up over my writing-table, and sat down, and that was the beginning of my fourth era of Gastein! Since then I have had more perturbations of another kind, which I cannot tell in a letter, they being too long and stupid; having relation only to telegraph messages and missing relatives. In short, the story is: letter on Saturday night from my dear sister, in Salzburg, giving *no* address of hotel! all Sunday spent in vain attempts to telegraph to her there; finally I am rewarded by the information that Madame H—— had been there, but gone, and left her trunk at the Bankers Trauner. This is the advantage of being of one family! I being the Madame H—— who had left a trunk in charge of the Bankers Trauner; and my sister being all the while sitting quiet and unhappy in the Hotel Nelboeck, quite unaware that she never dated her letter. At last, late at night, I get track of her through Dr. Proell's brother, who lives in Salzburg, and to whom the doctor had telegraphed to go to *all hotels* in the city and look her up. But I am not much happier than before; the message is, "We leave for Munich to-morrow morning." Such are the contingencies and vicissitudes, my dear people, of being "round loose" in this part of the world. How would you like it? To see your dearest friends whisked off in that way from under your nose and eyes is a test of one's patience. If my sister had dated her letter I should have taken post-horses and dashed down to Salzburg to see her; but as the postmark of the letter was the only proof I had of her being there, I had not quite courage to go on the venture, not being yet able to speak *more* than two thousand words of German.

Tuesday Eve, August 17. — Who ever thought I should live to do what I have been doing to-night, and who ever could guess what it is? Lighting candles in honor of the Emperor of Austria's birthday! Ah, my people, if you could but have seen the little town an hour ago, and the Villa Proell, — for that is what we on this height are called. Every house in town was gayly lit from roof to cellar, and rockets going up among the fir-trees, and I patting about the village with the doctor looking at it all. We were very proud of our house, which was by far the gayest, having lights on the balconies behind the lattice-work, and at every window, and having the Austrian flag at one corner and the Hungarian at the other. I lit the candles on the upper balcony and at my windows with my own hands, just to say that I did it, not out of any love for the Emperor. But the waterfall was the wonder of the night; it is one of the sights I shall never forget, — lit at bottom by a fiery red light and at top by a brilliant blue. Can you try to fancy how a foaming cascade three hundred feet high would look, lit with blue and red, the foam sparkling off like stars of a rocket, and the fir-trees standing out in the glow, as if they were drawn with a fiery pencil on the sky? Then the moon came up from behind one of the mountains and gave an atmosphere of peace to the whole. Very thrifty are the good German people, though, with all their patriotism; they are beginning already to blow out the candles, and it is not nine o'clock; here comes the servant past my window blowing out ours. I do not think more than three inches of the candles have been burnt up.

Now I shall give you an exact list of the things which are suspended on the front of this house. You will not believe me, but it will be true. Nobody could believe, till they saw it, the childlikeness of these Germans. From first balcony, a yellow fuzzy hearth-rug; on top of it a flower-pot with gay paper round it and an imitation lemon-tree in it. From second balcony, a blue and white tablecloth; pinned in centre of the tablecloth something cut out of colored paper, which I take to be a coat of arms; above tablecloth, a white sheet on a *frame*, with F. J. in large gilt-paper letters; above these, on the white sheet, two worsted mats, one crimson and one green (a present to the doctor from an English lady yesterday, for *his* birthday is also to-day). These have a very striking effect as an outdoor decoration. On the third balcony, a black and yellow tablecloth, the Austrian flag in one corner, with a green bough at end of it and the Hungarian flag in the other corner. Now, do you believe me? Because if you don't I will tell you something droller still. Last night the doctor and his brother, and brother's wife, and Baroness Strauss, who are visiting him, had a small festivity in honor of his birthday, and this morning he sent up to my room two of the adornments of his office on the occasion. One was a wreath of purple thistles, and the other was a large oval of white paper wreathed with oats, plantain-leaves, may-weed, and grass, with two small carrots, tops and all, at bottom. Ophelia herself could not have tied up anything crazier. In the centre of this a shockingly bad photograph of the doctor, and around it written, "This likeness is considered beautiful, Don Juan." Now, if you do not believe this, I cannot tell you anything more. I for my part, am heartily in love with their simple-heartedness, and I feel so ashamed of myself to have outgrown thistle-wreaths and carrots and tablecloths. It is a new experience for me to see people pleased with even smaller things than please me.

Wednesday, August 18. — Really now, dear souls, the letter must go. I know it is a patchwork, and

I am afraid to look at the seams. I am at end of my paper too, and have cribbed these last sheets from Dr. Proell's office. I ought to tell you more about him, but it would be a tale by itself. I have just come from dinner, and he has given me a little German verse which his brother wrote, as part of the birthday sport; his brother is the first advocate in Linz, and as clever in his profession as Dr. Gustave in his.

> "If in high heaven happy saints had need
>   Of some good, wise, and faithful soul
> For doctor, God would surely send with speed
>   For this dear man, Gustavus Proell.
> But since in heaven haste is not allowed,
>   And since to blessed sweet Gastein
> The sick of nations come in yearly crowd,
>   God leaves him here. But if Divine
> Compassion could but see how o'er the roads he springs,
> He quickly would provide him with a pair of wings."

What do you think of my progress in German, my first effort at translation? For a six weeks' scholar is it not good, considering that my only teachers have been waiters, chambermaids, and landlords? How stupid to waste room on such nonsense! Of course I only translated it by having it read to me. Now do you have an idea of how I am getting naturalized here? I should take root in Germany much more easily than in Italy, with all its beauty. This morning I have been with Miss S—— to hear the grand mass for the Emperor, in the little stone chapel of St. Nicolai, which you will see in the picture. There were two grand dignitaries there with the Order of the Golden Fleece. If I had only known it beforehand I would have looked harder at them; but as it was, I looked at a poor peasant woman who knelt on the stone floor by their side from beginning to end of the mass. Afterwards we drove up towards the Kötschackthal, which you will also see. It is a delight to send you these pictures. I wonder I never thought of it before; when I come home it will be such a pleasure to me to see them again. I only wish I could spend twenty dollars a month in photographs and bring home all the places I see.

Here comes Marie the housekeeper with a little bunch of flowers for me, because it is the 18th of August, day of St. Helena, and the doctor has told her it is my "name-day," as they call it. Marie is an old family servant, in whose arms the doctor's mother died, and she keeps house for him, and looks after his interests as if he were a child of her own. She is always, so far as I can judge, either locking up or unlocking some of his goods. Good by, and good by, with love and love.

BAD-GASTEIN, Sunday morning, September 5, 1869.

DEAREST PEOPLE: Behold me still in Gastein. Shall I ever go away? The Fates have it settled, I suppose; but I should not dream of saying that I knew I should do anything so against nature as to leave this eagle's-nest. Rooms are engaged for the S——s and for me at the Bayerischer Hof, in Munich, on Monday, the 13th of September. A good man with an einspanner is engaged to take me to Salzburg next Friday and Saturday; but whether I go or not I shall doubt up to the last minute. Think of coming to stay four days, and staying five weeks. It has been a lesson to me in the matter of clothes; my black travelling dress has come to be to me as much like my skin as if I were a chamois and it were my fur; to be sure, my wrapper has come out at both elbows, and the washerwomen have torn each of my two nightgowns. There are inconveniences attending the living for five weeks in the clothing intended for four days, it must be owned; but to have found out that one can do it is something. I find myself thinking with some dismay of the big trunk of superfluous things I own in Salzburg.

Now what shall I tell you about since I have to write a second letter from Gastein? Did I put in all the mountains and the waterfalls in my last letter? Bless their grand old faces! if I wrote you a letter every day and all about them, I should never get them in. They are never twice alike. Yesterday they were so cold and stern that it would have been easy to be afraid. To-day they are so soft and warm that they bring tears into my eyes. If they look like this the day

I go away it will break my heart. I must put more
pictures into this letter to try and show you a little
more of this wonderful blessed spot. But there is no
picture of the view I want most to send you, and that
is the view from the balconies of this house. I do not
sleep on the balcony, but that is the only thing I do not
do on it. I live and move and have my being on it.
The town is at my feet, — that you can understand from
the picture; but you cannot understand how the opposite side of the valley — that is, the east wall—looks, and
that is the glory of all. It is the whole of a mountain,
and to the south and north of it are other mountains,
and they have their feet braced and interlocked with
each other in that wonderful way which mountains
have, whereby are made depths of valleys and ravine
beds for streams. Into three such valleys — no, not
into them, but *across* them — I look now; they come
down at nearly right angles into the Gastein and the
Böckstein valley; and to-day they are all so flooded
with sun, that way up, almost to the very top, I can
see the shadow of each fir-tree thrown on the ground.
We have not had so delicious a sun for a week; my
feet are toasting in it at this moment as before a wood-
fire. I am afraid I shall have to draw them in from the
lattice-work of the balcony (which makes my best
cricket), for I think the thermometer would be about
110° just at my toes; and yet the air is so cool that I
like a shawl, or even a waterproof, over my shoulders;
and at six o'clock to-night I shall have a wood-fire in
my stove.

O, how shall I tell you about this opposite hillside!
It cries out to me to let it alone, that not even an
artist could paint it, it is enough that it *is;* but I am
restless with my desire to make you see it. It is
eight thousand feet high, to begin with. At top it
is bald and bleak, many days snowy; but, so far up that
I cannot distinguish the points of the fir-trees, it is
green, green as a field of spring wheat. Fancy it! Half

forest, half pasture; little brown threads of fence lining it off here and there, and here and there a little brown house or barn. One third of the way up is a small white house, the Windischgrätz Café. Up to that I climbed, day before yesterday, with poor little E—— K—— carried in a *trag-sessel* (sedan-chair). Ever since I have been here it has been beckoning me up there, but the day never came for it until Friday. I thought I knew how high it was; but when I got there and looked down into the valley of Hof-Gastein on one side, and Böckstein on the other, and saw all the village of *my* Gastein in a little confused dark mass at my feet, and the Villa Pröll, which I thought in the clouds, down almost out of sight under a wood, then I found out how high the Windischgrätz Coffee-house is; and now you can remember that I tell you that it is certainly not more than one third of the way up the mountain wall, out on which I look all day; and, remembering this, can you begin to see what I see? In the early morning, when the sun is but just above it, it is all in soft mist, great broad beams of mist such as we see when we say "the sun is drawing water." Until eleven o'clock I always think that this is its most beautiful time; then it is in clear sun, and I can count every shadow of every tree, and almost see down to the very roots of the trees in the forests, and I think that is the most beautiful time; and then in the late afternoon, when it darkens again, and the fir-trees look black and the fields look gray, I think that is the most beautiful time. This is the way with lovers. Do you not pity me that I go away? If I do not suffer a little at first, like a transplanted tree, it will be strange. Have you any wonder what I do in this valley that I love it so? I should think you would have, but I am afraid I shall be as puzzled as the fir-trees to tell. In the morning at seven, Marie, the housekeeper, comes and gives a shadowy little knock at my door, thinking perhaps I may be asleep, though she has

Q

never yet found me so in all these four weeks. She
comes in with a jingle like a sleigh, for she has the
keys of everything hanging at her waist. "Kiss the
hand, madame," she says. "Slept well? O, good,
good!" and "Fine weather," she adds, if she can, and
if she can't, she holds her tongue like a Christian,
and don't mention the weather at all. Then I tell her
what I will have for breakfast, and as I lumber out
the words worse and worse each time, she says,
"Ah! madame speaks very good Dutch, very good."
Meantime, Irma, who is the little chambermaid, has
brought me two enormous great brown jugs of water,
and a wooden tub, and a decanter of the warm spring-
water, with which I am trying faithfully to treat my
throat; the dear enthusiast Dr. Pröll having assured
me over and over that if I will only gargle the throat
with this water several times a day, I will never, no,
never, have another sore-throat. Believing that my
"chief end" was to have sore-throats, and not believing very firmly in any kind of mineral waters, I naturally
do not remember to gargle my throat so many times a
day as I might; so when the next sore-throat arrives,
Dr. Pröll will be entitled to the benefit of the doubt
as to whether it would have come if Gastein water had
been faithfully used. Breakfast comes in on a tray
covered with a snow-clean napkin, — tiny little white
teapot of tea, tinier white teapot of hot water, baby-
house pitcher of milk, — teapot has a silver strainer at
nose, and is as pretty as a picture; but the nose is all
wrong, and the tea runs anywhere but in the strainer.

"I wish one thing to the man that has made these
teapots," says Dr. Pröll, "that he might be condemned
for two thousand of years to *do a pour* out of one of
them."

Besides the tea, I have a glass of milk, which Marie
has strained into the tumbler the night before, so there
is thick cream on the top; a plate of "house bread,"
which is brown and hard, and has anise seeds in it; a

plate of white bread, which is as good as anything which is not home-made bread can be; a saucer of raspberries or blueberries, or an egg, and the last evening Post; — that is my breakfast. After breakfast, Marie comes to take the tray, then I pay for my breakfast, and make her laugh at my German numerals, as I insist on adding it all up myself. How much does it cost? Butter, 7 kreutzers; milk, 6; bread, 7; tea, 20; raspberries, 8, — 48 kreutzers in all, — and a kreutzer is, as near as I can make out, about three fifths of a cent. Then, when I have paid for my breakfast, comes the ordering of dinner; this takes dictionary, and Marie and I have great fun over it. There is n't much more variety about my dinners than about my gowns. So far as the meat is concerned, it is beefsteak or chicken; then on many days comes what Marie calls "ros-bif," and that is simply beefsteak cut from another part of the ox and cooked the same way. They call nothing a steak, except what we call "porter-house steaks." I have now brought Marie to the point of being able to bake potatoes, boil rice, and broil a steak "rare"; so I consider myself a missionary to the good doctor's kitchen. After Marie is disposed of I settle down in my corner of the balcony, and read or write all the morning; then I take a walk, and then comes dinner at one or at two. Sometimes the dinner is in the doctor's office, because just at present a very grand Hungarian countess has the saloon; sometimes it is in the "pavilion." That sounds grand. Well, now that the woodbine has turned to crimson and yellow and white, it *is* grander than any royal pavilion in the world; but except for the woodbine it is only a little rough wooden house with two sides open, a plank floor over the rock, and wooden chairs and a table. To-day we dined there, and the sun shone through the wall of woodbine, filling the air with reds which cannot be uttered.

While we are dining, come messengers from the north, south, east, and west, to call the doctor; never yet have I seen him left ten minutes uninterrupted. "Ah!" he says, "at the gate St. Peter will say, 'Who are you?' 'I have been physician at Gastein.' 'Then you can come in immediately; you need not go to purgatory. You have had it already!'"

After dinner a snatch of German legend, or an experience from Dr. Pröll's own life, which is all like a legend; and then he is off again for the rest of the day and most of the night. This wonderful man, fifty-three years old, walks seven and eight hours a day, seeing patients, and talks sometimes with sixty people in one day, for all the peasants flock to him; *runs* this lodging-house with only a faithful old housekeeper to help him; keeps all the meteorological records of Gastein; writes till midnight and after; and then is up, and down in the town at 5 A. M., to see to people in the vapor-bath! It is such a pity that some story-wright should not have had this month under Dr. Pröll's roof that I have had; it would make a good foundation for a novel. But I have been so stupid, I have sat dreaming away over the mountains and have not written out the stories I have heard and the people I have seen; and next week will come Munich and pictures, and then Vienna and more pictures, and the woodbine pavilion will fade away. That is the thing that grieves one most in Europe, that the pictures will, in spite of you, wipe each other out. Venice has grown dim already. I see that by the time I come home these letters will be as interesting to me as they can ever have been to you. Well, in the afternoon is either a drive or a walk, and then the sunset, and then bed, after another season with Marie on the subject of supper, — which consists, if I am frugal, of bread and butter and milk; if I am extravagant, of trout and bread and butter and beer.

This is all there is to a day at Gastein, but when I go away next Friday, I shall have spent thirty-five such days in perfect content; and if I acted out my heartiest impulse I should stay thirty-five more. How many of you will understand it, I wonder, that with Munich and Vienna on the "boards," I cling to Gastein? Nobody of you all, except you who have been with me at Bethlehem.

Yesterday we went to Böckstein, the little village three miles farther up the valley, or rather three miles farther on, in a valley of its own, which used, like this Gastein valley, to be a lake. "We" means Mrs. K——, and her poor little daughter E——, who cannot walk, Miss S——, their cousin, and I, in a big carriage; and Dr. Pröll and Mr. H—— in an einspanner. I cannot tell you about the machinery of the gold-mill, which was what we went to see, for I do not remember the names of the "things"; but if I could only make you see the old water-wheels which are standing still there! Really they look as if Shem, Ham, and Japhet had set them up in the days of the beginning of water-privileges, and had soon got tired of the business and sold out. Black, crumbling, and moss-grown, there the wheels stand and drip, drip, drip, — for the water still runs, as it ran in the days when the Weitmosers worked the gold-mine, through big water-pipes and sluices through the middle of the village. You can see, in the picture of the village, that in the middle of it the houses all seem to join; that is where the gold-mill and the long galleries and water-pipes are. All the machinery looked as if it were aching to fall apart, so old and so tired! It seemed somehow unchristian to let it stay unburied. An old workman went about with us and explained where the gold-stones were broken, and where the quicksilver was put in pans, and where it was all melted over fire. Above the furnace was an old dial-plate like a clock, with figures and hands to mark the heat which the metal had reached in boiling, — how more than mute it looked! — and on the edges of the furnace were mouldy fungus growths. After this was over, being in Germany, we thought of eating, and drew up before the little inn. Carriages were standing in the yard, and people drinking beer round tables in front of the windows.

Could we have trout? No. Chicken? No. Beefsteak? No. What could we have? Veal and eggs. The strangers from Gastein had eaten up everything else which the Böckstein inn possessed. Veal and eggs are the two staple delights of the German stomach; the veal steaming with fat and mustard, and the eggs horrible with butter and garlic. Ugh! All my life I shall remember the egg-salad which dear Marie added to our dinner yesterday, and of which I tasted, to appear civil, but was positively obliged to swallow hastily, like calomel, by help of great mouthfuls of beer. I thought I had tasted of bad things in Italy, but I give Germany the unquestioned palm. I am anxious to know whether the great students and thinkers of Germany eat the same sorts of food which I have seen in Berchtesgaden and Gastein. If they do, it is plain that for the German nation has been made by the Creator some peculiar and especial provision by which brains are independent of stomachs; yet dyspepsia is a rare disease here.

After we had to abandon the idea of a supper at the inn, Dr. Pröll took me in the einspanner, and the K—— party drove back disconsolate to Gastein; but I—ah, where did I go then? To the end of civilized roads, up, up, up, through the ravine that you see in the picture, to the very end of the road. It was the wildest spot I have ever seen. Look carefully at the picture, and there will be no need of my describing it. Beyond this, there is no getting out of this valley except by two very dangerous passes, on foot or on horseback, over into Carinthia. By one of these, Venice can be reached in three days and a half, my guide-book says. I think it means three years and a half. I know I am no nearer than that to the Grand Canal and Luigi.

Here comes Marie with a moss-basket full of forget-me-nots and crimson adonis and strawberry-leaves. Marie is a weather-beaten old woman of fifty, but she has youth in her soul for flowers. Everywhere that she can set a pot she has flowers growing, and fine fuchsias in among her beets! The garden, which is a collection of bits of soil tucked in among rocks and on steps, is her special province, and twinkles in the sun like her own quick-winking eyes. I always think, when I look out of my window, that it is going up the hill, and will be out of sight presently, there is so much more staircase to it than anything else. Wild ferns and pink heath are here and there in unreclaimed corners of it, and great piles of mossy rock, with fir-trees, and the pavilion, and a tent, and an arbor, and a sun-dial, and a barometer, and a rain-measurer, and I do not know what not. And Marie's sister, who is a rough peasant, but is a true clairvoyant, and has given the doctor most wonderful experimental tests of the "Od," — doing and saying and revealing things which she no more understood than if she had spoken in Greek, — is always to be seen groping about purposelessly and giving little pulls to the beets and peas and potatoes, as if she were pulling invisible wires and sounding bells beneath. She never pulls them up, so far as I can see. The doctor says, "She likes to do it." How much he pays her a week for this work I have not asked. She has her face bound up in a white handkerchief, and wears list shoes which make no noise. Marie always gives her a shove, I notice, when she comes near her, and this is all I perceive. But I ought to tell about Marie. Eighteen years ago she was a patient of the doctor's here in Gastein. At the same time a very poor old woman was dying in a hut here, of a horrible disease. When the doctor told Marie of her, she went instantly to the hut, and (sick herself) stayed and nursed the old woman till she died. The old woman lay on straw. Marie, when she lay anywhere,

lay on the bare boards of the top of a chest. From
that day Marie has been the protector of the sick and
dying of the doctor's family. She went to Venice,
and for several years nursed a paralytic uncle who
could not even feed himself. He died in her arms.
Then she went to Nice and nursed his brother through
three years' dying of consumption; he died in her arms.
Then his mother last of all, and she, with almost her
last breath, blessed Marie. Now Marie will never
leave the doctor himself, and so strong is her passion
for nursing, that I believe in the bottom of her heart
she feels a kind of divine satisfaction when she sees the
last illness approaching. I know she took more comfort in a sore-throat that I had for two days than in
anything else that has happened since I came. She
has given her whole heart to me, because I am the
"only lady she ever had in the house who was as nice
as a gentleman!" This sounds like equivocal praise,
but it is not. She loves me because she sees that she
pleases me in all her ways. Every day she makes
some new kind of German pudding for dinner, and
eyes me like a hawk while I take the first mouthful;
and every day, now she knows I am going away, she
sighs and says, "It will be sorrow to Marie when
madame goes." So I add her to Marianina in my book
of remembrance; and, if it came to being sick, I should
like Marianina to look at, but Marie to take care of
me. On the 18th of August (that was the day after
the Emperor's birthday, and the illumination, etc., of
which I wrote you), Marie came in to dinner bringing
a bunch of roses and forget-me-nots, and laid them by
my plate, looking shyly at the doctor, who explained
for her, "Marie thinks to give you a pleasure because
it is your *name* day." It seems that in Germany the
Catholics think more of the day which is called by the
name of the saint whose name you bear, than they
do of your birthday. 18th of August, I shall never
forget now, is "St. Helen's" day. (Glad there's been a

St. Helen already, because one of a name is enough. So I need not —) But next St. Helen's day there will be no Marie to bring me roses and forget-me-nots. How the forget-me-nots hold on here! You can't imagine! They flower and flower, and grow and grow; there does n't seem to be any *die* to them. I have had them in a tumbler for ten days at a time, growing taller and taller, and as blue at the last as at the beginning.

Wednesday, 8th. — There is nothing new to tell you to-day, except what the sun did this morning. At seven o'clock the whole valley was filled dense and thick with solid white clouds; it fairly seemed to roll in between the slats of the lattice-work of my balcony. I have seen nothing like it before. Newport's densest is not·so white, so solid. All of a sudden it lit up as if fires were kindled behind it. The sun had got fairly up over the mountain, and was driving all before him. In a few moments there began to come rifts in it, through which I could see bits of fir-wood and pasture on the mountains, gleaming with sunshine. Then the tops of the mountains came out clear, and the solid banks of cloud rolled and piled and struggled below. Some were gray, some were silver-white, some were yellow, and some were pale pink. No sunset ever was so beautiful. For an hour they went up and down and back and forth along the whole mountain wall, to east and south and north, as far as I could see. Gradually the colors died out, and the clouds grew fleecier and fleecier, till only little floating films were left here and there, and the whole valley was full of sunlight. I feel as if I had seen a world made. This afternoon I have been in the Platz, buying some more pictures to send to you, and some curious bone boxes made by the peasantry here. I hope those of you to whom I bring one will not scorn it for being scooped out of a cow's horn, and tattooed with ink in queer figures and mottoes. "Gastein" is written on all of them, and that makes them sacred to

me, but I am afraid you will not have the same romance
about it. On the way down I had an interview with
the man who is to take me to Salzburg. He is the man
who drives a carriage for Dr. Pröll; perfectly trust-
worthy and good, and has an uncommonly keen and
honest face; but really he looked to me so like my worst
enemy I could hardly speak peaceably to him.

O, here is the time for me to tell you about an
einspanner, for that is the thing I am going in, —
only I am going in an uncommonly fine one, which càn
be shut up in case of rain, and is painted in bright
green, in imitation of straw-work, on the sides. But,
after all, the greatest thing about a einspanner is not the
einspanner at all, but the way the horse is put in. The
carriage is like one of our common buggies, only very
low, and instead of a dasher in front is a tiny low seat
with no back, no front, no anything to it, and on this
the driver sits, with his feet dangling over among the
legs of the horse, or tucked up on the pole. I was just
going to say whiffletree, which would have been a
great joke, seeing that there is n't anything approaching to one about the whole concern. Now for the
horse. Out of the centre of your einspanner comes a
pole, just as if it were intended for two horses. On the
left side of this pole is your horse, fastened by traces
which are leather only half-way, and the rest of the
way small rope twisted and tied, — and frayed, as like
as not. No breeching, — nothing under heaven to
prevent your horse from stepping out of the traces on
the off side, nothing for him to hold back by, going
down hill, — so on the gentlest slopes they lock two of
the wheels and put on a brake, and you grind down
safely in spite of the cord traces flapping round the
horse's heels. The first time I rode in one I was positively afraid, which was a new sensation for me on
wheels; but now I am hardened to them, and feel as
comfortable as if I were in the most approved of high-
top buggies on the Bloomingdale road. Fancy me

dashing along for a day and a half all alone in one of them. Really, the things one does in Europe would seem extraordinary at home. If I started to take a journey of seventy miles in an open wagon, it would sound preposterous there, but here I think nothing of it. I am even thinking of going a little longer way to see some new places. I shall put my letter away now, and add just a few pages after I reach Munich. I think you will like it better if it is not *all Gastein*, so I shall not send it off, as I had intended, before starting. I cannot expect you all to be Gastein-mad, as I am, and I dare say I shall not be so myself after a few days in a picture-gallery again.

Saturday Eve. — Did I not say that I had need to be careful about saying that I would do anything so against nature as to leave Gastein? Behold me returned again to sleep in my attic, after having been as far as Hof-Gastein on my way to Salzburg! O, how I am laughing, and how queer it all is, and how glad I am of one more sunrise on these mountains! But this is the way it came about. Till the last minute I had put off starting. At three o'clock this afternoon it was to be. At three o'clock the carriage was here, — a nice little einspanner, which can be shut up tight like a cab. Marie cried hard, and I cried a little. At the last minute she appears with a big basket of raw tomatoes and peaches, and a bottle of strong beef-tea, which I taught her to make when I had my sore-throat, and which she considers, I believe, to be a standard American beverage. These are for the journey. A great round bouquet, gorgeous with verbenas, china-asters, pansies, phlox, yellow buttercups, and asparagus, and white openwork tissue paper, comes behind in Irma's little grimy fingers; another little bunch of roses, fuchsias, and forget-me-nots from Marie's own treasures; the big one is from the flower-store, and I very much fear that Marie gave a whole gulden for it. The doctor goes before, having promised to drive as far as Hof-Gastein with me. What

is my surprise to see him suddenly fly into the most
tremendous rage, and begin to talk loud and gesticulate
furiously to some invisible person behind the fir-trees!
I run on to see what has happened, for a voluble German in a rage is a sight to make you quicken your steps
any day; sure enough, there, instead of the good, faithful, steady-going owner of the einspanner, who had
promised to take me, was his boy, sixteen years old,
who is the most deliciously careless little grinning rascal I ever drove behind. The other day, in the space
of three hours, he twice ran into a fence, one time coming very near killing his horse, and the other time still
nearer smashing the wagon; but he only laughed, and
jumped down and tugged away at the back wheels till
he got us into the road again. This was a charming
escort on a seventy-mile journey. However, I said,
"Allah il Allah — I go!" So off we started. The
carriage was partly shut up, for already a drizzling rain
was setting in. Just before we reached Hof-Gastein it
grew colder, and the rain began to drive in at each side.
Where were the window pieces? O, he had not
brought them! Then you should have seen the holy
fury of Dr. Pröll! I am rather glad to have discovered that he can grow red in the face, and abuse people, like other mortals, because he always seemed a
little too much like a saint before. There I was; nothing to do but to come back, for to go on in an Alpine
storm with the carriage open would be madness; and
the most provoking thing was, that it had only been
to save a few pounds' additional weight for his horse,
that the man had left the side pieces at home. O, how
disconsolate and black the boy looked when he was
ordered to turn round and come back to Gastein!
Every few minutes the exasperated doctor would break
out with some hotter and heavier sentence, which
sounded like something more fearful than the preceding
one. Really, angry German is the most horrible sound
I ever heard in my life. Incantation, maledictions, su-

pernatural thunderings, and sputterings are in it. When I arrived at the house, Marie, Irma, Rupert, all came running with astonishment so great that their faces looked all eyes. Irma takes out the bouquets and disappears with them; Marie claps her hands, and says "Good, good, it is good, — that now I will not go at all"; Rubert lugs up my hat-box; the boy with the green einspanner drives off more crestfallen than I thought he could look; and here am I at my old writing-table, with a fire in my stove, and candles lit at six o'clock of a September evening. I believe there must be some special providence in the thing, for the storm has increased so fearfully it is almost a gale of rain. I should have been drenched even in a closed carriage before seven o'clock. Now what is to be done next I do not know. I fear the doctor and the einspanner man are now so angry that I have no chance in that green chariot again. I await the news with which the doctor will return to-night from the Platz. In the mean time you have two more pages of Gastein, after all. I should n't wonder if to-morrow there were to arrive a letter or a telegram from somebody, I can't imagine who or what, but somebody or something which should keep me here another month. It would be no odder than my having stayed here this month and having come back to-night. .... Here comes the doctor, his face all aglow with delight. "Such a miracle!" he says; "do I not tell you all is miracle? A storm is raging out at the end of the valley such as has not been seen for weeks and weeks." I should have driven directly into it and have been at six o'clock in the Klamme, the narrow pass of which I wrote you; no, I did not either. Well, it is the wildest sort of a pass; just room for the road and a river, and tremendous precipices above, on one hand, and below, on the other.. In many places the road is on a plank shelf, held on, I don't know how, to the side of the rocky cliffs. It makes me shudder to think of having been overtaken there by this storm, with the grinning boy for driver. But more good luck yet. A carriage is here from Salzburg, anxious to get a passenger to return, a good carriage and two horses, for which I pay but one gulden more than for the einspanner, and the driver is a trusty old man who has been on the road for twenty years, and is well known to everybody. At half past six to-morrow morning I start once more, and this time I think it will really be a success.

MUNICH, *Wednesday, 15th.* — Yes, it was a success, if anything can be called so which takes one away from the Gastein valley. Two such days as I had, all alone in my big carriage, with the fatherly old driver, who will puzzle his head to his dying day, I believe, to make out why it was that I went by myself, and what under heaven made me look so delighted all the way. It was such sunshine and such beauty, I even forgot that each mile took me farther from Gastein. Zell-am-See, Saalfelden, Reichenhall, Salzburg; but I was two days doing it, and I said everything that was needful at the odd little German inns; and I climbed down into the Seissenberger Klamme, which is the one spot on earth where chaos reigns; and my flowers never wilted by a shade during the whole two days, the wonderful Gastein blossoms! And when I walked into the grand Hotel Europa at Salzburg, I felt like one in a dream,— waiters with white cravats again, mushroom-sauce, and clothes to be seen on all sides! Heigh-ho! I slipped my shoulder under the strap once more, and picked up the burden of belonging to the world's people. Gastein, Gastein, farewell! Then came telegraphings between Salzburg and Innspruck, and, of course, misunderstandings; and did n't I come on here to Munich stark staring alone, instead of having met my friends at Rosenheim, as I should have done if I had properly understood the arrangement! At the station here, a providential man who spoke English! Always I find one when I am in straits, and this time the straits were dreadful. I shudder to think what I should have done without that man. In the country I don't mind; with my dictionary I get on; but at a railroad station in a city! I should have turned and run away, I think, and never been heard of more. Two hours later, by the next train, arrived poor P—— and N——, equally bewildered and unhappy at not finding me. Now we are settled, and have seen the Prince of Prussia. We came out of the hotel ahead of him too. Four black horses, riders in blue and silver on the two near horses, riders in blue and silver high up behind coach in blue and silver, rider in blue and silver on another black horse galloping before! The prince wore a stove-pipe hat, and looked, as every man looks who wears a stove-pipe hat, like any other man's barber; but the horses and the blue and silver were gay to see.

Munich looks to me, after three hours' driving in it, about as interesting as a brick-kiln, and more like it than anything else. Bricks unbaked and all stamped same pattern. But all that this century can do in the way of pictures is to be seen here now, so I mean to look. Carpaccio's St. Ursula is worth more than the whole of it, I suspect.

Good by, and good by, and good by.

MUNICH, Monday, October 4, 1869.

DEAR PEOPLE: Behold me, once more alone, left to myself for four days in this German city. The girls have just started on their journey southward,—Innspruck, Botzen, Verona, Florence, Rome. It sounds better than my programme, does it not? mine being Nuremberg, Cologne, Rotterdam, London. But, ah, how joyful I am, to be, at last, moving to the North! I had planned to set out at the same time they did, i. e. nine o'clock this morning; but at the last moment the dear Fräulein Hahlreiner, in whose house we lodged for two weeks, said if I would wait until Friday she would go with me. This I was but too glad to do, for of the only two women I could find who spoke English and were willing to take the journey, I could not tell which I disliked the more. One wished to go as my bosom-friend, and the other was a simpleton. But the Fraulein! You'll have enough of her, though, before you are done, for my letter will be full of her.

I cannot tell you very much about Munich, I think. See New York Independent for my opinions as to the outside look of it, and did I not tell you in the last letter also? I forget. But all I shall bring away from Munich will be pictures. Think of my having seen, in this short time, nearly four thousand! Of course I do not remember distinctly one hundred of them, but I have learned the different touch of the different painters, and know whom I love.

More and more I wonder what art would have done if Christ and his mother Mary had not lived on the earth. More than one gospel we owe them. Nobody will ever paint anything so sweet as Bellini's and Van Dyck's Madonnas, or so pure and strong as Fra Angelico believed the old saints to be. The only Christs I have seen at which I can look are Van Dyck's. One was a head in an old palace at Genoa. I wrote you about it. It had a look of John Weiss made martyr. The other is a crucifixion here in the Pinakothek. Van Dyck dares to make his Christ dark and strong and stern with suffering. Everybody else paints him a gentle, inefficient-looking creature, with long hair parted in the middle. It is something I cannot understand. The type began in the old seventh-century frescos, and from that day to this, so far as I can see, Van Dyck is the only man who has departed from it.

Now, for these four days, I shall do only two things, — write, and go to the Pinakothek. I have *done* the Exposition (and you can all read it in the Independent), and now I am going to spend three whole forenoons with Albert Dürer, Van Dyck, Rembrandt, Gerard Dow, Murillo, Teniers, Van der Werff, Cuyp, Paul Potter, Titian, Veronese, and Raphael, Holbein, Meister William of Cologne, and half a dozen more whose names I won't write. Don't think I look at everybody's pictures out of the four thousand, or at first one and then another man's, as most people do. I look at such people (and they are everybody) with perfect astonishment. I can't do it, any more than I could read fifty books at a time, a few lines from one and then from another, and so on. That would be precisely the same thing. I look at Murillo, for instance, for a day, and at nobody else. There are six lovely pictures of his in the Pinakothek. Such delicious beggars, and such a good time as they have! There is one boy with a great mouthful of melon in one cheek that I shall never forget; and another with his head thrown back, eating grapes. I had seen the engravings before; but they are nothing, the coloring is all.

But I write to you too much about pictures. I remember I used to think it the most stupid reading in the world, other people's notions of pictures which I had not seen.

Thursday Morning, October 14, 1869. — On the Rhine, four hours above Rotterdam; rolled up in blankets to keep warm.

Ah, but it's a great thing to have come down the Rhine! O, how shall I ever tell you the worry and the strain of it! With any less of a genius than my Fräulein I should never have got through. I shudder when I think of the time I should have had with the simpleton or the bosom companion. But I will begin back. Last Friday morning we left Munich for Nuremberg. I had read in Murray that the Wittelsbacher Hof was "good, clean, and moderate," so I telegraphed from the station at Munich to the Wittelsbacher Hof for two rooms. Arrived in Nuremberg at 9 P. M., confidently we said to men in crowd, "We go to the Wittelsbacher Hof." Crowd lifted up its voice, and said there was no Wittelsbacher Hof. I, being by nature obstinate, and having Murray in my hand, said there was. Poor Fräulein, in despair, dumped me in the waiting-room and went off to see. She came back with, "My dear lady, she do not exist these now four years, the Hotel Wittelsbacher." So we followed a small boy, with a glass of beer in his hand, down the square to the Würtemberger Hof, to which we found our telegram had been sent, and which is the very worst hotel I have seen in Europe. Next day it was a pouring rain. Nevertheless, I saw Nuremberg. A carriage, which might have been at Albert Dürer's funeral, I think, and two skeleton horses, and the Fräulein and I lumbering in and out under umbrellas, the Nuremberghers saw in their streets for five hours that day.

Old frescos by Durer, old dungeons worse than any in Venice, most wonderful old churches, (I send you pictures of all,) such instruments of torture as I have read of, but never fairly believed in, Albert Dürer's grave and statue, Hans Sach's grave, the castle, street after street of odd old houses, with windows to make your mouth water, fountains by Peter Vischer, shops of such worsted miracles and silver carvings and amber necklaces, — O, I am wretched now to think that I could not spend $100 in five minutes in those shops!

Never any of you try to see Nuremberg in a day. It is a place to ramble in for a week, to study corners and doorsteps and odd shadowy places, and in St. Lawrence's and St. Sebald's churches to spend mornings and evenings. I must go back some day with some of you. Who speaks? That Iron Virgin I must tell you about. It is gray stone, and the picture is exactly like it. It is in the last chamber of a series of dungeons under the wall of the city. Those two doors swing open. Inside they are set with horrible iron spikes in the head and the chest. When the person was placed inside, the doors were pressed slowly together by a great iron bar which comes from the wall opposite. It could not take many seconds to kill one so; that was the only consolation to think of; it was not really so cruel as some of the simpler-looking methods. Under the feet is a trap-door through which the body fell, eight feet down into the canal, and so out into the river. I looked down; but poor Fräulein said, "Mein Gott, mein Gott!" and turned so pale that I was afraid the great hearty creature would faint away, and how should we ever have got her out of those winding stone caverns! Everywhere she said such striking things that I was lost in astonishment at her. But I can't tell them to you here, because if I do you will none of you care anything about my story which I am going to make of her as soon as I get to London. Blessed old darling! I only wish I could take her for the rest of my life, wherever I go.

From Nuremberg to Mayence, nothing worth telling. From Mayence to Cologne, first day on the Rhine! Ha, my people, do you think I am going to send you a letter full of ecstasies about the Rhine? Not I. When the boat first pushed off from Mayence I said to myself — No! I won't tell you what I said; but for several hours I was the most damped creature you ever saw. The Fraulein had never before seen it, never before been in a large boat. "O, my lady, find you not this boat very large?" And when I told her that I was only astonished to find it so small, she was dumb with incredulous surprise. There were three American women on the deck, who were "doing" the Rhine so zealously, reading aloud from Murray at every ruin and castle, that somehow I took a sudden perverse disgust to the whole thing, and for the first time in my whole year I played the *blasé* traveller. The truth is, that one should never see the Coliseum and the tomb of Cecilia Metella before seeing the ruins on the Rhine; after them, nothing else this side of Palestine can look like more than a middle-aged house "out of repair." And, above all, one should not come from Tyrol *down* the Rhine; remember that, all of you who mean Rhine and Tyrol some day. Go *to* the Tyrol, *up* the Rhine, and then perhaps you will *get* a Rhine! I honestly own I have not had any. It won't "take." Well, we went on shore at Cologne. .... (O, I must not forget to tell you that they have built up a nice new old arch where Roland's real old, old arch fell down last year. It looks quite well against the sky, after you get far enough off, and the island below is really just as lovely as the ninety-nine thousand tourists have said.)

At Cologne we were splendidly lodged at the Hotel du Nord, in which I had to sleep with my head to the south; bright and early we set out to find the man who sold tickets "through" to London. If there is any creature in the world that rouses my ire, it is the porter in a first-class European city hotel. Their assistance is odious to me even in my greatest extremity, and their politeness so flavored with impudence that I boil. I have n't yet fathomed the mystery. I do not understand the species. Such a one I met in the doorway. Would he give me the address of the agent for the steamboat line for Rotterdam and London?

"Madame wished to go to London?" with a bow and a smile.

"Can you give me the address?"

"The agent will be here at eleven o'clock; he comes every day to make all the arrangements for passengers for our house."

"I do not wish to wait, I wish to see him at once; will you give me the address?"

"I can give you all the information, madame, myself, and save you the trouble of going to the office."

"Will you, or will you not, give me the address?" said I, — *thundered* I, would be more true, for O, how mad I was! Then I got it, and the porter went back into his office, muttering to himself, I suppose, that Americanerins were all bears.

Poor Fräulein stood by, silent and aghast. "Find you that man respectful, my lady?" she said, after we were in the street.

"O no," said I, "quite impertinent."

"I thought so," she said. "O, but I hate these people in this north country!"

Well, we drove to No. 12 Frederick William Strasse; grand office; "London, Calais, and Dover R. R." over the door. "O dear!" thinks I. "However, I'll ask." Grand cockney in white vest. "I wish to make some inquiries about the route to London via Rotterdam, and I was sent here; is this the place?"

"You wish to go to London?"

"Well," said I to myself, "Yankees are not alone in asking needless questions." However, I thought best to conciliate this bull, and I said I did, for reasons best known to myself, wish to do that very thing. "But I certainly would not go via Rotterdam." *Their* line, via Ostend, was so much shorter, quicker, etc., — a ten minutes' harangue from a prospectus. At last I got out of him the address of the office of the Netherlands Steamship Company, and down to the wharves we drove. A little box of a building, and a mild, surprised young man, and "O yes, they *did* sell through tickets to London, but no direct line through except on Sunday morning. Yes, I could wait at Rotterdam, or take a run up to Sweden and Norway, or somewhere, and in eight days I could be in London." I was in despair; at last I said, "But there is surely another company?" "O yes; the Cologne and Dusseldorf." "Ah, where was that?" He told me, bowed blandly, and resumed his writing as if such little conversations were frequent at his desk.

More wharves, another little box building, another clerk selling tickets to people that looked like emigrants. This seemed more promising. Could I get a through ticket to London? "O yes; but I would have to wait in Rotterdam over one day." Just what I wished. Then I was passed over to another man, an old man with big benevolence in the forehead, and he explained to me that I could go at 3 P. M. that day to Dusseldorf, at 8 A. M. next day to Arnheim, and there, whether there would or could not be a boat he could not say, but, at any rate, I could take cars to Rotterdam from there, and the whole ticket was so cheap I did not mind that at all, and I felt all the safer because he did not guarantee where he was not sure. He believed there would be a boat at Arnheim. Could he check my big trunk for London? Yes. So I bought my ticket; only 40 francs for me to London, and Fräulein to Arnheim! Remember that, you who mean to come, you can get from London to Cologne for $7 less this way.

Then I set out to see Cologne, took a look at the church where St. Ursula's Virgins' bones are laid, (this

I did for love of dear old Carpaccio's pictures in Venice. You remember?) then St. Gereon, which is a grand old church; here were skulls of martyrs set over doorways, behind railings, skulls set back side to the front, or else the eyes and nose and mouth were all wrapped in red velvet or damask, I could not make out which it was: then the house where Rubens lived and Marie de Medicis died; and then the Gurzenich, which is a handsome stone building, and has two nice old fellows in stone set under pent-house roofs in the front. And then the Apostles' Church, and the house near by, where are two stone heads of horses looking out of the third-story window, to commemorate the coming to life of Mrs. Somebody who was buried in that church, and, not being dead, returned quickly to her home and walked in on Mr. Somebody before he had decided what to do about it, and says he, "You are not my wife any more than my horses can be up in the third-story room"; and pop! out come the horses' heads, at that very minute, out of the third-story window; and the stone heads are there still to prove the story, which of course they do.

Then a dinner at a café; poor Fräulein turning white with horror at the prices and the quality.

"O my lady, find you this chicken good? She are old, old chicken; never had I courage to give old chicken in my house. Now I give. O, I win much money from this journey!"

After dinner, the cathedral, two hours free for it. Those of you who have seen it will not wonder that I have nothing to say about it; those of you who have not must forgive me. I cannot say one word. It is more wonderful than any words. If I said that by miracle a stone mountain had flowered in spire and arch and statue till there was not room for one single flower more to be set, that is my nearest word to what I saw, and so near that I think that somebody else must have said it before me.

At half past two behold Fräulein and me down on wharf again, (O, I forgot to say that there are now 17,000 different smells in Cologne, besides the Farina!) and at the little box-office door. Women and babies and bundles round the doorstep. I felt like Castle Garden. No old man of the morning, no clerk, no boat. One mortal hour passed; old man arrived; in half an hour more the boat. Things and people and we drizzled in as if all day were before us. I took a last, long, lingering look at my trunk, and tried to believe I should ever see it again. It must go by another boat to be sure of getting past Arnheim. Now I am sorry I did not bring it with me, but I was over-persuaded by the old man with benevolence big.

On deck I see an unmistakable *English* bonnet. The bonnet sprang up and said, "Oh! oh! do you know when this boat will start?"

"Immediately, I think."

"But there has been an accident to it."

"Oh! oh!" said I, and my heart sank.

"Yes; and each man says a different thing, and we have had no dinner, and I have just left a most beloved daughter at school at Neuwied, and I have cried the whole night, and I look like a fright," said she, lifting up her frightful black lace veil spotted with white, and showing a very pleasant, clean face.

"O, bless you!" thought I, "you are a godsend anyhow, if you are going to talk in this way."

Then came along the husband, a good-looking, brown-eyed, brown-whiskered man, who talked through his nose quite as much as any American I ever saw, and we fell to immediately and wondered what would turn up, and if we should ever get to Dusseldorf. In comes old man with big benevolence, and says, "We can tell in half an hour whether we can go on to-night or not!" Half-hour was one hour. O, how much that woman told me in that time!

Then we started for Dusseldorf. I, being half dead

with a cold which I had taken sleeping in the damp
layers of sodden flax which they call sheets in Cologne,
had to curl myself up in a corner of the cabin and make
the best of solitude and darkness. Every few minutes
came down the Fräulein to tell me what the English
lady had said, and to see how I got on. At 9 P. M.
Dusseldorf! English advocate said Hotel Europe was
the one they had selected to go to. Out we filed; two
men ahead carrying English advocate's valise and my
hat-box; English advocate's wife and I hugging on to
each other like old friends; Fräulein and English advocate roaming about loose on the outer edges of the procession; dark as midnight. Nobody seemed to know
exactly what we were to do; each thought somebody
else was taking responsibility.

"Halt!" Plump down go valises and hat-box in
middle of street; custom-house officer with lantern!

"Have you meat or sausage?" said he, twinkling his
eyes with fun to see how little we looked like sausage-
smugglers, and how scared we were at the idea of having trunks opened in the dead of night in the streets
of Dusseldorf.

Then he let us go on, having taken our word for all,
and not opened a single bag or box. "O Fräulein!"
said I, "did you tell that man you had no sausages in
your basket?" I knowing that she had at least six.

"O no, my lady, I did not make lie, I make diplomatique. He say, 'Have you meat or sausage?' and I
say, 'No, I have no meat!'"

Then we brought up at the Cologne Hof. Quite
cheery looked the hall, well lit up. Down went valise
and hat-box, and we stepped in, glad of a roof. "All
full! all full!" cried the landlord, running out from
the dining-room, "not a single room!"

Then rose a great babble of the porters and waiters,
and each said the name of a different house to which
we would better go. English advocate, who could n't
speak a word of German,— by the way, I don't know

how he had been getting on, — said we would go to the nearest, good or bad. Up and down, in and out, round and about, we went, full half a mile, and reached the Breidenbacher Hof, got in, and got rooms and got to bed.

"Call us at six; we go on board the boat for Arnheim at eight," said I.

"There is no boat in the morning," said the porter.

"There must be," said I, remembering the forehead of the old man in Cologne.

Porter was obstinate, knew there was no boat; the boat for Arnheim went at 11 P. M. every night. Then I ordered a commissioner to go to the office and see. In an hour he came back with the same story; still I did not believe, but I went to bed quite unhappy at the prospect of a long car ride the next day, and the thought of having been swindled by the big benevolence. At six and a half next morning I rang for water. Waiter says, with the air of one having an unimportant second thought, "O, there *is* a boat down this morning at half past eight, the porter says." Thinking the impressions of the employees of the Breidenbacher Hof quite too vacillating to be depended on, I pack poor Fräulein off in the cold twilight, down to the wharf, to ask. She comes back, pops her head in at my door, "Yes, my lady, he go," and is off again on some other mysterious errand of her own.

At breakfast comes the bill, presented by a pale, melancholy young man who spoke excellent English, (and whom I suspect of being a student at Dusseldorf,) with item of ten silver groschen for the services of commissioner. Would n't you have liked to have heard the English with which I declined paying for the services of the commissioner who had informed me that there was *no boat* that morning? Pale young man smiled a sickly smile, but struck off the item. I left a word of farewell and thanks to the voluble Mrs.

Advocate, and gave her my London address, and once more poor Fräulein (who began to look a little fagged by her new worries) and I took up our line of march. This boat proved not to be a boat for Arnheim at all, but direct for Rotterdam by way of Nimwegen. Much I fear that Big Benevolence did not know it would be at Dusseldorf on Wednesday morning. However, the tickets were as good on it as on any other, and we need not go off it at all, and we shall be in Rotterdam at half past one. So all is well that ends well. If I had my big trunk I should be content. But if you could once imagine how cold it is. A drizzling rain and a cold wind and no fire. Last night the Fräulein and I slept on mattresses in the captain's cabin. We, being the only women on board, had it to ourselves. I wore all my clothes which are not *black*, my woollen wrapper, a heavy cloth sack trimmed with astrachan, and I had three blankets above me. Now I have a jug of hot water at my feet, and two blankets rolled around me to the knees, and am just comfortable, except my hands, which are icy cold in spite of all I can do. I see Holland going by in oval strips through the three cabin windows opposite me. It is chiefly windmills, and the ships look like Chinese junks. Every few minutes we pass small steamers towing five and six of them up stream. The outer cabin had six Dutchmen in it, all smoking like furnaces. So I have coaxed the conductor to let me stay in his cabin, and he is writing away at his round table on invoices, etc. Last night I had the washbowl, pitcher, etc., on the same table, and this morning he had to come in to get at his books before I had finished washing my hands. He only knows two English words, " all right," and he says them whenever he comes in or goes out, and pulls off his shiny black silk cap and bows to me. He cannot imagine what I am writing. The Fräulein told him her lady would recommend his boat everywhere, and so I do. All of you remember that if you want to get from Rotterdam up the Rhine, you will do best to take the *Netherlands* line, not the Cologne and Dusseldorf. Such good things to eat as we have had for this day and a half, such clean sheets and blankets to sleep in, and such kind and pleasant service, I have not seen since we left Munich. Last night the waiter brought in a light for us to burn all night, lest we might be afraid. Such a contrivance as it was! A tumbler half full of oil, floating on it a *thing* made of three round bits of cork, and in the middle what looked like a thin white wafer with a bit of candle-wick in it; and burn, burn, burn, it burned all night, with a queer little glimmer which only showed how dark the cabin was. Whenever I half waked up and saw it I said, "Twinkle, twinkle, little star, how I wonder what you are!" and dozed off again, thinking of Alice in Wonder Land. By the way, did I tell you — you who know that delicious book — that "Lewis Carroll" is a woman, quite young, who never wrote anything else but "Alice"?

ROTTERDAM, *Friday Morning.* — I suppose there must be some reason why it is best that I should not see the Hague, as I had intended to do to-day; but I must own I was in a rebellious frame of mind to find, when I waked up this morning, solid sheets of rain pouring down. As if there were not water enough in Rotterdam! So there is nothing to do but wait quietly for my ship for London to-morrow morning. Poor Fräulein is the picture of woe. She has read all her magazines, and now has fallen back on an old almanac which she borrowed of the waiter. To sit still is as great a misery for her as if she were five years old instead of fifty-two, and she is so near-sighted that she cannot amuse herself by looking out of the windows as I do.

These Dutch women are the drollest figures I have seen yet. They are running back and forth in this rain with white fluted caps on their heads, and white wooden shoes turned up at the toes like Chinese junks, — just such as the poorest peasants wear in the Tyrol in wet weather. And such scrubbing as goes on in the morning here, never did I see! Opposite my windows — in all the rain — a woman with pails and pails and pails of water, and a broom, and a mop, and cloths, scrubbing the sidewalks and the doorstep for two whole hours! O, if I were an artist, would I not have made a picture, "A Wet Morning in Rotterdam," — the shop door and the windows, and this woman flooding the sidewalk with water, and scouring away with her mop, and all the time the rain pouring down on her fluted cap and into her wooden shoes!

Now I go out in a close carriage to see Rotterdam. It is too bad! so much I should have enjoyed running up to the Hague this morning, and loafing in these streets this afternoon! I must be forgiven for this one little grumble. Poor Fräulein is fast asleep on the sofa. She looks much older when she is asleep, I see. When she is awake, and her eyes and her dimples at work, nobody would think her over forty. When she came in yesterday, she said, "O my lady, what think you a man said on me? When I go on the post-office for your letter, five men they sit by table to play cards, and each man he have — *so*, in his mouth, (making one very big cheek with her tongue, to indicate a tobacco plug!) and one man he say, 'Dunderwetter, but that wife is fat!' and I make my eyes not to right, not to left, as if I nothing hear, but I feel my get very red in the face!"

Never have I seen any human being with such talent for mimicry as this Fräulein. On the stage she would have made her fortune. I have laughed more in these seven days' journeying with her than in the whole last year put together. There is no human thing she cannot *become* in one second. The changes in her face, when she is telling a story, sometimes almost frighten me. Last night she told me about an interview with a priest; and the sanctimonious priestly face that she lengthened out into in one second, and the drawl and whine, were such as I never have seen outdone on any stage.

Farewell, now, my dear souls, till I get to London.

Evening. — But I must tell you a little about my day. The first thing to be done was to get some money. Mons. Ezekiels was the prophetic name on my letter of credit. Were the banking-houses open all day?

"O yes; all day."

O the things that people don't know about their own city! I wonder a dozen times a month if I should lie so, in giving a stranger information about New York. I suppose I should.

Well, to Ezekiels we went. To get anywhere in Rotterdam you drive a long way up one side of a canal, till you come to a bridge that has n't a ship going through, and then, after you have crossed that bridge, you drive a long way down the other side of the canal, and through a narrow lane out on the banks of another canal, and cross that, and then you cross the first canal once or twice more, and drive up and down on the shores of the second, and then you *get* there! This is the way it *looks*. I suppose the canals and lanes really are far apart from each other, and called by different names, but they all feel alike, and you can see your face in every bit of window-glass or door-bell along the way. There is n't any place left for godliness next to cleanliness in Rotterdam, I am sure; cleanliness has taken all the room!

A long, low, stone-paved, stone-arched passage-way led to Ezekiels's counting-room at the back of his house; his cellar and kitchen were on the same floor; a woman in wooden shoes was scrubbing his floor; and such shining pans and kettles filled his kitchen, they almost lit the stone gallery. No Ezekiels! *Loquitur*, young man with a yard of Jew nose, "All banking-houses in Rotterdam shut from twelve till three!"

So I drove off. Saw old Admiral de Witt in stone in the St. Lawrence Church, and the funny high seats with tent-roofs over them, where the burgomasters sit of a Sunday; bought some photographs; saw statue of Erasmus; and back again to the Jew's. Five Jew noses all turned and pointed at me as I went in. "I will take gold," I said. "O, we have no gold; we will give you good Dutch currency." "But I am going to England. I do not want Dutch currency." All five of the Jew noses sniffed at the idea of a benighted individual's preferring gold to Dutch currency, and the young man said, "You can get it changed for gold on the Boompjes." (Wish you all joy pronouncing that word.) So I patiently took my bundle of flabby Dutch currency, and bowed to all five of the Jew noses, and drove off, up and down half a dozen more alternating strips of canal and street, and found another Jew who gave me gold for my paper. This is the first banking-house in which I have had to do such a clumsy and absurd thing.

Now all is packed and strapped and ready for the morrow. I have a big ache at leaving my great Fraulein. I shall feel like a swallow pushed out of the nest to fly alone.

On board steamer, nine o'clock, A. M., *Saturday, October* 11. — Lest I forget some of the scenes of the last half-hour, I have taken out my pen and inkstand and paper (to the stewardess's great surprise), and while the boat only rocks a little, I shall try to tell you what sort of a time we have had. Dear Fräulein's train for Cologne was to start at eight o'clock this morning, the boat for London not till nine.

"O my dear lady, could you not go on board at half past seven, that I see you all comfortable before I go?" So, to please her, I ordered breakfast at half past six, and down to the boat we came at seven. A more surprised stewardess was never seen, nor a darker, colder den than the ladies' cabin. However, I saw the wisdom of the Fräulein's plan in the increased respect of the stewardess's manner. She stood by with wide eyes to see the great splendid Fräulein crying and kissing my hands. Really I have not had such a parting for years. I did not know the good soul had so taken me to heart.

After she went off the boat, the stewardess was overwhelmingly polite, much more than she would have ordinarily been to a lady as went "hout by 'erself." But the Fräulein told her that she had come all the way from Munich to bring me, and that my friends were to meet me in London, and so she thinks I am "quality"; and would I 'ave this berth or that? This one would "perhaps 'ave too much hair" for me. ("The best one I could go into," thinks I to myself.)

At last I persuaded her to let me have a stateroom in the gentlemen's cabin, out of which the den called ladies' cabin opens, and not a stateroom in it! Think of that, woman's rights people! So I am to pay for two berths, and for once in my life count as good as two men!

"Who are you, who are you, I should like to know?" screamed out a great gray parrot in a cage above the table. Then a canary-bird, in another cage, set up the shrillest sort of song before I could reply to the parrot, and "Can't you speak, — don't you know your name?" said the parrot; "I'm pretty Poll, — pretty Poll; what's your name?"

"Well," thought I, "you're very funny for once, but eighteen hours of you will be quite too much," and I curled myself up on a sofa, and rolled my feet up in a blanket, and thought I would take a nap before the boat started. The steward and clerk and stewardess were eating their breakfast in the outer cabin, and looking at me through the open door.

"Dirty weather," said the steward.

"Yes, beastly," said the stewardess; "but the captain says there's no use waiting; it won't be any better to-morrow."

This was cheerful. I, in my innocence, thought it

only a quiet drizzle, but I see it is going to be another affair when we get outside.

Presently I heard the gayest little bird-laugh in the cabin, and "Dear mamma, let me come with you." "No, dear, stay there till I come back"; and a tall, fair English lady came into the cabin, looking for her berths. She had a sweet voice and face, and the little girl's voice was like a bird's. In a few moments more the little thing came tripping in. Such a head of curls, and such gray eyes, and such a jolly little straw hat tipped on one side of her head! I involuntarily exclaimed, "O you dear little lady!" She skipped along, laughing, and took no notice of me.

"Do you like the steamboat?" said I, as she ran about, looking into every corner.

"Yes," said she, quite shortly, and then, turning back suddenly, she said, "How *dare* you look out that way!" I could not imagine what she meant, and I said, "I don't understand you; look out *what* way?"

"Why, at *me*," she said; "you should n't stare. I hate staring people."

Fancy me! I laughed till the tears rolled, and then I said: "I 'll tell you why I stared so. It is because I love little children so much. When I see a little boy or girl coming, I can't help looking at them. Is n't that a good reason?"

"Yes," she said, reflectively, looking a little appeased, "but I hate staring people."

However, she came up close to me presently, and put her little cold paws on mine, and said, pointing to my bag and bundle, which were at my feet, "You can't have those in here; it is not allowed, I am quite sure."

"O my!" said I; "how old are you?"

"Three and a quarter," said she, dancing off and laughing. Then she grew quite friendly, and invited me to go with her and look at the little bed in their corner; and then her mamma bundled her up, and took her on deck, for it has stopped raining, and for people who have not horrible colds that is the best place.

Then came a stir at the door, and a man appeared bringing in his arms a girl, perhaps twenty years old, with the most glorious auburn hair I ever saw. Two other girls followed with pillows and bundles, and all the paraphernalia of an invalid. O, such a terrible time as it was to get her into the narrow berth! There was evidently a mystery about it all. One sister whispered to the stewardess, who grew frightened-looking at once, and the other sister held the invalid's hands, and a fearful instinct seized me that the girl was insane. How I pitied the poor elder sister who had her in charge! I never saw a difficult place better filled. There is a gentleman with them, who is either brother or doctor, I cannot make out which. They are Germans, but speak English perfectly. She is quiet, but looks wildly about from time to time. Then came in a great sofa, which they are carrying about with them, and then a trunk, which must be there too, and the whole cabin hardly big enough to turn round in. How that elder girl did manage the stewardess, and how I did thank my stars that I had secured a stateroom in the outer cabin! Next were produced from the trunk three long narrow black bags, like umbrella cages, and "Has the ice been brought on board?" said they. "O yes, mum, the hice is 'ere," said the stewardess.

"Well, these bags are for sea-sickness, to prevent sea-sickness, to be applied to the spine," said the elder young lady, and then followed the drollest sort of a discussion between the stewardess and her. I had to put my veil over my face.

"Well, mum, I'll put the hice in, but the screwing up part of it you'll 'ave to do yourself; and if you all gets bad to once, I don't know who'll be a puttin' of these 'ere to your *speings*."

Then came in a pretty German woman, with a nurse and baby, and, "Stewardess, if I am sick, will you just take my baby a little; and a few drops of *this* in the bottle if he is hungry."

At this crisis I picked myself out and came away. The stewardess put my bag and shawl in my stateroom, and I said to her, "I fear you are going to have a terrible night, stewardess, with the sick lady and the baby."

"Well, mum, you may well say so, and *I* am to feed the baby, you know, while the nurse keeps quiet in her berth," with a toss of her head; "it's more than 'uman nature can bear sometimes, is it, in these ships, mum, and the poor young lady is not right in her 'ead, and it's such nasty weather."

Luckily there are only two other ladies in the cabin besides those I have named, but I do not see . . . .

LONDON, *Monday*, 18*th*. — In less than an hour after that last sentence, I was the sickest mortal you ever saw. Heaven forbid that I should tell you the horrors of that voyage! From twelve o'clock Saturday noon till twelve o'clock Sunday noon, I lay in my berth in a condition of which I never even conceived. Never but once have they known so rough a passage. There was no real danger, they said, but O the misery! Now, at last, I know what sea-sickness means. Except that the captain said it never *could* be so bad on the Atlantic Ocean, I would never come home. The channel boils all ways at once. You are lifted endwise, sidewise, and whopped over in a second. For six hours every wave hit the boat like an iron wall, and broke over it; the winds howled like devils; and the sailors' cries sounded like the wails of lost spirits; and till eleven o'clock at night that fiendish parrot never stopped its silly screeching!

At one o'clock, Sunday noon, I landed; at three I was eating cold mutton and drinking ale in the E——s's pleasant parlor, and had forgotten all about the sea-sickness, so like a miracle does it pass off. Then in the evening came darling S—— C—— and stayed till eleven o'clock. Think of the good luck of my just catching her! She and Miss F—— go to Paris to-day.

It is so dark I can but just see at this writing,— about two in the afternoon. Howie, the dear little fellow, says, "O, this is nothing! You should have seen the fog last week. They lit candles at twelve of the *noon*."

Now, London! It looks well; all but weather, and that I knew I could not get. I have a lovely little parlor and bedroom, and the E——s also have a parlor and two bedrooms, and we are to buy our beef and mutton, and the landlady has it cooked.

"Economical Funeral" was one of the first signs I saw yesterday, as I drove up from the boat!

Fifteen letters awaited me here! Bless you, all who wrote. Good by. Peace be with you.

P. S. — Particulars of the eclipse next time. It is n't quite so dark as I thought it would be.

GREAT MALVERN, December 13, 1869.

DEAR PEOPLE: How shall I make my tale of bricks this time, having come away from all sorts of straw? But you will none of you believe me if I say there is nothing to write about in Malvern; and you will all of you be vexed with me if I send you, for once, a short letter. It has just dawned upon me that I have spoiled you horribly in this one year. It is high time I left off my monthly sermon. I know just how the ministers feel on Friday: I see the fifteenth standing and staring me in the face just like a Sunday, and for the life of me I can't, as the children say, "think of anything to say!" But now, as I go on, a misgiving seizes me that I am the one who is spoiled after all, thinking that there is nothing worth telling you about because I am not up to my ears in sights of the technical order. Yes, I am the one who is spoiled, and I am ashamed of myself — here in this lovely, quiet, green English country, and on such a hillside as you may look America through for and not find — to have said there was nothing to tell you.

To tell the truth, I have just come to you from reading the saga of Grettir the Strong, translated by dear, delicious William Morris; and somehow to-day the simply being alive, and not killing anybody, nor sailing across any sea, seems not worth speaking about, unless there were Morris and Magnussen to tell it in fashion of sagas.

Well, now I'll go and get the Malvern Guide, and see what it says about Malvern. I hate to leave my fire a minute, and I don't know where the book is; but it is somewhere about the house, and unless I have that open before me, I shall be sure to tell some lie or other about ". . . . feet above the sea," etc.

"Malvern, so interesting to the geologist, lover of nature, botanist, and antiquarian, possesses unique and attractive historical reminiscences. In ancient mediæval, as well as modern times, the tall brow of its bard-hill was an object of much interest." "The town of Malvern strangely contrasts with that vulgar succession of streets, courts, alleys, etc., that are usually so denominated. In place of streets it has a succession of fashionable mansions; in place of courts and alleys it has villas, crescents, and terraces; and, though town in fact, it is little like one in external aspect. It has few buildings consecutively joined together, and consists chiefly of separate and distinct residences."

There are one hundred and seventy-two pages of this, my people! Think of my having thoughtlessly said there was nothing to be told about Malvern, and yet this valuable work had been lying for two weeks on my table. I am more than ever impressed by the style of it, as I look it over with a view of making quotations. Some slight ambiguities I observe, here and there, owing to the size of the words, which appear to overlap each other a little. For instance, to a practical mind it might occur that it would be troublesome getting about in a town where there were no streets, and only "a succession of fashionable mansions." But sleighs drawn by reindeer, after the pattern of that in which Darley drew St. Nicholas, glide without difficulty over the chimney-tops; and for pedestrian excursions stilts, made by the boot-maker of Jack's giant, enable us to step over the "villas and residences" which obstruct our way.

"Another feature that greatly distinguishes the climate of Malvern is the perfect dryness and elasticity of the air."

Here the ambiguity which characterizes the style of the author of the Malvern Guide seems really, though

I shrink from saying anything harsh, to run into something which is usually called by a severer name. I have only been in the town three weeks, to be sure, so perhaps my observations are too limited to be set against his; but it is fourteen days now since we have seen the sun, except for one half-hour day before yesterday, and another this morning. On all those fourteen days the whole county of Worcestershire, which lies spread out in a beautiful meadow map below Malvern, has been wrapped in impenetrable fogs, which much of the time have climbed the hill, walling our house in with a dead-white sort of ground-glass-looking substance, which has slowly oozed and trickled and drizzled down on the tops of our umbrellas, without which we have never been out. Had enough guide-book? Then I 'll tell you why we came, and when.

We came up on the 22d November, five days after I mailed my last letter to you. That was the when. And the why? Because we were persuaded that if we were only once well washed in our lives we should become as little children.

I came on ahead by a few hours and looked up lodgings. Ah, my people, don't believe one word you hear written or said against "lodgings"! It is the ideal way of living, and England is the country of comfort. If I were to set forth, in as glowing language as I might, how comfortable we are, you would all say, "O, that is only her enthusiastic way of describing things; it can't be as she says!" But listen now to naked facts.

We are in one of the houses in Malvern, but whether it is a "mansion" or a "villa" or a "residence," I don't know. It is called, however, "Holyrood House." So perhaps it is something grander than any of those three other kinds. At any rate, it is n't a "crescent" or a "terrace." I am sure of that. Holyrood House is kept by Mr. and Mrs. Brown, who have been, I think, chief butler and housekeeper in some noble family in days gone by. There are five apartments in it; that is, there are five sitting-rooms, with bedrooms to match, — some with one, some with two.

I pay for a nice little parlor and bedroom, and a blazing coal-fire all day in each, twenty-eight shillings a week ($7 in gold). Think of that, ye unfortunate New-Yorkers, who could n't get a back-stoop in Sixth Avenue for that money. The E——s have a parlor and two bedrooms on the same floor for ten shillings more.

We pay three shillings and sixpence for the kitchen fire; we pay one shilling a week for the hall gas. Then we buy what we want to eat, and Mrs. Brown cooks it for us; and we have our own private table and especial housekeeping and undisturbed life, just as safe and secure as if we were in a great house all to ourselves, with five servants. We pay for the washing of each thing we use, table and bedroom linen; so we can have all we like. The service is admirable. O the quiet and order and gentleness of these English servants! It is as good as soothing-syrup to tired nerves to see them moving about. The china and silver are all not only good, but nice and pretty and abundant. We can have three or four friends to tea as satisfactorily as in our own house, and thus far it has never cost us over one pound a week each for the living, aside from the rent.

How in the world the down-stairs part of it is managed, I cannot imagine. Why we don't eat Dr. Mauprat's butter, and the Rev. Mr. Dickey does n't get our herring, is a mystery to me. But Mrs. Brown says I may go down stairs some day, and see her pantry, and then I shall understand. She has shelves numbered with the numbers of the rooms, and our cold mutton is always set in our corner, above our sugar, and below our bread and carrots. When I get the exact run of it, I shall write an article for the Independent about the system, in the wild, baseless hope of setting somebody to do likewise in America. Think of the contrast between the privacy, comfort, and economy of such an arrangement as this, and the dens of high-priced misery called boarding-houses, in New York or Boston. It is a bewildering thing that we in America, with every facility for being more comfortable than any other nation in the world, should be less so in this one matter of living. If into these comfortable, well-ordered English lodging-houses could be brought our Indian corn, our oysters, our squashes, our poultry, our tomatoes, our apples, our cracked wheat, and if through their great clean windows could shine our sun, life, so far as the body goes, would be perfect. I remember, before I came abroad, I used every now and then to read in the papers a despairing wail from somebody or other about the superiority of the foreign methods of living in apartments in comparison with boarding, but I never quite believed it. I thought there would prove to be a screw loose somewhere when I came to try it; and so there is, for that matter, when it is in Rome that you do it, and have to have your dinner come in on a man's head, from a horrible "trattoria." It is not absolute perfection, either, in Munich, even in my beloved Fraulein's house, where, do her best, she cannot be other than a *German* cook. I believe it is only in old England that the climax of success is reached; and, my people, you should taste the mutton! Can't you believe that a sheep that had eaten purple thyme steadily for four months would taste marvellously well at the end of that time? I have seen as good roast beef in America as can be bought here, say what they will about their national dish; but mutton! Give up! We never tasted it in America. I did not know what it could be. And they broil it, too, O friends, if it is in the shape of a chop you have it. Even in the little inns in out-of-the-way places, where you stop for a lunch, your chop is broiled, and your plate is hot. A fried chop on a cold plate,—that perpetual insult, that unchristian outrage, which pursues the traveller in New England, from Monday morning till Saturday night, — it would make an English landlord stand still in wonder to see.

A week ago last Friday we drove over to a lovely little village eight miles from Malvern, went to the village church, roamed about the graveyard, and dined at the inn. From the outside of it we felt misgiving, it was so very small and humble. The whole village street had not more than twenty houses, and they were the houses of laborers. Our dinner was laid in the one room beside the kitchen, — bare wooden floor, wooden settle, wooden chairs, old cherry sideboard, tiny little windows high up in the wall; but the landlord pinned on a white napkin to wait on us, and served us with the ease of an old butler, — broiled chops, broiled bacon, potatoes white and mealy to the point of crumbling, good bread, delicious butter, home-brewed ale, and a hot apple-tart, whose crust would not have dishonored any table, and whose flavor of lemon and mace might well be remembered among the apple-tarts of one's youth. O, how we abused our native land round that table, when the landlord was out of the room! how we said to each other, "Fancy the dinner we should have had in any New England town no larger than this,— the soggy potatoes, the saleratus bread, the pickles, the doughnuts, and the gravy! Who will head a subscription for Blot's lectures to be delivered throughout the land, and the governors to compel all heads of families to attend? Who will lift up her voice, or his, and write, write, write in all newspapers till we have better things to eat? Now slavery is no more, we might be free from dyspepsia!" So we said; and then we went over to call at the vicar's house, he having politely asked us to lunch with him, fearing we might not be well fed at the inn; and we found him a pale, sickly, dyspeptic-looking man, just having taken a wishy cup of tea, and an egg, and some dark-looking bread and white butter. Were n't we glad we did n't accept his invitation to lunch, if his page did have 1,733 buttons on the front of his body?

But I have run on in a way befitting "gluttons and wine-bibbers." You would not wonder, however, if you knew what it was to come into luxurious eating and drinking after having lived a year on old stones and oil paint. I think I shall not escape for some months from a perpetual sort of undercurrent of consciousness, like a refrain to a song which won't get out of one's head, "Beef, mutton, oatmeal, oatmeal, mutton, beef"; and as for the fires, I shall spend half my time, till spring, poking them to see the flames shoot up.

Now I will tell you a little of the routine of the life of a water-cure patient; a water-cure *im*patient would be nearer the truth. Life under the water-treatment is a series of interruptions, unbuttonings and buttonings up, and we all know what drove that Frenchman to suicide. Interruption first is of your morning naps. If one is to be packed in wet sheets for one hour, dress, and walk for fifteen minutes, and then sit still for fifteen minutes, all before a nine-o'clock breakfast, it is plain, to be sure, that quarter before seven is the latest possible minute for beginning. Quarter before seven is an hour and a quarter before light just now, even on this eastern hillside, which gets the first wink of the sun. When Annie, the silent chambermaid, with a smutty Honiton-lace cap on her head, comes into my room at half past six to make my fire, I always think that something has happened in the way of accident, and that I am being summoned in a hurry. "O Annie, what is the matter?" I said regularly for the first ten days, but now I only groan, "O Annie!" This is the only thing I do not like in the water-treatment. To be waked up out of sleep has always seemed to me a crowning insult and outrage to Nature.

Then comes Maria, my good bath-woman, for whom

I have already conceived a sentiment nine parts veneration and one affection. Of course I can't help loving her a little, she is so kind and energetic in my behalf, so generally good-natured and straightforward, and so sure I shall get to be a giant of strength and health. But, dear me, my love is so put upon by my awe! This woman, of like passions with myself, and not much older, who comes three times a day into my presence as the representative of a system from which I can no more escape than I can from grim death; authoritative as Dr. Gully himself; no more mindful of my naked and helpless body than was the mother who bore me whenever I needed washing or whipping! — laughing at my screams; holding her old snail of a watch in her hand, and declaring it is only four minutes when I say it must be ten, — O, we have very funny times together, Maria and I! She little dreams how my soul is on its marrowbones before her. When she says, "Indeed, mum, you mus' n't," I no more think of persisting than if Parliament were at her back; and when she looks at me reflectively as she ties on a compress over the "upper stomach" (did you know we had more than one? I keep forgetting to ask Dr. Gully if camels have the most, or we) I feel as if her glance reached the inmost secrets of my bosom, and she must know all about the lies I told, and never got found out in, in my infancy. "Maria," said I, "did you ever see two human bodies alike?" one day when I felt a little sentimental, and was thinking more than ever how she was getting possession of me in all this wet and dry scrubbing. "O Lor, mum, I s'pose not, for the matter of that, if you looked close. But they 're all alike to me. Not but what I 'd rather rub the fat ones than they that 's all bones," she added, reflectively, with a half-chuckle and sigh, I suppose at the thought of some recent vertebræ that she had scraped her hands over. Fourteen years she has been at it, this faithful soul; and she has given out and away so much of her own animal heat and electric vital force that she is not strong as she was. My own theory is, that half the benefit comes from the splendid rubbing after the baths. It sets every nerve and pore in your skin on to the full gallop of doing their duty. Well, as I say, this getting into a whole or a part "pack" is your morning interruption. Then you turn over, mummy that you are, and look out and watch the dawn, if you are a person of nerves, with the most delicious sense of being under no more responsibility about yourself for the next hour than if you were one of the fleecy clouds which are drifting in the wind. If you are of adipose make, you go to sleep again, and at the end of an hour have another interruption, and are ordered into a "shallow," that is, a long bath-tub with six inches of water in it,—at 65°, if the doctor is merciful; "stone-cold," if he is n't. I have mine at 65°. Into this you are plunged, smoking hot, and for one or two minutes are scrubbed with towels; then out, and rubbed for ten or fifteen minutes more, till you are "red as a rose is she," by the author of "Cometh up as a Flower"! Then you hurry on your clothes, and take a walk of ten or fifteen or thirty minutes before breakfast. This was the one thing I thought I could never do; "never had been *able to*," as women always say to the long-suffering doctor, who knows a thousand times better than they do. But already I like it so much that I think I shall never again breakfast on food before I have had a little breakfast on air; I walk, usually on the piazza,—for Holyrood House has a fine piazza on two sides, one looking off eastward over this glorious great valley. There are three ravens which always come at this time, and flap and bustle about in a great bare linden-tree in the garden. They usually arrive about five minutes after I do; never have missed a morning yet. What they are at, I can't make out, but there is a solemn jollity or jolly solemnity about their behavior that interests me mightily. They would do for Odin's two ravens, "Thought and Memory," if I were bent on romantic sentiment at that hour in the morning.

At half past twelve, noon, just as I get well under way with my writing, comes second interruption, — Maria's head, peering round the corner of my parlor door, and "If you please, mum." Then it is either "spinal washing," that is, the washing of the whole length of the spine with cold water for four minutes,— the most delicious thing of all, making your brain feel as suddenly fine and clear as if it had been changed in a second from curds to spun glass; or a "lamp bath," which is, sitting in a wooden chair, rolled up in several hundred-weight of blankets, and a spirit-lamp burning you up from underneath, till you are drenched in perspiration, and then out into a "shallow" of cold water, and scrubbed and rubbed as in the morning. This is about like a Turkish Bath.

Or a rose douche, or the inch-and-a-half douche, or the two together!

These are infinitely surprising, I cannot say pleasing. I took them but twice; they did not suit me. These cannot be taken at home. You go to the bath-house, undress in one cupboard, then step into another, which is set with mysterious bars and pulleys and faucets, reminding one of Nuremberg torture-dungeons. You have to let the thing on yourself, for the bath-woman would get wet if she came in. Perhaps you think you can thereby play possum, and not take the full force of the water. Ha! there is a small round hole in the wall, between inner and outer cupboard, and there glares, like the palpable eye of Omniscience, the eye of Maria! "Indeed, mum, you must stay under!" and back you bob as spry and guilty as if you'd been caught stealing. If you think you know what the real duration of a minute is, you're mistaken, unless you have had a stream of water an inch and a half in diameter fall on your back and loins for that length of time, and you wanting to "stand from under," and not daring to.

Sitting before a daguerreotype man after you have "assumed an easy and natural expression" is less than nothing to it. Whichever of these or other noon treatments you undergo will take, all told, an hour. Then you must walk from half an hour to an hour. Then dinner. Then a little lounging and talking, and then, perhaps, you go to make a call on a friend, and as you are just in the midst of a fine talk, she says, "Now, I know, as you are a patient yourself, you will excuse me, but my bath-woman has come for me to take a foot-bath." "O dear!" say you, "then probably my woman is at this moment waiting for me." Sure enough, it is half past five o'clock, and you are now to sit for twelve minutes in a sitz-bath-tub of water at 65°, and then have a little more scrubbing. Then you dress for the evening, eat a good supper, and by nine o'clock are so sleepy, you wish you had gone to bed immediately after the sitz-bath, and made that second undressing answer.

This is an average routine of an average patient at the present day under the water-treatment. The old horrors and severities are done away with, unless it may be in some of the German establishments, where tortures are still in vogue. Also the diet is no more restricted than it ought to be for all Christians in or out of water-treatment. We can eat anything we ought to like, and we do eat. Such hunger as results from it all, and from the electric Malvern air! We misgive whether a pound a week will feed us much longer.

We are a little concerned about our Christmas. Our English cronies are going away before that time, and we sha' n't be asked out to dinner, we know. We have bought big boughs of mistletoe to hang up over our doors, and propose to kiss each other under it. It is an uncanny, scrambling-looking thing. I am a little afraid of its spidery shape, but the berries are lovely. If a white currant were to marry a snowberry, their babies would be like these. Now do you know how they look? You see through them, and you don't; they quiver, and yet are firm-planted as the bough itself; they are uncanny too, like the rest.

We have thought of putting an advertisement in the newspapers to the following effect: —

"An intelligent American family would like to spend the Christmas holidays in an English house, where the Christmas customs and festivities will be well observed. No objection to noblemen."

But I fear it is now too late. Some dear English souls in London want us, but that is too far. So we shall console ourselves by having a plum-pudding, and trying to keep little Howie from realizing that he is all alone for a holiday. Good by.

THE END.

Cambridge: Printed by Welch, Bigelow, & Co.

www.ingramcontent.com/pod-product-compliance
Lightning Source LLC
Chambersburg PA
CBHW022026240426
43667CB00042B/1201